This is an authoritative and acces
crime. It offers timely insights wh
ers across the world, and its reflections on hate crime terminology, p
practice have much to offer anyone interested in the challenges surrounding
effective community engagement and law enforcement.

Professor Neil Chakraborti, *Department of Criminology, University of Leicester,*
UK

This book is a welcome addition to the expanding literature on hate crime. At a
time where the importance of effective law enforcement responses to hate has
rarely been greater, this book offers valuable insights into the myriad of complexities inherently associated with the policing of hate crime and responding to
the needs of diverse communities.

Dr Nathan Hall, *Associate Head (Academic) and Postgraduate Programme Area*
Leader, Institute of Criminal Justice Studies, University of Portsmouth, UK

Policing Hate Crime: Understanding Communities and Prejudice is an innovative contribution to the literature in the field. Drawing upon a unique research
partnership between police and academics, this book entwines current law
enforcement responses with key debates on the meaning of hate crime to explore
the potential for misunderstandings of hate crime between police and communities. In looking at both sides of the equation, it offers new insight into the
dynamics of policing hate crime. Significantly, it does not stop at simply laying
bare the problems. It also highlights ways in which these communication difficulties might be overcome.

Professor Barbara Perry, *Faculty of Social Science and Humanities, University of*
Ontario Institute of Technology, Canada

In this illuminating book the authors examine an issue at the cutting edge of contemporary social and political debates: the policing of hate crime. Drawing upon
the findings from an innovative police–academic research partnership, the authors
document the history of the relationships between the police and hate crime
victim communities that have often been fractured by poor communication and
breakdowns in trust and confidence. Crucially though, the authors also offer con-
structive organisational and operational policing ideas for how to improve these
relationships, making this book an essential read for academics, practitioners and
policymakers working in the areas of hate crime and policing.

Professor Jon Garland, *Department of Sociology, University of Surrey, UK*

Policing Hate Crime

In a contemporary setting of increasing social division and marginalisation, Policing Hate Crime interrogates the complexities of prejudice motivated crime and effective policing practices. Hate crime has become a barometer for contemporary police relations with vulnerable and marginalised communities. But how do police effectively lead conversations with such communities about problems arising from prejudice?

Contemporary police are expected to be active agents in the pursuit of social justice and human rights by stamping out prejudice and group-based animosity. At the same time, police have been criticised in over-policing targeted communities as potential perpetrators, as well as under-policing these same communities as victims of crime. Despite this history, the demand for impartial law enforcement requires police to change their engagement with targeted communities and kindle trust as priorities in strengthening their response to hate crime.

Drawing upon a research partnership between police and academics, this book entwines current law enforcement responses with key debates on the meaning of hate crime to explore the potential for misunderstandings of hate crime between police and communities, and illuminates ways to overcome communication difficulties. This book will be important reading for students taking courses in hate crime, as well as victimology, policing, and crime and community.

Gail Mason is Professor of Criminology at the University of Sydney.

JaneMaree Maher is Professor in the Centre for Women's Studies and Gender Research, Sociology at Monash University.

Jude McCulloch is Professor of Criminology at Monash University.

Sharon Pickering is Professor of Criminology at Monash University.

Rebecca Wickes is Associate Professor at the School of Social Sciences, Monash University.

Carolyn McKay lectures in criminal law, procedure and the legal profession at the University of Sydney.

Routledge Frontiers of Criminal Justice

Policing Hate Crime

Understanding Communities and Prejudice

Gail Mason, JaneMaree Maher,
Jude McCulloch, Sharon Pickering,
Rebecca Wickes and Carolyn McKay

Routledge
Taylor & Francis Group

LONDON AND NEW YORK

First published 2017 by Routledge

2 Park Square, Milton Park, Abingdon, Oxfordshire OX14 4RN
52 Vanderbilt Avenue, New York, NY 10017

Routledge is an imprint of the Taylor & Francis Group, an informa business

First issued in paperback 2019

British Library Cataloguing in Publication Data
A catalogue record for this book is available from the British Library

Library of Congress Cataloging in Publication Data
A catalogue record for this book has been requested

ISBN: 978-1-138-90424-8 (hbk)
ISBN: 978-0-367-22659-6 (pbk)

Typeset in Times New Roman
by Wearset Ltd, Boldon, Tyne and Wear

Contents

Figures

Tables

Notes on the authors

Gail Mason is Professor of Criminology at the University of Sydney. Her research centres on crime, social justice and exclusion, particularly: racist and homophobic violence; hate crime law and punishment; and the legal construction of hatred. She is co-ordinator of the Australian Hate Crime Network and is involved in funded research exploring hate crime laws and cyber racism. She has published her work in many books and journal articles and has editorial roles for several leading international journals.

JaneMaree Maher is Professor in the Centre for Women's Studies and Gender Research in the School of Social Sciences, and Director of the Social and Political Sciences Graduate Research Program at Monash University. Her research interests include gender and targeted crime, as well as families, women's careers and motherhood. Her research has been published in numerous books, research reports and international journals, and she has been involved in major Australian Research Council funded projects.

Jude McCulloch is Professor of Criminology at Monash University. Her research focus includes policing, counter-terrorism laws and the growing indistinction between war and crime, with a concern for human rights and social justice. She has published widely in leading scholarly journals and written five books and more than 50 chapters elsewhere. Prior to taking up a position in academia, she practised as a lawyer providing legal services to disadvantaged members of the community.

Sharon Pickering is Professor of Criminology at Monash University. She researches irregular border crossing and has written in the areas of refugees and trafficking with a focus on gender and human rights. She leads a series of Australian Research Council projects focusing on the intersections of security and migration, deportation, and police and community responses to prejudice motivated crimes. She has recently taken up an Australian Research Council Future Fellowship on Border Policing and Security.

Rebecca Wickes is Associate Professor at the School of Social Sciences, Monash University. Her research interests include criminological theory; communities and crime; informal social control and social disorganisation;

and social exclusion. She is the lead investigator for the Australian Community Capacity Study.

Carolyn McKay has recently completed her PhD at Sydney Law School, examining video link technologies in criminal justice. She lectures in criminal law, the legal profession and legal research at the University of Sydney and is an academic member of the New South Wales Bar Association. Her research has been published in several international journals and in book chapters.

Acknowledgements

This book would not have been possible without the support of the Australian Research Council for our project 'Targeted crime: policing and social inclusion', a collaborative, criminological study of the policing of crimes motivated by prejudice or hatred. We are particularly indebted to Victoria Police for the initiation of and ongoing contributions to this project as well as openness to engaging in such critical research.

Regarding our research assistants, we would like to thank: Kristin Macintosh for research assistance for Chapter 8; Andrew Dyer for research assistance and original analysis of the legal material upon which Chapter 8 is based; and Kathryn Benier who helped with the quantitative analyses of the Victoria Police incident data in Chapter 7. We also thank Lorraine Mazerolle and Toby Miles-Johnson for their valuable contribution to the recruit study in Chapter 6.

Thank you to all our universities for their research support, specifically University of Sydney, Monash University and University of Queensland.

This book contains material published in:

Gail Mason, Jude McCulloch and JaneMaree Maher (2015) 'Policing hate crime: markers for negotiating common ground in policy implementation', *Policing and Society*, Publisher Taylor & Francis Ltd. (www.tandfonline.com), reprinted by permission of the publisher.

Rebecca Wickes, Sharon Pickering, Gail Mason, JaneMaree Maher and Jude McCulloch (2015) 'From hate to prejudice: does the new terminology of prejudice motivated crime change perceptions and reporting actions?', *British Journal of Criminology* (DOI: 10.1093/bjc/azv041), Oxford University Press, reprinted by permission of the publisher.

Part I

Introduction

1   Introduction

A prejudice motivated crime is a criminal act which is motivated (wholly or partly) by hatred for or prejudice against a group of people with common characteristics with which the victim was associated or with which the offender believed the victim was associated.

(Victoria Police 2010)

I think it's just a word that is only made for those people who can understand it, so the community wouldn't understand what it actually means.

(Focus group participant)

Every nation has a story to tell about the vexed and sometimes violent relations between the police who uphold its authority and the minority communities who, in different ways, live in its margins. In recent decades, law enforcement agencies in many Western countries have sought to rewrite the ending to this predictably gloomy narrative by introducing policies to promote trust and confidence amongst diverse communities. Hate crime initiatives are part of this larger community policing trend. In an environment where some forms of social division and marginalisation seem to be intensifying rather than diminishing, hate crime has become a barometer for contemporary police relations with minority communities. But how do police effectively lead conversations about the problems experienced by vulnerable and marginalised communities arising from prejudice? The proposition at the heart of this book is that successful dialogue between police and diverse victim groups depends upon the will to negotiate common understandings of the injustice, harm and human rights violations that are implicit to hate crime. While such dialogue has its roots in long-standing debates about the terminology and language that we use to talk about hate crime, it ultimately calls for a symbiotic relationship that encourages the attribution of shared and negotiated meaning around the nature and significance of hate crime. Such dialogue is central to the legitimacy of policing in this domain.

Policing has always been a core driver of the hate crime movement. As demonstrated by the Stephen Lawrence Inquiry in the UK (Macpherson 1999), inadequate operational and institutional responses from policing agencies both to crime committed against minority communities and complaints from those communities about prejudice-fuelled crime have provided much of the impetus for hate crime policy and law reform since the 1980s. In the context of larger concerns about the over-criminalisation and under-protection of vulnerable populations, hate crime now represents a highly charged interface between policing agencies and their communities. In *Policing Hate Crime: Understanding Communities and Prejudice*, we aim to interrogate the complexities of effective policing practices and prejudice motivated crime. We consider the value of different language and terminology around hate crime. A common vocabulary to identify, talk about and respond to hate crime provides an opportunity to address sometimes fractured lines of communication between police and those communities experiencing hate crime. While such language is valuable, it is only the first step in the larger goal of achieving a congruent understanding through which to confront prejudice and hate. When different actors construct diverging meanings of hate crime, these definitional mismatches undermine community trust and confidence in policing. Such divergences in narrative create fundamental challenges for police organisations and the pursuit of social justice.

In this book, we explore the potential for misunderstandings of hate crime between police and community and illuminate ways to overcome communication difficulties. Contemporary police are expected to be active agents in the pursuit of social justice and human rights by stamping out prejudice and group-based animosity. At the same time, police themselves have been the vectors of such animosity and violence, reflecting entrenched attitudes and underpinning over-policing of targeted communities as potential perpetrators, as well as under-policing of these same communities as victims of crime. Despite this history, the demand for impartial and democratic forms of law enforcement requires police to challenge prejudice in their own practices and simultaneously respond effectively to hate crime in vulnerable communities.

What is hate crime?

Hate crime has emerged globally as a significant social, political and legal concern. Despite much ambiguity, the concept loosely signifies crime that is motivated or otherwise fuelled by bigotry, bias, hostility, prejudice or hatred towards members of particular groups and communities. For better or worse, it has come to encompass a myriad of prejudice against: racial and ethnic minorities, including black, Asian, Indigenous, Latino/a and Roma communities (Alfieri 2013; Hall *et al.* 2015; James 2015; Johnson and Cuevas Ingram 2012); disabled people (Hamilton and Trickett 2015; Sin 2015); lesbian, gay, bisexual, transgender, and gender non-conforming people (Moran 2015; Woods and Herman 2015); religious minorities, including Jewish (Rich 2015) and Muslim people (Chakraborti and Zempi 2012; Noble 2009) and sectarianism in Northern Ireland (Duggan 2015). While some forms of group hostility, such as racism, have received recognition as hate crime from the very beginning, others, such as gender-based animosity towards women, have come up against much more resistance (Hodge 2011).

Victims of hate crime report significant psychological and emotional harm (Barnes and Ephross 1994; Boeckmann and Turpin-Petrosino 2002; Herek *et al.* 1999; Iganksi 2008), and there is some, albeit contested, research to suggest that they experience more extreme levels of violence compared with non-hate crime victims (VEOHRC 2010). Hate crime sends a 'powerful message of intolerance and discrimination' that can have a 'general terrorizing effect on all members of the target group' (Sentencing Advisory Council 2009). As an extreme manifestation of a larger continuum of discriminatory and bigoted behaviour, hate crime can attack the security and confidence of entire communities, undermining multiculturalism, equality and harmony (Boyd *et al.* 1996; Finn 1988; VEOHRC 2010) and tearing at the fabric of democracy (Lawrence 1999).

In effect, hate crime is a human rights concept (Chakraborti 2015) constructed around hierarchies of difference and otherness (Garland 2014; Iganski 2008; Perry 2010a) and largely geared towards acts of violence and intimidation against minority communities (Perry 2001). It is a concept that has become institutionalised in the criminal justice systems of many liberal democracies. The creation of new hate crime offences, the development of policing and prosecutorial policy and the emergence of treatment interventions have all changed the landscape for responding to offenders who are motivated by group-based hostility. This new legislative and policy terrain means that responsibility for hate crime offences is now core business for law enforcement. While ideally the adoption of principles of human rights and procedural justice can help support police in meeting this responsibility (Weber *et al.* 2014), embedding such principles into prejudice-sensitive policing for vulnerable and marginalised communities has proven more elusive.

Since its inception in the 1980s, and as we explore in more detail in the next chapter, there has been considerable debate about the utility of the concept of hate crime, with many law enforcement agencies favouring less emotive terms, such as bias crime, targeted crime or prejudice motivated crime. To take one example, Stanko (2004) has cogently argued that the most conceptually useful way to consider criminal and other anti-social incidents motivated by racial, religious, sexual or gendered prejudice is through its denotation as 'targeted crime and incidents'. This allows more effective government and non-government responses to assist a range of vulnerable groups without singling them out as specific targets. These debates are about more than the merits of competing terminology. They embody beliefs about the aetiology of the problem, the way it should be represented and constructed, and how the criminal justice system should respond. While the terminology used to label such forms of crime and violence is central to this book, language is ever only a conceptual scaffold or practical instrument that facilitates, and hopefully enhances, the real work of negotiating common ground and meaning between law enforcement and a diverse body of marginal and vulnerable communities. This is our principal concern in this book.

An international snapshot of hate crime victimisation

Hate crime is conceptually ambiguous. It has no singular, historical or universal definition, much less an agreed-upon mode of measurement. In the absence of a mutual framework, the meaning of hate crime depends on how it is defined, interpreted and construed by different communities and authorities, and in different criminal justice domains (Iganksi 2008; Perry 2010a). Divisions between hate crime scholars, policy makers, practitioners and the public result in competing narratives, which impact on a synthesised approach to policy and practice (Chakraborti and Garland 2014; Perry 2016b). As well as definitional variances, there are qualitative distinctions between jurisdictions in how hate crime is recorded, generating statistical inconsistencies. This makes it difficult to form a comprehensive, quantifiable and 'real' picture of the problem or to make meaningful international comparisons (Chakraborti 2015). With these qualifications in mind, we offer a snapshot of hate crime victimisation in a number of broad geographical regions.

The United Kingdom

In 2000, the Association of Chief Police Officers (now the College of Policing) began to refer to hate crime as 'a crime where the perpetrator's prejudice against any identifiable group of people is a factor in determining *who* is victimised' (ACPO Guide 2000). The perception of the victim or any other person became a core ingredient in this definition (ACPO Guide 2005). Thus, in 2005, a hate crime was defined as '[a]ny hate incident, which constitutes a criminal offence, perceived by the victim or any other person, as being motivated by prejudice or hate' (ibid.). A hate incident has the same characteristics except that it may or may not constitute a criminal offence. More specifically, a racist incident for example is 'any incident which is perceived to be racist by the victim or any other person' (ACPO Guide 2000). In 2007, criminal justice agencies in England and Wales adopted a comparably broad, operational definition of hate crime, applying it to five recognised strands of hate crime. Under this definition, a hate crime is any criminal offence which is perceived by the victim or any other person to be motivated by a hostility or prejudice based on a person's race, religion, sexual orientation, disability or transgender identity (or their perceived status as such) (College of Policing 2014). This definition, which is used primarily for recording purposes by police and the Crown Prosecution Service, is not an exact replica of the legislative definitions of hate crime in England and Wales, but its use of the phrase 'hostility' rather than 'hatred' does make it more consistent with these statutes. Although these definitions have remained fairly constant, it can be seen that the 2014 Association of Chief Police Officers (ACPO) guide now favours concepts of 'hostility and prejudice' over 'prejudice or hate' (Chakraborti and Garland 2015). It continues to use the language of hate crime, hate incident and hate motivation, rather than other concepts such as targeted violence (ACPO Guide 2014).

In 2013–2014, there were 44,480 hate crimes recorded by the police in England and Wales, an increase of 5 per cent compared with 2012–2013 (Office for National Statistics 2014). These official hate crimes comprise the five monitored strands, of which 84 per cent (37,484) were based on race, 10 per cent (4,462) on sexual orientation, 5 per cent (2,273) on religion, 4 per cent (1,985) on disability and 1 per cent (555) on transgender (Home Office 2013–2014). Discrepancies between the hate crime figures recorded by police and the results from victim surveys make it difficult to be certain about the size of the problem. For example, Giannasi (2015b) compares data from the 2011–2012 British Crime Survey, which shows that there were 260,000 actual hate crimes, with the official police records of only 43,000. Giannasi notes similar disparities with the US Bureau of Justice figures and argues that data from these two states is compelling evidence as to why under-recording should be considered to be one of the greatest operational challenges for police. He claims that the closing of the gap between these two sets of data is the clearest indication of state progress (ibid.).

While racial (Phillips and Bowling 2012) and homophobic victimisation (Beyond Barriers 2003; Robinson and Williams 2003; Williams and Robinson 2004, 2007) have long been recognised in the UK, the problem of religious hate crime, particularly Islamophobia, is increasingly documented (Chakraborti and Zempi 2012; Taras 2013). Recent large studies of hate crime victimisation, such as the All Wales Hate Crime Project and the Leicester Hate Crime Project, have also recognised the traumatic impact of targeted violence on the basis of other victim characteristics (Williams and Tregidga 2014; see also Milne *et al.* 2013). For example, the Leicester Hate Crime Project reported on hundreds of victims who referred to being routinely ignored, stared at, abused, threatened and spoken to in a belittling and derogatory manner on the basis of their identity or perceived 'difference'. For many, these experiences formed a routine feature of their daily lives and had a profound emotional and psychological impact upon them (University of Leicester 2014). Victims made reference to a wide range of identity characteristics with race and ethnicity being the most frequently cited, at 33 per cent (ibid.). However, 21 per cent felt that they were targeted because of their dress and appearance, 17 per cent cited their religion, 14 per cent their gender, 10 per cent their age, 9 per cent their learning disability, 8 per cent their physical disability and 7 per cent their sexual orientation (ibid.). A small but significant proportion of the survey sample (13 per cent) considered they were targeted for 'other' reasons (ibid.). Within this group many aspects of 'difference' were identified such as having a distinctive or strong accent, a lack of religion, body shape or weight, education status, homelessness, immigration status and social status (ibid.). The question of which victim attributes warrant recognition in the criminal justice system has garnered considerable controversy in the UK (Ashworth 2013, 2014; Heard 2013, 2014; Law Commission 2014), contributing to the devolution of greater discretion to local policing authorities to make decisions about appropriate recording categories for hate crime victimisation (HM Government 2012).

The United States

In the US, for the purposes of collecting statistics, Congress has defined a hate crime as a 'criminal offense against a person or property motivated in whole or in part by an offender's bias against a race, religion, disability, ethnic origin or sexual orientation' (FBI 2015). Hate crime laws have taken many forms throughout the US, with statutes proscribing criminal penalties for civil rights violations, 'ethnic intimidation' and 'malicious harassment' offences, and enhanced penalties if an extant crime is committed for bias or prejudicial reasons (Grattet and Jenness 2008). Hate crime laws in the US also vary in terms of the groups that are protected, covering race, religion, colour, ethnicity, ancestry, national origin, sexual orientation, gender, age, disability, creed, marital status, political affiliation, involvement in civil or human rights, and armed service personnel (ibid.). Some states also require authorities to collect data on hate or bias motivated crime, implement law enforcement training and provide for victim compensation (ibid.). The statutory 'mandate to enforce hate crime law' brings with it definitional ambiguities (particularly in establishing motive), political controversy and criticism of 'political correctness' and, for law enforcement, 'organizational dilemmas connected to agency structures, resource allocation decisions, and workplace culture' (ibid.). All of these dynamics have been influential in the policing and prosecution of hate crime in the US (Grattet and Jenness 2005, 2008).

The most common forms of targeted crimes reported in the United States have historically been harassment and/or intimidation (Byers and Zeller 1997). Racial violence and discrimination against African Americans and Latina/os has been a continuing problem, intimately linked with a volatile national debate on immigration policy (Alfieri 2013; Johnson and Cuevas Ingram 2012). Hate crime statistics from the Federal Bureau of Investigation for 2013 report 5,928 hate crime incidents involving 6,933 offences, 7,230 victims and 5,808 known offenders (FBI 2014). These statistics show that 49.2 per cent of hate crimes were racially motivated. The FBI figures evidence sexual-orientation bias as the second-most common form (20.3 per cent), followed by religious hate crime, particularly anti-Semitism (16.8 per cent), ethnicity (11.5 per cent, centred on Hispanics), disability (1.3 per cent), gender identity (0.5 per cent) and gender bias (0.4 per cent) (ibid.). Amongst the 6,933 hate crime offences reported, 63.9 per cent were crimes against persons, 35 per cent were crimes against property, and the remaining offences were crimes against society such as drug or narcotic offences or prostitution (ibid.). In terms of victim types, amongst the reported 6933 hate crime offences, 82 per cent were directed at individuals, 4.4 per cent were against businesses or financial institutions, 2.6 per cent were against government, 2.6 were against religious organisations and 1.1 per cent were against society or the public; the remaining 7.3 per cent were directed at other/unknown/multiple victim types (ibid.). As with the UK, a disparity between FBI figures and the USA Victimization Study has also been found (Martin 1999; Turpin-Petrosino 2015) and Meli argues that the FBI statistics do not reveal the full extent of the problem, which may be 19 to 31 times greater, according to Bureau of Justice Statistics (2014). Turpin-Petrosino points out the considerable difference in the statistics makes it clear that a single source of national data cannot be viewed as sufficient to gauge the true scope of hate crime prevalence (2015).

Europe

Although the harm caused by hate crime has a long history of recognition by some European governments (Whine 2015), the term 'hate crime' was used officially for the first time by the Organization for Security and Co-operation in Europe (OSCE) in 2003. Chakraborti and Garland (2015) point out that the concept has struggled to establish itself in many of the EU nations, even though the ODIHR has developed a definition of hate crime for all of the 57 countries in the OSCE, including the 27 EU member states (ibid.). According to the ODIHR, hate crimes have two key aspects: they must constitute a criminal offence, and the victim must have been deliberately targeted 'because of [their] ethnicity, "race", religion or other status' (ODIHR 2013). ODIHR also uses the term 'bias', rather than the more extreme concept of hate, and states that 'bias' does not need to be the primary motive for the offence (ODIHR 2013). Even in the face of concerted initiatives within the EU to harmonise hate crime laws, numerous approaches are evident in hate crime statutes (Chakraborti and Garland 2015; Whine 2015). For example, in Germany, an incident is a hate crime if either hate or bias is the primary motive of the offence (Chakraborti and Garland 2015). On the other hand, in Sweden, where the concept of hate crime is comparatively new, the National Council for Crime Prevention's definition of hate crimes is that they are 'motivated by fear of or hostility or hate towards the victim based on skin colour, nationality or ethnic background, religious belief, sexual orientation or transgender identity of expression' (ibid.).

Data collection, capacity building, regulation and policy functions are performed by a number of European agencies including the European Commission Against Racism and Intolerance (Council of Europe), the ODIHR, the European Union Agency for Fundamental Rights (FRA) and the European Court of Human Rights, which has ruled that member states have an obligation to 'unmask' the motive behind racial and religious hate crime (Whine 2015). Despite significant effort, collecting hate crime data from a diverse range of countries, each with its own understandings of the term and different policy priorities, continues to prove problematic (ODIHR 2013; Whine 2015). Hence, the monitoring of hate crime and the collation of statistics are carried out in a far from uniform manner across Europe. For example, 25 EU states officially record racist/xenophobic crime; 12 states monitor anti-Semitic crime; eight monitor homophobic crime, and six monitor religiously motivated and Islamophobic crime, while only four monitor transphobic or disablist crime (Chakraborti and Garland 2015). This produces a big range in hate crimes recorded and prosecuted by EU countries. In

2012 the UK recorded 50,688 hate crimes and 19,802 prosecutions; Germany recorded 4,020 hate crimes (but no data recorded for prosecutions in 2012); Sweden recorded 5,493 hate crimes and 347 prosecutions; the Czech Republic 238 hate crimes and 246 prosecutions; Austria 57 hate crimes and 38 prosecutions; and Poland 222 hate crimes and 43 prosecutions (Chakraborti and Garland 2015). Ukraine recorded only five hate crimes and two prosecutions for 2012 (ibid.). Despite low reporting rates, inconsistencies in recording practices and a lack of political will in some nations (Whine 2015), the extensive work being conducted by inter-governmental and non-governmental agencies promises to generate measures capable of garnering a more consistent picture of hate crime victimisation across Europe in the future.

Canada

In Canada, subss. 318–319 of the Criminal Code cover 'hate propaganda' and incitement to hatred. These provisions were adopted by the Canadian parliament as early as 1970. Hate propaganda crimes include advocating genocide, public incitement of hatred, and wilful promotion of hatred against persons of an identifiable group (Turpin-Petrosino 2015). Identifiable groups include persons distinguished by colour, race, religion, ethnicity or sexual orientation (ibid.). The second category of hate crime laws are defined as offences motivated solely or in part by hatred, bias or prejudice regarding a person's race, ethnicity/nationality, language, colour, religion, sex, age, mental or physical disability, age or sexual orientation (ibid.). In 2012, there were 1,414 police-reported criminal incidents motivated by hate (Allen 2014). About half of all hate crimes (704 incidents or 51 per cent) were motivated by hatred towards a race or ethnicity (or ancestry) such as black, Asian, Arab or Aboriginal populations (ibid.). Four hundred and nineteen incidents, or 30 per cent of incidents, were motivated by hatred towards a religious group, including hate crimes targeting Jewish, Muslim, Catholic and other religious populations (ibid.). An additional 13 per cent (185 incidents) were motivated by hatred of a sexual orientation. The remaining 6 per cent of hate crimes were motivated by language, mental or physical disability, sex, age or some other characteristic, such as occupation or political beliefs (ibid.).

Chakraborti and Garland note that the number of hate crimes in Canada is a surprisingly low figure for a country, like the US, which developed some of the earliest multicultural policies and legal interventions in the area of hate crime (2015). In part, this may be because the Canadian legislation is framed so that a police officer needs to obtain written consent from the Attorney General before s/he can proceed with charges for these offences, causing severe delays in some cases (ibid.). Given that people of colour continue to experience both over- and under-policing in their communities, Perry is less surprised that victims of hate crime are reluctant to report victimisation (2010a). For example, only 15–20 per cent of such victimisations are reported to the police, often because the victims anticipate either lack of concern or some form of secondary victimisation (ibid.).

Allen (2014) reports that the majority of victims in police-reported violent hate crimes were male (72 per cent), and 40 per cent were under the age of 25 (ibid.). The majority of victims sustained no physical injuries (68 per cent), while just under one-third (30 per cent) had minor physical injuries, and 2 per cent sustained major injuries (ibid.). Most victims of violent hate crimes (62 per cent) did not know the accused (in incidents where an accused was identified) (ibid.).

Asia

In comparison to the West, the concept of hate crime has been adopted only minimally in Asian nations. Turpin-Petrosino (2015), however, points to the emergence of some important studies. In India, for example, Sharma (2015) investigated the effect of economic disparity between upper and lower classes or castes and concluded there was a positive relationship between the narrowing of the economic gap between the two and hate crime incidence. When legal barriers preventing Northeast Indians and other ethnic groups' access to education and job activities were removed, these groups moved to metropolitan areas seeking new opportunities. Hate-motivated victimisations against lower caste groups became regular occurrences, including aggravated assaults, sexual assaults, rape, murder and human trafficking as well as conventional discriminatory practices (Turpin-Petrosino 2015, citing Chandra 2012). The perpetrators of these crimes and other forms of harassment are often from the more dominant upper classes (Turpin-Petrosino 2015, citing Sharma 2015). Although the caste system has been officially dismantled in India, it appears that equal opportunity has not been prioritised (Turpin-Petrosino 2015). In relation to China, some have argued that the cultural practice of devaluing female infants fits the theoretical definition of hate crime but, as Turpin-Petrosino (2015) points out, the different dynamics of this practice outweigh the similarities with more accepted forms of hate crime.

A snapshot of hate crime perpetrators

Far more empirical research has been conducted on the experiences of hate crime victims than perpetrators. Yet, official statistics in some nations do provide basic demographic information about hate crime offenders who come to the attention of the criminal justice system and about the offences they commit. For example, data from the Crown Prosecution Service in England and Wales shows that in 2013–2014 (CPS 2014), the majority of defendants across all hate crime strands were men (83.9 per cent) and 70.5 per cent of defendants were identified as belonging to the White British category. Defendants between 25–29 years of age comprised 61.1 per cent and those 18–24 comprised 24.9 per cent (CPS 2014). The most commonly prosecuted crimes were offences against the person (52.4 per cent) and public order offences (31.4 per cent) (ibid.). Although broadly similar patterns for defendants can be seen between the Crown Prosecution Service data and the British Crime Survey data, a recent review of the international literature concluded that there is a lack of rigorous, evidence-based information on perpetrators of hate crime (Roberts *et al.* 2013). Many of the accounts that do exist are based on information collected from victims, so they do not provide adequate insight into individual offender perspectives or the socio-economic and psycho-social dynamics of perpetration (ibid.). Although there is some literature from the US to indicate that the socio-demographic profiles of hate crime offenders tend to match the demographics of the population of a given area (ibid.), data from Northern Ireland and London indicates that there is an over-representation of unemployed or economically inactive hate crime offenders. For example, of those prosecuted for sectarian offences in Northern Ireland, 25 per cent were unemployed, while 60 per cent of those accused of homophobic hate crimes in London were also unemployed (Iganski and Smith 2011).

While some case studies provide valuable insight into the psychological profile of individuals labelled as hate crime offenders (Gadd and Dixon 2012), there have been only a few systematic analyses of offenders at the collective level. US research has proposed a typology of hate crime perpetrators that divides them according to categories of motive: thrill, reactive (or defensive), mission and retaliatory crimes (Levin and McDevitt 1993; McDevitt *et al.* 2003). Thrill crimes are described as criminal behaviour 'set off by a desire for excitement and power' (McDevitt *et al.* 2003) and 'to stir up a little excitement' (Levin and McDevitt 1993). Reactive (or defensive) crimes consist of those where offenders feel threatened by outsiders encroaching on their 'community, means of livelihood, or way of life' (ibid.). Mission crimes are those in which the offender believes the victim is 'evil' and needs to be destroyed, often involving allegiance to a bias group or ideology (ibid.) and are said to be sparked by 'a desire to avenge a perceived degradation or assault on their group' (McDevitt *et al.* 2003). Retaliatory crimes referred 'specifically to incidents in which offenders act in response to a [real or perceived] hate crime' (ibid.). Roberts *et al.* (2013) argue that this categorisation is useful, in so far as it clarifies that hate crime offenders are not a homogenous category.

However, more recent attempts to replicate this typology have found that it cannot be generalised to the wider population of hate crime offenders (Phillips 2009). In a study of cases referred for prosecution by the New Jersey bias unit, Phillips found 30 per cent of cases were simply unclassifiable according to the typology, often because the bias did not seem to be the primary motivation for the crime (ibid.). The 'classic' portrayal of the hate crime offender has been a person motivated by some individual level of hostility or 'animus' to a group, attacking strangers perceived to represent that group (Roberts *et al.* 2013). This is a narrow portrayal which may hold true in some cases, but the literature makes it clear that the 'violent stranger' attack is not the modal form (Bowling 1999; Mason 2005; Roberts *et al.* 2013; Stanko 2001).

Hate crime in Australia

A number of government inquiries in the late 1980s and early 1990s exposed the problem of hate crime in Australia. In 1987, the Australian federal government initiated a royal commission into Aboriginal deaths in custody in an attempt to address the deplorable rate of mortality amongst Indigenous people in police lock ups and correctional centres (Royal Commission into Aboriginal Deaths in Custody 1991). One of the most significant findings of the commission was that the over-representation of Aboriginal people in all forms of custody was largely a result of alcohol-related street offences, rather than offences against persons or property (ibid.). Like other institutions, this finding implicated police in the reinforcement of the broader social subordination of Aboriginal people and undermined public perceptions of institutional legitimacy (ibid.). The royal commission was followed in 1990 by the National Inquiry into Racist Violence, conducted by the Australian Human Rights Commission, the first comprehensive exposure of the problems of violence on the basis of racial and ethnic identity (Human Rights and Equal Opportunity Commission 1991). The inquiry found that racism permeates the day-to-day lives of Aboriginal people and people from culturally or linguistically diverse backgrounds, such as Vietnamese and Arabic communities, either through direct acts of violence, intimidation and racist abuse, or through the processes of discrimination (ibid.). Evidence in the inquiry also suggested that racist violence against people from non-English speaking backgrounds usually takes the form of harassment and intimidation rather than physical assault (ibid.). Significantly, the inquiry heard much evidence that the police were often the perpetrators of this violence and racism.

The national inquiry recommended that the *Federal Crimes Act* be amended to create a new criminal offence of racist violence and intimidation, as well as a clearly identified offence of incitement to racist violence and racial hatred which is likely to lead to violence (ibid.). The inquiry also generated a number of recommendations for law enforcement, including the need to record and monitor racist violence so as to 'enable the extent of the problem to be more accurately understood' (Human Rights and Equal Opportunity Commission 1991). Further, it was recommended that statutory codes of practice be developed for police in relation to Aborigines and Torres Strait Islanders and people of non-English speaking background to ensure better protection of the human rights of these people (ibid.). Unfortunately, these proposals were largely ignored by police at the time (Cunneen 2009). In 1995, however, the federal government did amend the *Race Discrimination Act* to prohibit – but not criminalise – racial hate speech. In the context of concerns about far right activity and racist media commentary, a number of Australian states and territories also moved to introduce civil and criminal racial vilification laws, some of which have been extended to outlaw hate speech based on other characteristics such as religion, sexual orientation and transgender status (McNamara 2002). Subsequent research has provided compelling evidence of the problem of racist violence throughout Australia (Babacan *et al.* 2010; Cunneen *et al.* 1997; Cunneen and White 2002; Dunn *et al.* 2007; Fraser, Noble 2009; Melhelm and Yacoub 1997; Poynting and Noble 2004).

In the late 1980s, a number of community organisations also became active in documenting specific forms of targeted violence and hostility through self-report and victimisation surveys. For instance, the Executive Council of Australian Jewry started collecting statistics on anti-Semitic incidents, which now include data on physical attacks, abuse, harassment or intimidation, property damage, vandalism, graffiti and threats in emails, Facebook, postal mail, telephone, text, fax, leaflets, stickers and posters (Executive Council of Australian Jewry 2014). The 2014 Anti-Semitism Report demonstrated a 35 per cent increase in the overall number of reported anti-Semitic incidents over the previous year, suggesting that much of the increase was due to hostile media and other reactions to the 2014 Israel–Gaza war (ibid.).

Around the same time, the gay and lesbian community, particularly in New South Wales (NSW) and Victoria, also began documenting homophobic violence and discrimination through community victimisation surveys and self-reporting (Asquith 2004; Mason 1993; Tomsen 2010). These initiatives were a direct response to community concern about prejudiced and unresponsive policing. Surveys of these communities have consistently found that lesbians and gay men are significantly more likely to encounter abuse and violence compared to heterosexual men and women (Tomsen 2010). For example, more than half (56 per cent) of the respondents to a 2003 survey on homophobic abuse and violence reported having experienced one or more forms of abuse, harassment or violence in the past 12 months (NSW Attorney-General's Department 2003). Eighty-five per cent had at some time experienced such abuse, harassment or violence (ibid.). In their study of policing and the transgender community, Moran and Sharpe (2002) report on two victimisation surveys in NSW that found 'a very disturbing picture of public and domestic violence against transgenders', with approximately half of all respondents reporting physical and sexual assault, particularly amongst sex workers and, in some instances, by police (ibid.). The greatest factor in the under-reporting of transgendered violence appears to be an almost universal experience of negative police attitudes (ibid.). Moran and Sharpe conclude that bias against gender and sexual minorities within police culture and the criminal justice system more broadly gives form to harassment and intimidation by individual police officers (ibid.). Although disability hate crime has been documented in Australia (Sherry 2010), unfortunately there is little systematic research in this area.

Following the 2001 September 11 attacks in the US and the 2002 Bali bombings, a number of studies began to document the rise of ethnically motivated hostility towards Muslim and Middle Eastern Australians (a trend which had also been observed in the early 1990s in the context of the First Gulf War). The Australian Arab Council reported a twentyfold increase in reports of vilification of Arab Australians following September 11 (Poynting 2002), with women more likely than men to report racism, abuse or violence (HREOC 2004). Dunn (2003) found that residents living in particular regions in Sydney and Brisbane reported strong anti-Muslim sentiment, as well as an ongoing intolerance of Asians, Jews and Indigenous Australians. The depth of this sentiment was borne out in 2005 in what became known as the 'Cronulla riot', when several thousand people gathered on Cronulla Beach in Sydney to vent hostility towards young Lebanese men who were perceived to have been disrespectful towards 'Aussie icons', namely surf lifesavers. Although a subsequent inquiry by the NSW Police Force found that people were encouraged to go to Cronulla Beach to 'support "Leb and wog bashing day"' and that victims were selected for intimidation and violence because of their Middle Eastern appearance (Strike Force Neil 2006), many state and federal parliamentarians were quick to deny that racism was involved (Asquith 2015; Dunn 2009). For example, the then Australian prime minister, John Howard, stated, 'I do not accept that there is underlying racism in this country … yesterday's behaviour was completely unacceptable but I'm not going to put a general tag [of] racism on the Australian community' (NineMSN 2005). More recently, claims of racist violence against Indian nationals studying at tertiary institutions in Australia, particularly in the state of Victoria, attracted global condemnation in 2009, placing pressure on police and politicians to acknowledge the racial dimension of this victimisation, and generating a plethora of government interventions to protect Australia's international education industry (Mason 2012b). Although Victoria Police did acknowledge that Indian victims were over-represented in their complaint data, they initially rejected the claim that this was due to racial targeting (ABC News 2009), giving rise to community dissatisfaction that police were genuinely committed to guiding principles of procedural justice and human rights. In 2010, both Victoria Police and the Victorian Government were rebuked by the United Nations for ignoring the potential racial motivations behind the victimisation of Indian students in Australia (Flitton 2010).

Determining the prevalence of hate crime is always difficult and, although there is ample Australian research documenting the problem of hate crime, only a few studies have used official statistics or a population-based sample to examine such incidents. Tomsen (2002) found 74 anti-homosexual killings with male victims between 1990 and 2000. Most victims were middle-aged or older males, with perpetrators at least 10 years younger in 17 killings and 20 or more years younger in a further 25 homicides (ibid.). Many of these offences were notable for their 'exceptional brutality and the frenzied form of attacks, with victims tormented and wounded repeatedly' (ibid.). Mouzos and Thompson (2000) also examined gay hate-related homicides in NSW between 1989 and 1999. During this period, on average, they report that approximately four men were killed each year in attacks related to homophobia and masculinity (ibid.). The most likely cause of death for gay hate-related homicide victims was beating, whereas other male homicide victims most likely died of a stab wound, meaning that gay hate-related incidents were significantly more likely to involve a high level of brutality (Mouzos and Thompson 2000).

Other Australian research has focused on the differences in ethnically motivated victimisation. Using International Crime Victimisation Survey data, Johnson (2005a) found that, compared to the general population sample, the level of victimisation believed to be racially motivated was higher in the Middle Eastern and Vietnamese migrant populations. More recently, a rigorous study of crimes against international students conducted by the Australian Institute of

Criminology matched names and dates of birth from student visa information held by the Department of Immigration and Citizenship against police victim records for the years 2005–2009 (Joudo Larsen *et al.* 2011). Examining three key offence types – assault, robbery and other theft – the study concluded that, with some variations, international students – from India, China, Korea, Malaysia and the United States – 'are no more likely than Australian reference populations to be the victim of assault or other theft', and, in fact, 'were often less likely to be the victims of these crimes' (ibid.). However, the study *did* find that students from India were 'significantly more likely to be the victims of robbery compared with other international students and the Australian reference populations' (ibid.). This heightened vulnerability to robbery amongst male and female Indian students was explained, in part, by the fact that Indian students have a level of English proficiency which means they are more likely to find employment that comes 'with an increased risk of crime' (whether at work or while travelling to and from work), such as clerks in late-night convenience stores, attendants at service stations and as taxi drivers (ibid.). The authors of the study are clear, however, that their methods of analysis did not permit them to arrive at a conclusion as to whether the over-representation of Indian students as the victims of robbery could be attributed to racial motivations on the part of the offenders. A subsequent qualitative study of court decisions and media reports found compelling evidence of racially prejudiced elements in some crimes where Indian students were targeted (Mason 2012b). It also highlighted the far-reaching harm that the denial of racism by police and politicians inflicts on community confidence (ibid.).

Police–minority community relations: the challenge of policing hate crime

Crimes motivated by bias, prejudice or hate towards members of specific communities emerged as a pressing and public concern for police largely during the 1970s and 1980s (which we discuss in more detail in Chapter 3). Such crimes are said to require a distinct law enforcement approach, as it is not just the individual victim who experiences the harm but also the targeted community as a whole (ODIHR 2013; Perry 2010a). Existing community feelings of vulnerability, anxiety and anger can be amplified if police are reluctant to acknowledge and record the prejudicial element of victimisation (Mason 2012b; Perry 2001). Public statements of denial and deflection invalidate victims' experiences and generate a distrust of police and authority figures (Asquith 2015; HREOC 2004; Mason 2012b). Consequently, police and criminal justice agencies have invited regular criticism for failing to meet the expectations of targeted communities in terms of their immediate responses to individual incidents, the provision of support for victims and their groups, and long-term prevention. In the UK, for example, the Stephen Lawrence Inquiry (Macpherson 1999) has been identified as the most significant driver for the recognition of targeted victimisation (Giannasi 2014; Hall 2014) and much subsequent policy and statutory reform has been a response to the institutional failures and racism it exposed within the Metropolitan Police Service (Hall *et al.* 2015; Storry 2000).

Conceptual and practical issues plague effective policing of hate crime. The relative newness of this criminal category means that ambiguity can surround what actually constitutes a hate crime. Even where legislative reform has been transformed into hate crime policing policy, there is still considerable uncertainty at the operational level (Bell 2004; Cronin *et al.* 2007; Grattet and Jenness 2005, 2008; Nolan and Akiyama 1999; ODIHR 2013; Whine 2015). Although such policies constitute concrete operational plans through which law enforcement may become something more than symbolic – i.e. instrumental – specific agency and community variables shape the capacity of policy to encourage reporting and recording (FRA 2016; Grattet and Jenness 2008). This is compounded by the fact that policing authorities have not traditionally needed to recognise the group identity of victims nor the motives of perpetrators prior to recording incidents, making classification difficult. There is often a lack of detail included in police incident reports, as the type of data needed to record, track and understand hate crime is not typically collected by investigating officers. This can make it difficult to distinguish between hate crimes and so-called opportunistic crimes. Furthermore, hate crimes are not as common as many other types of crime, meaning that many operational police only undertake this process of identification sporadically (Cronin *et al.* 2007; Cunneen *et al.* 1997; Jenness and Grattet 2001; Stanko 2001). As a result of conceptual ambiguity and practical inexperience, police officers may apply a restrictive definition of prejudice motivated crime and submit potentially bias motivated crimes to a high level of scrutiny before recording (Cronin *et al.* 2007). This leads to under-recording as police tend to focus on the most extreme incidents and the most extreme perpetrators (Kielinger and Paterson 2007). Institutional attempts to address this by minimising police discretion in recording, for example, through policies that place identification solely in the hands of victims or witnesses, can lead to over-recording (Mason *et al.* 2015).

Under-reporting by victims is also prevalent (Asquith 2015; FRA 2016; Harlow 2005; Martin 1996; VEOHRC 2010), and this has a negative impact on the ability of police to understand and respond to hate crime. A 2010 study by the Victorian Equal Opportunity and Human Rights Commission, which we return to later in the book, found that 57 per cent of respondents who had experienced a prejudice motivated crime did not report the incident to a formal agency. Of those who did report, only 23 per cent reported to Victoria Police. Problems of under-reporting are also reflected in international studies. For example, European research suggests that there are many reasons people do not report hate crime to police, including a belief that reporting will not help. However, a lack of trust in police is one of the key reasons for under-reporting, particularly concerns that police will not be sympathetic and may share the discriminatory attitudes of offenders (FRA 2016). In the US, it has been found that two-thirds of hate crimes go unreported to police (Fathi 2013). As hate crimes in the US are frequently related to migrant populations, under-reporting also occurs due to fears of deportation (Johnson and Cuevas

Ingram 2012; Singh *et al.* 2013). Victims of hate crime fail to report incidents for other reasons; for example, gay victims may fear their situation might not be treated seriously by police, and they may also fear further stigmatisation because of their sexuality (Perry 2003a). It is difficult for police to understand tensions in the community when hostile incidents are under-reported, representing one of the greatest operational challenges (Giannasi 2014).

Historically, police have typically responded to targeted crimes as detached incidents (Bartkowiak-Theron and Asquith 2015; Bowling 1999), without recognising the broader societal context within which such incidents occur and the processes of discrimination through which they are experienced. This can lead police to believe they have responded effectively to a complaint, while leaving survivors feeling unprotected, unconvinced and frequently disillusioned by the law enforcement effort. For example, in the context of Canada, Perry (2010a) argues that there has been a persistent failure of police to protect men and women of colour from racial violence, particularly by declining to record, investigate or charge such complaints as racist offences. Such failures implicitly condone the violence itself.

Police–minority relations are further undermined when police are themselves implicated in civil rights abuses (FRA 2016; Johnson and Cuevas Ingram 2013; Kim 2011). In the wake of the Stephen Lawrence Inquiry, UK police services were encouraged to address comparable issues through the idea of 'policing according to need' rather than policing homogenously (Home Office Police Standards Unit 2005). A 2005 strategy produced by the Home Office Police Standards Unit and ACPO functioned as a 'comprehensive step-by-step … textbook' through which individual police services could 'revisit and develop their own policy approaches and tactical options' for policing hate crime based upon 'good practice' across England, Wales and Northern Ireland (Home Office Police Standards Unit 2005). Detailed tactical and practical guidance was provided to enable a holistic, enhanced and consistent approach to investigation, victim satisfaction, enforcement and prevention (ibid.). For example, police discretion in the recording of hate crime was minimised so that racist incidents would be recorded even when minor in the overall scheme of crime and disorder (Home Office Police Standards Unit 2005). More recently, on the heels of a cross-government action plan which further 'frees' police to work closely with their communities (UK HM Government 2012), national guidelines published by the UK College of Policing emphasise the role of community engagement in addressing hate crime, building positive relationships with various communities, providing liaison officers and awareness training for staff where relevant, and encouraging third-party reporting schemes for certain targeted groups (College of Policing 2014; see also the Welsh Government's Hate Crime Framework for Action 2014 and FRA 2016). While post-Macpherson legislative and policy changes are said to situate the UK 'at the international forefront of state responses to hate crime', significant obstacles remain (Giannasi 2015a), especially at the operational (Chakraborti 2009), resourcing (Williams and Tregidga 2014) and institutional (Bartkowiak-Theron and Asquith 2015) levels.

In effect, efforts at policing hate crime must, first and foremost, build enhanced relationships between the police and the diverse communities they serve, prioritising improved community perceptions of law enforcement (Perry 2010a). If police are to be effective in responding to hate crime, citizens must also be prepared to trust them; that is, they must have confidence that police can and will assist them (FRA 2016; Meli 2014; Singh *et al.* 2013). A significant predictor of victim and community satisfaction with the police is procedural justice. In terms of policing practices, procedural justice is characterised by: (1) neutrality – that is, transparency and consistency in police decision-making; (2) respect – citizens are treated by police with dignity; (3) trustworthiness – a belief in police as trustworthy and caring; and (4) voice – the ability for citizens to expressively participate in situations and for police to listen (Burke and Leben 2007; Murphy and Barkworth 2014; Tyler and Murphy 2011). In the absence of these key elements, victims and communities may consider they have been treated unfairly, leading to feelings of marginalisation and negative attitudes towards law enforcement. Cumulatively, victim and community perceptions of unfair or unfavourable treatment lead to a decreased willingness to engage with police (Murphy and Barkworth 2014; Tankebe 2013). In essence, there is a correlation between notions of procedural justice, fairness and trust (McKernan and Weber 2016) and victims' willingness to report hate crime to police (FRA 2016).

An enhanced response to targeted crimes and incidents thus requires police, partner agencies and community groups to work closely together to measure, define and better understand the size and nature of the problem (Bensinger 1992; Sandroussi and Thompson 1995). Prejudice-sensitive policing calls for procedurally fair strategies that are alive to the voices and human rights of marginalised and vulnerable communities as victims of crime (not just offenders) and that appreciate that individual forms of hate crime fall within a larger spectrum of diversity and vulnerability (Bartkowiak-Theron and Asquith 2015). This is essential both to address community perceptions of police indifference and bias, which can manifest in under- and over-policing, and to boost the protection of these communities in the face of hate crime. This book will explore ways in which the mobilisation and negotiation of common understandings of hate crime can help foster such police–community co-operation and trust.

Victoria Police and hate crime: introducing the research case study

Australia is a federation of eight states and territories. Although there is an overarching tier of government at the federal level, each jurisdiction has its own criminal law and law enforcement agencies. In the state of Victoria, policing is the responsibility of Victoria Police, commonly referred to as VicPol. All states and territories in Australia have distinct policies and statutes governing multiculturalism, equality, discrimination and human rights. Yet few of these policies directly address hate-motivated crime. In 2011, VicPol became the first

Australian police service to acknowledge the importance of a comprehensive and specific policy statement for the policing of prejudice motivated crime when it launched its Prejudice Motivated Crime (PMC) Strategy. The strategy, which we discuss in more detail in Chapter 4, addresses under-reporting of hate crime, focusing on individual victims and community responses, and adopts an integrated and coordinated approach to hate crime policing (Victoria Police 2010). Ultimately, it aims to reduce hate crime victimisation by improving police understanding and recording of PMC, and by increasing community trust in the police (Mason *et al.* 2014).

Other Australian police forces have initiatives and protocols that recognise and address prejudice motivated crime to varying degrees, but they have yet to introduce an all-round hate crime policy. For instance, New South Wales has a designed Bias Crime Unit and a set of Standard Operating Procedures but no public policy to match, relying instead on a range of more generic policies on multiculturalism, sexual diversity and Aboriginality. Some of these address hate crime by aiming to increase community reporting, enabling police to identify prejudice motivated offences, educating police to respond in culturally appropriate ways, and encouraging police to methodically record hate crime evidence (Asquith 2015). For example, the NSW Police Force's 'Priorities for working in a culturally, linguistically and religiously diverse society plan for 2011–2014' acknowledges the importance of monitoring hate crimes, particularly those involving racial, political or religious bias or in the context of counter-terrorism (NSW Police Force 2011b). The Queensland Police Service has its Multicultural Action Plan 2011–2012 to strengthen satisfaction with and confidence in the QPS amongst diverse communities. The action required to achieve this goal includes, amongst other things, 'enhanced investigations of alleged "hate crimes" and racially motivated incidents, including referral to the Anti-Discrimination Commission Queensland (ADCQ) as appropriate' (Queensland Government 2011a). The QPS Good Practice Guide for Interaction with Transgender Clients (Queensland Police Service 2011b) also promotes respect, equality and trust between members of the QPS and the transgender community. In short, law enforcement agencies in Australia have responded to targeted crime to varying degrees, but these responses are, at best, patchy.

In this environment, Victoria stands out as a suitable jurisdiction to form the case study for this book for several reasons. First, for more than a decade, VicPol has actively pursued community and neighbourhood policing strategies that facilitate closer engagement with local communities (Nixon and Chandler 2011). Much of this has been geared towards crime reduction and enhanced confidence and trust amongst vulnerable and marginal communities, who are not just the targets of victimisation but also implicated as offenders themselves (Fleming 2010; Pickering *et al.* 2008). Second, VicPol has a history of over-policing, racial profiling and brutality with racial minority communities, including the Indigenous, Asian and African communities, but also with the gay, lesbian and transgender populations (Cunneen 2001; Fitzroy Legal Service 2010; Flemington Legal Service 2013; Nicholls 2014). Third, it was only in 2011 that VicPol moved to formally introduce its PMC Strategy. This provided an opening to track the emergence of a new hate crime strategy in the policing domain and the impact of its mobilisation on community relations, particularly with minority communities likely to bear the brunt of targeted violence, some of whom have a long history of vexed relationships with police. Fourth, VicPol's decision to introduce the PMC Strategy was not mandated by the need to operationalise statutory offences. Unlike many jurisdictions where policing agencies have been the subject of academic research on hate crime (Bell 2002; Grattet and Jenness 2008; Hall 2014), there is effectively no specific offence in Victoria that police can use to charge hate crime offenders. The PMC Strategy thus might be understood as a show of good will towards minority communities, despite some serious deficits in policing–minority relations in Victoria. The absence of a legislative imperative surrounding this policy represents both a unique opportunity, in terms of the freedom it gives to police to define and construct the meaning of hate crime, and a unique challenge, in terms of the absence of legal or statutory guidance for such definitions. Finally, VicPol chose to adopt a distinctive vocabulary in the development of its strategy to address problems of targeted violence against racial, religious, sexual, disabled and comparable minorities, namely, 'prejudice motivated crime'. While concepts of hate crime, bias crime and targeted crime have all attained different degrees of currency in law enforcement agencies, as we discuss in Chapter 2, the term 'prejudice motivated crime' is far less common. On the one hand, it is a phrase that risks splintering into multiple and divergent meanings in the hands of different communities and institutions. On the other hand, it opens up a pathway for negotiating and advancing congruent perspectives around PMC with marginalised and vulnerable communities.

For all these reasons, Victoria and its law enforcement agency, Victoria Police, provides a fertile context for examining the complexities and nuances of initiating, interpreting and operationalising a hate crime policy in an environment that is conducive to the ideals of community policing and the principles of human rights but simultaneously cognisant of the realities of police–minority tensions.

As we explain further in Chapter 4, the research conducted for this book grew out of a partnership, beginning in 2009, between VicPol and the authors (funded by the Australian Research Council). In a period of significant public scrutiny around police–minority relations, most notably with regards to claims of racist violence against Indian students described above, VicPol sponsored the authors to conduct an independent research study into best practice for the policing of hate crime. As the project grew, VicPol launched its Prejudice Motivated Crime Strategy in 2011, and this strategy became a focal point for the project. Over the next few years, and taking a mixed-methods approach, we conducted the following empirical research:

- focus groups ($n=9$) and individual interviews ($n=5$) with a total of 53 participants from high-priority victim communities in Victoria, including African, Muslim, Jewish, Indian, LGBTI (Lesbian, Gay, Bisexual, Transgender and/or Intersex), Indigenous, migrant youth and homeless groups

- a survey of VicPol officers ($n=1609$) evaluating the impact of hate crime training on new recruits
- an analysis of 25 reported and unreported cases under sentencing legislation in Victoria and the two other Australian jurisdictions (New South Wales and the Northern Territory) that make comparable provision in their sentencing statutes for hate crime offences
- a time series quantitative analysis of the impact of VicPol's PMC Strategy on reporting
- 'exit' interviews ($n=3$) with key VicPol personnel on the implementation and impact of the PMC Strategy over the five-year period since it was launched.

This research provides the basis of the case study for this book. In most instances, chapters are organised around one of these discrete pieces of research, and further methodological detail is provided in each of the relevant chapters, with the exception of the exit interviews with VicPol personnel, which offer insider information pertinent to the whole book and can be found woven throughout different chapters.

From the beginning, VicPol recognised the importance of flexibility when attributing meaning to hate crime (Mason *et al.* 2012). As the PMC Strategy was rolled out, questions over how to define and understand prejudice motivated crime came to the fore. Interviews we conducted with senior VicPol personnel five years after the launch of the strategy reveal that the biggest challenge has been 'understanding what is … a PMC' and, more specifically, 'understanding the importance of listening' to communities who 'are still saying, "Well, we identify it; do you identify it?"' (Commander, Priority Communities Division, VicPol, interview 6 May 2016). The hurdles involved in arriving at an understanding of prejudice motivated crime that resonates with both targeted communities and front-line officers have had an impact on training, recording and investigation of hate crime in Victoria. Furthermore, achieving this 'consistency of message' continues to remain a key challenge in the policing of hate crime (Senior Operational Officer, VicPol, interview 6 May 2016) and thus a priority tactic for ensuring that 'the difference between community expectations and organisation expectations are minimised' (Commander, Priority Communities Division, VicPol, interview 6 May 2016). We adopt this challenge as the core organising principle for this book. We explore and critique the lessons learnt from VicPol's journey in working towards a common framework for understanding prejudice motivated crime, one that is shared and valued by those communities who are most vulnerable to targeted hostility.

Situated within a broad context of global criminological responses to hate crime, the VicPol case study that forms the backbone of this book has international significance. Policing represents an essential dimension of criminal justice strategies designed to tackle hate crime and has been the subject of some influential studies examining the operational implications of hate crime law and policy. In *Policing Hate Crime: Understanding Communities and Prejudice*, we seek to build on these by offering a multi-dimensional empirical analysis of the challenges facing law enforcement in this field. Defining and achieving mutual understandings of hate crime has been identified as one of these challenges (Giannasi 2015b). The Victoria Police case study offers lessons and insights into how law enforcement agencies might develop a shared framework amongst their own members and with their communities about the nature and significance of hate crimes and, in so doing, contribute meaningfully to social justice, human rights and legitimacy in the policing domain.

Overview of the book

Following this Introduction, Chapters 2 through 4 are designed to set the scene for our analysis of the empirical research, which we present in subsequent chapters. We begin in Chapter 2 with an examination of the diversity of terminology and meaning in hate crime policy and scholarship. Concepts such as hate crime, bias crime and targeted crime are in operation in different jurisdictions and often grounded in competing assessments of the merits and implications of each term. Sometimes such concepts are used interchangeably. Our concern here is the particular implications for policing of these different concepts. What are the impacts of the multiple understandings attached to these terms in different jurisdictions and contexts, especially when it comes to achieving a common framework between law enforcement agencies and communities? We explore the particular implications of terminology and meaning in the context of the PMC Strategy adopted by VicPol. We conclude that little is known about how different terms impact on the success of policing hate crime. Without a common, comprehensive and simple understanding of hate crime, it is difficult for policing agencies to track and monitor hate crime incidents across jurisdictions. For enforcement agencies and the communities they serve, such ambiguity undermines the potential for shared perspectives on hate crime, crucial for successful enforcement and the effective achievement of the objectives of hate crime legislation and policies.

Chapter 3 examines the mobilisation of hate crime law and policy through policing. Effective implementation of hate crime laws and policies requires that police identify, record, investigate and respond to such crimes in line with the provisions and intent of hate crime initiatives. The chapter focuses on the challenges that frequently impede the effective police implementation of hate crime protocols and examines the policing strategies deployed or recommended to overcome these challenges. It also considers the relevance and role of community policing and human rights frameworks in policing hate crime, critically evaluating the potential of these to support implementation of hate crime laws and policy by ameliorating the long-standing trust deficit between police and marginalised communities. In this chapter, we emphasise the utility and challenges of developing shared perspectives between police and communities about the significance and nature of hate crime.

Chapter 4 explains the case study, detailing a local policing response to the pressures raised by minority group experiences of crime and violence. It traces the legal, socio-economic and political drivers for the development and subsequent implementation of the Victoria Police Prejudice Motivated Crime Strategy through 2010. It sets out the aims and objectives of the strategy, the significance and implications of the adoption of the term 'prejudice motivated crime', and the nature and genesis of the research partnership between the authors and VicPol. It also locates the strategy within the context of Victoria Police's history of, and avowed commitment to, community policing and human rights, as well as ongoing controversy over police racism, prejudice and excessive use of force against minority communities.

Responses to hate crime are very much dependant on how it is conceptualised and what it is seen to encompass (Jacobs and Potter 1998). Yet, there is an absence of a universal language or agreed meaning across jurisdictions or between law enforcement agencies and targeted communities. Disturbingly, it is often those who most require the protection of relevant interventions that may have a limited understanding of the terminology. Having charted the introduction and use of the term 'prejudice motivated crime' by VicPol, Chapter 5 examines how high-priority community groups in the state of Victoria make sense of this new terminology. An integral part of our study involved focus groups and interviews with: migrant youth; the African community; homeless people; people with disabilities; Muslim women; the Jewish community; the Asian community; LGBTI people; and the Indigenous community. These respondents spoke of the importance of shared understanding and vocabularies in local contexts to suggest that the PMC terminology does not fully capture the nature of incidents, victims' experiences or the required criminal justice responses. The problems of terminology are important yet, as we assert throughout this book, a mutual language around hate crime must be accompanied by procedurally just treatment by police. In this regard, a critical issue that arose from the focus groups and interviews was the lack of trust between these marginalised communities and police. The effective policing of PMC incidents thus requires a shared understanding of the concept between police and high-priority communities, plus procedurally just policing practices to engender communities' and victims' confidence in reporting incidents driven by prejudice.

Hate crime laws and strategies rely on police for effective implementation. In the case of Victoria, police leaders have communicated a commitment to policing hate crime by developing the PMC Strategy. The effectiveness of the strategy depends largely on the willingness and ability of front-line police to adopt its core values and actively pursue its objectives. The barriers to this relate to the difficulty of recognising hate crime, the complexities of dealing with marginal communities, and the low priority such crimes often receive amongst operational police (Hall 2012). One challenging aspect is that police often perceive marginalised communities as potential offenders rather than as potential victims. Police training, then, is critical in overcoming entrenched prejudices that lead police to overlook or underplay hate crime as a serious policing issue. The aim of such training is to reinforce the imperative for officers to see hate crime as 'real crime' and to respond consistently and effectively to community expectations.

A second critical element of training is to communicate to operational police how to recognise, record and investigate hate crime. In this chapter, we consider how police make sense of hate crime and, more broadly, how it relates to perceptions of trust, respect, professional conduct and ethical training in the context of working with and providing services to diverse communities. Based on extensive survey material with over 1,500 new recruits, this chapter charts how officers understand prejudice motivated crime pre- and post-training. It examines how these understandings conflict with their own prejudices and influence their capacity to recognise and record hate crime. Chapter 6 exposes the challenges for police in delivering training that can demonstrate positive improvements in understandings of hate crime amongst front-line members.

For VicPol, generating a compatible understanding of prejudice motivated crime is key to addressing the under-reporting of relevant instances to the police. Despite the rollout of the strategy in 2011, there is a concern that under-reporting remains extremely common amongst victims. As we noted above, a study (2010) conducted by the Victorian Equal Opportunity and Human Rights Commission (VEOHRC), reveals that 57 per cent of respondents who had experienced a prejudice motivated crime did not report these incidents to any formal agency. Of those who did report, only 23 per cent reported the incident to Victoria Police. In Chapter 7, we employ time series modelling with aggregated monthly police incident information before and after the official rollout of the strategy to ascertain whether or not reporting has increased. Here, we focus on the influence of the strategy on reporting behaviours for different victim groups (for example, Australian-born, Aboriginal, Middle Eastern, Asian), prejudice motivations (like political beliefs, religion or physical features of the victim) and crime types (such as violence or property damage). This analysis shows that victims are more likely to report PMC events to police if they involve overt violence, such as assault, and if they are based on racial or ethnic prejudice. The seriousness of the offence is determinative of victims' reporting, so that low-level prejudice incidents are more likely to go unreported. This comes back to the problem of framing hate crimes as cumulative and longitudinal incidents whereas, despite the PMC Strategy, both victims and police still have a tendency to consider serious assaults in isolation from ongoing, low-level incidents. It is a key finding that VicPol's PMC Strategy has not influenced reporting behaviours. We canvas the possible reasons for the downturn in reporting and reinforce the need for victims and communities to, first, understand what PMC means and, second, trust police to record, investigate, prosecute and gather relevant information for the purposes of sentencing. Victims and marginalised communities value certainty and a meaningful response from police.

Chapter 8 focuses on the opportunities and limitations for policing hate crime in a jurisdiction where the absence of defined offences, and therefore of a prosecutorial imperative, means that the enactment of the PMC Strategy is an atypically proactive position for police. As our research with communities and key stakeholders showed, differences in meaning have effects on the success and value of hate crime strategies. Such differences also have significant implications for police as first responders and as the gatherers of the evidence necessary for recording and sentencing. After analysing the impact of these divergences, we propose that VicPol has an opportunity to respond to community perspectives by engaging in negotiation over the meaning of prejudice motivated crime. Working towards a shared understanding can help facilitate the implementation of the PMC Strategy, while acknowledging different perceptions of the problem in the eyes of law enforcement and targeted communities. We advance a series of flexible, rather than prescriptive, markers, based on existing Australian case law and expectations amongst vulnerable and marginalised communities, which can provide operational police with a practical guide for identifying PMC. We argue VicPol can build legally grounded but community-oriented markers to support a transparent framework for mediating an understanding between stakeholders about the nature and significance of prejudice motivated crime. Such transparency is necessary for minority communities to develop the confidence and trust in police that in turn will support reporting.

The development and implementation by VicPol of its strategy in 2011 provided a unique set of opportunities and challenges in relation to building trust and legitimacy with marginalised communities and enhancing social inclusion. In the concluding chapter of this book, we bring together the previous analyses by charting out a range of challenges and options for moving forward that are relevant, not just to policing in the state of Victoria but to international law enforcement agencies. Through our partnership with VicPol, we have sought to contribute insights that complement, rather than reproduce, existing policing guidelines from Europe, the UK and the US. Our research shows the need for operational police to 'dive deep' into their engagement with affected communities to develop a mutuality of understanding and collaboration. An effective dialogue requires authentic conversation – a process of law enforcement officers speaking *with*, not *at*, victims and vulnerable communities. It is impossible to enact cultural change without acknowledging the nature and source of the problem. Police need to be prepared to both name prejudice within their own ranks and use concepts and strategies that resonate with communities most vulnerable to group hostility. This does not require a singular or universal definition of hate crime, but it does require common meeting points in definition and conceptualisation that facilitate a mutual framework, yet one that is simultaneously capable of accommodating different perspectives. Policing hate is more than just recording, investigating and building a case for prosecution or sentencing. It must be procedurally just and victim-focused, and procedures must reflect an awareness of a victim's minority status. As relationships between minority groups and police are often strained and characterised by distrust, changing the way in which police engage with vulnerable groups more broadly, and their responses to targeted victimisation specifically, must be a priority for any policy initiative that is concerned with legitimating its response to hate crime.

Part II

Context for policing hate crime in Victoria

2 Hate crime terminology and meaning

Setting the scene

Introduction

Hate crime legislation and enforcement responses reflect the trend across Western societies towards 'particularizing protections against abuse' (Feenan 2006) for groups that are commonly perceived to be marginalised or especially vulnerable, with the broader objective of promoting values of tolerance, inclusion and human rights (see Mason 2009b). Yet hate crime policy and scholarship have been plagued by disagreements over terminology and meaning since their inception (Garland and Chakraborti 2012). Concepts such as hate crime, bias crime and targeted crime are and have been championed in different jurisdictions at different times amid a plethora of competing arguments about the merits and implications of each (Jacobs and Potter 1998; Jenness and Grattet 2001; Perry 2001; Hall 2013). Although the term 'hate crime' has gained the greatest traction, its meaning is specific to the socio-legal domain in which it is used (Iganski 2008); the term has therefore numerous definitions (Chakraborti 2015). Existing confusion and ambiguity surrounding the various definitions, however, have greater significance than a lack of 'clarity and uniformity' in the field (Brudholm 2015). These differences illuminate the difficulty of creating common meanings that can be shared by communities, governance structures and legislators. Such differences underpin variations in the type of legislation that is understood to address hate crimes effectively, and diversity and complexity in court interpretations in different jurisdictions (Mason 2014). This diversity and difference have particular implications for policing. Without a mutual, comprehensive and simple understanding of hate crime, it is difficult for policing agencies to track and monitor hate crime incidents across jurisdictions (ODIHR 2014); jurisdictional comparisons and enforcement responses are potentially compromised. The communal, expressive and symbolic purposes of hate crime legislation, central to the justification for the introduction of such legislation, cannot be realised when compatibility over what constitutes a hate crime between police forces and their local communities is lacking. In fact, one of the key informants in our study indicated that the greatest value of the Victoria Police PMC Strategy was to create a 'conduit' or pathway for communication and understanding. She argued this pathway could assist even where relationships between police and their communities were conflicted or uneasy (Senior Operational Officer, VicPol, interview 6 May 2016).

In this chapter, we examine the existence of competing and/or divergent hate crime terminologies, and the meanings attached to these terms, in a range of Western jurisdictions. Guided by our research findings, we begin to examine the implications for policing practice. We explore the way different terminological and legislative frameworks have developed and the critiques that exist of such concepts. One of our central concerns here is how contests between concepts such as hate, prejudice or hostility are translated first into shared or common social and legal understandings and then in turn into policing practices. Yet there is little direct research on how different terms operationally influence policing and enforcement approaches, and whether some terms, and the meanings they imply, better support the enforcement of hate crimes legislation objectives. This gap is significant given, as discussed in Chapter 3, many legislative and policing responses emerge in response to specific and horrifying incidents such as the death of Stephen Lawrence in the United Kingdom and of Matthew Byrd in the United States.

In the first section, we review the terms currently circulating to describe and define hate crimes and we link them to jurisdictions where they are the preferred terms. We explore the meanings attributed to different terminologies and how these perspectives shape the operation of legislation or policy in these jurisdictions. The chapter then examines the use of 'group' or 'identity' as a dominant mechanism to define hate crime (Mason 2015) and other contrasting discussions which emphasise violence against 'difference' as a better framework for understanding such crimes (Garland 2010, 2012; Perry 2001). Our interest is how such conceptual mechanisms link to both legislative and policing challenges in the hate crime context. What are the impacts of these multiple meanings and terms attached to 'hate crime' in different jurisdictions and contexts, especially in relation to achieving a needed common language between law enforcement agencies and communities? How do ideas about the identification of victims shape the meaning and impact of hate crime legislation, especially for the communities these schemas are designed to serve? Broad concepts such as hate crime can offer a collective framework that connects different forms of discriminatory violence, including racism, anti-Semitism, disablism and homophobia. But the utility of any term can only be assessed against the frameworks developed by lawmakers and, crucially, the extent to which they are shared between police and the communities with whom they interact. A negotiated perspective on hate crime terminology is critical; however, it must also align and interact with procedural justice measures to legitimate and engender trust in policing practices. A nexus between hate incidents and events reported, recorded, investigated and prosecuted is thus crucial for the effective and sustained operation of enforcement in this complex area and to help fulfil these procedural justice objectives. In the final section of the chapter, we focus specifically on the use of the term 'prejudice motivated crime' by the police force in Victoria, Australia. Exploring the development of policy language and its operation in terms of policing is a crucial stage in the processes of negotiating, building and assigning communal meaning and operational weight to hate crimes legislation. Yet, as we argue, little is directly known about how different terms and their meanings shape and influence policing and the effectiveness of enforcement responses.

Development of the concepts of hate crime, bias crime and targeted crime

> At first blush it might seem relatively easy to define a species of crime based upon prejudice or bigotry. Upon inspection, this is not at all the case. What is hate? What is prejudice? What prejudices transform ordinary crime into hate crime? How strong a motivating factor must the prejudice be? The answers to these questions determine the nature and extent of the problem.
>
> (Jacobs and Potter 1998)

Hate crimes are most often characterised as offences committed with a bias or prejudice motive and are not restricted to one particular form of criminal act. Many jurisdictions in developed Western nations now incorporate hate crime provisions into legislation (Bakalis 2015). Hate crimes range from acts of intimidation, to property damage, to violent assaults and murder. They are a conceptual type of crime rather than a specific offence, the key distinguishing factor being the motive of the perpetrator (ODIHR 2009), although the extent to which an offender's hateful or prejudiced motive is an explicit and necessary element in hate crime laws varies considerably between jurisdictions. Hate crimes are also 'message' crimes that may seek to fracture or divide communities (ODIHR 2014). As Perry has observed, the effect of such a crime 'reaches into the community to create fear, hostility and suspicion' (2003a). The determining aspect of a hate crime, therefore, is arguably its meaning, both in terms of the intent of the offender and the impact(s) on the victim(s) and connected communities.

Mason (2015) examines the global evolution of hate crime laws, as well as contemporary legislative responses and interventions. She finds that there are broad discernible patterns in law reform that suggest a strengthening of hate crime discourse and responses (ibid.). Mason (2009a) identifies three models that serve to capture key features of hate crime laws across jurisdictions: the penalty enhancement model; the sentence aggravation model; and the substantive offence model. However, she points out that the 'multiple, contradictory and shifting ways in which law articulates hate crime' (Mason 2015) underpin the contingent nature of the concept itself and lead to inconsistent enforcement responses internationally. In addition, the models for legislation do not exhaust the models of policing and enforcement practice that evolve in relation to such models. In the following discussion, we explore the diverse conditions and contexts for defining these types of crimes as they have developed across Western jurisdictions. We examine some of the extant contests over creating categories of crime related to hatred or bias and how these contests produce differing terminologies, legislative outcomes and enforcement schemas. For each of the dominant terms – hate, bias and prejudice – we offer a key definition, an outline of jurisdictions where the term is used, and thoughts on how terminologies and their underlying meanings, whether shared or not, might be understood to influence policing.

'Hate crime'

> The question of 'what is hate crime?' is fraught with difficulties. Like other crimes, hate crime is a social construct, but there is no consensus amongst academics, policy-makers or practitioners about what hate crime actually is.
>
> (Hall 2005)

Coined by the anti-hate crime movement in the United States in the 1980s (Hall 2005; Jacob and Potter 1998; Jenness 2001, 2002; Whine 2015), the term 'hate crime' generally refers to the perpetration of violence that is 'motivated by prejudice, bias or hatred towards a particular group of which the victim is presumed to be a member' (Mason 1993). The European-based Office for the Democratic Institutions and Human Rights (ODIHR) defines hate crime as 'a criminal act committed with a bias motive' (Chakraborti 2015; ODIHR 2009, 2014). In this respect, and as described by Jacobs and Potter (1998), it can be argued that hate crime 'is not really about hate, but about bias or prejudice'. The motive or element of hate may be based upon the victim's nationality, ethnicity, religion, gender, sexual orientation, physical disability, mental disability or other factors, thereby locating a victim within a specific population. Hate crimes are generally understood to arise from motivations that are linked to or 'based on a characteristic that represents a deep and fundamental part of a shared group identity' (ODIHR 2014). As is immediately apparent, common definitions of hate crime itself rely on other terms, such as bias and prejudice that are used alongside and sometimes interchangeably with hate crime. These interlinking definitions contribute to the complexities in the field of law enforcement and to the challenges of developing shared or mutual perspectives.

It is commonly accepted in hate crimes discourse that the individual victim may not be significant to the perpetrator except as a member of the targeted group (Mason 1993; Morgan 2002; ODIHR 2009; Perry 2001). As such, hate crimes not only achieve individual victimisation but are understood to inflict secondary harm upon the broader community of which the victim is a member (Lawrence 1999). Hate crimes thus affect both the victim and the victim's community and may be described as 'symbolic crimes' (ODIHR 2009). As we shall later discuss, however, such elements are also routinely attributed to other dominant terms in this area such as bias and/or prejudice crimes.

The term 'hate crime', although 'firmly entrenched in contemporary discourse on crime' (Mason 2005) has been critiqued for a wide range of reasons (Hall 2005; Iganski 2008; Perry 2003a, 2010b; Ray and Smith 2001; Stanko 2001; Sullivan 1999). Some critiques suggest that the term 'hate crime' has become too broad and problematically assumes violent and pathological elements in the offence and the offender. The term might be misconstrued as suggesting that hate itself is the crime, whereas it is the behaviour motivated by emotions or attitudes including hate, prejudice or bias that constitute the offence. As Ray and Smith argue (2001) the term 'encourages a view of racism and violence as the result of the presence of pathological individuals, rather than as embedded in institutional practices and offending communities'. It has also been identified as dramatising offending behaviour (Iganski 2008; Perry 2003a; Ray and Smith 2001), as simplifying the causes of offending (Hall 2005) and, in particular, as implying that strangers are the perpetrators rather than persons known to the victim (Stanko 2001). As Mason (2005) has suggested, such assumptions can influence what incidents or events are accepted and understood as hate crimes, which may in turn impact policing and enforcement. There is considerable empirical research that reveals that, in many racist incidents, relationships between victims and perpetrators are not easily characterised as either one of strangers or one of familiars (Mason 2005; see also Bowling 1999).

More recently, Perry has argued persuasively for the need to expand accounts of hate crime beyond individual incidents and events. Perry's framework recognises societal oppressions and power dynamics that 'other' marginalised communities and reinforce hegemonies (Chakraborti 2015; Perry 2015). She argues that hate crimes are a critical way of 'doing difference' – that is, regulating raced, sexed and gendered differences – in contemporary societies. Perry defines hate crime as follows:

> It involves acts of violence and intimidation, usually directed toward already stigmatized and marginalized groups. As such, it is a mechanism of power, intended to reaffirm the precarious hierarchies that characterize a given social order. It attempts to recreate simultaneously the threatened (real or imagined) hegemony of the perpetrator's group and the 'appropriate' subordinate identity of the victim's group.
>
> (Perry 2001)

For Chakraborti, Perry's 'conceptual framework is arguably the most influential' discourse in contemporary hate crime scholarship (2015).

Jurisdictional use of 'hate crime'

The term 'hate crime' is used consistently throughout the UK by the Home Office, Crown Prosecution Service (CPS), Victim Support (London), South Wales Police, ACPO, National Offender Management Service and the London Metropolitan Police Service (MPS). Across these platforms, common elements of the definition focus on motivation and perceptions of prejudice.

> A Hate Crime is defined as:
> Any hate incident, which constitutes a criminal offence, perceived by the victim or any other person, as being motivated by prejudice or hate.
>
> (ACPO 2005)

In the UK, a distinction is drawn between a 'hate incident' and a 'hate crime'. The former are any incidents that are perceived by the victim or any other person to be motivated by prejudice or hate, while the latter are confined to those incidents that are also criminal offences. A hate incident is defined as:

> any incident, which may or may not constitute a criminal offence, which is perceived by the victim or any other person, as being motivated by prejudice or hate.
>
> (Home Office 2005; Williams and Tregidga 2013)

Police in the UK are required to collect comprehensive and robust data on *both* hate incidents and crimes (Home Office Police Standards Unit 2005).

There has been continued recognition in the United Kingdom of the need for a clear understanding and robust definition of hate crime (ACPO 2005). Most recently, the 2005 ACPO Hate Crime Manual was replaced by the 2014 College of Policing National Strategy and Operational Guidance. In this document, hate crime is defined as follows:

> A hate crime is any criminal offence, which is perceived, by the victim or any other person, to be motivated by a hostility or prejudice based on a person's race or perceived race/religion or perceived religion, sexual orientation or perceived sexual orientation/disability or perceived disability/transgender identity or perceived transgender identity.

In common with earlier definitions of hate crime, the Home Office continues to refer to 'any criminal offence which is perceived, by the victim or any other person, to be motivated by hostility or prejudice towards someone based on a personal characteristic' (Home Office 2013–2014). As is evident in the above outline, five strands of hate crime are recognised in England and Wales: race or ethnicity; religion or beliefs; sexual orientation; disability; and transgender identity (Clement *et al.* 2011; Home Office 2013–2014; 2014).

Each of these definitions contains considerable detail, while maintaining a focus on crimes or incidents that are perceived by the victim to be 'motivated by a hostility or prejudice based on' one of key areas (for example, a person's disability) that have been cited as monitored strands (2014). The Leicester Hate Crime Project (2014), however, defines hate crime more broadly than the College of Policing, as 'acts of violence, hostility and intimidation directed towards people because of their identity or perceived "difference"'. In this way, the project seeks to 'capture acts of hate, prejudice and targeted hostility directed towards *anyone*, from *any background*' (ibid.). This emphasis on 'difference', rather than group identity, as the ground for defining hate crime is one that Garland (2010, 2012) and Chakraborti (2015), as noted above, have identified as a much-needed development in hate crimes discourse and criminal justice responses. We will return to this point towards the end of the chapter.

Williams and Tregidga have examined the 'patchwork' of UK legislation relevant to the five identified strands: disability, race, religion, sexual orientation and transgender: the Crime and Disorder Act 1998 for racial and religious aggravated crimes; the Public Order Act 1986 for incitement; and the Criminal Justice Act 2003 for aggravated sentencing in relation to disability, sexual orientation and transgender identity (2014). In their study, the All Wales Hate Crime Research project, they adopted the 2005 ACPO definition (Williams and Tregidga 2013) and found there was a considerable 'disjuncture' between victim-centred reporting processes and evidence-driven criminal prosecution procedures (2013, 2014). For Williams and Tregidga, this gap emphasised the challenges in using the words 'hate' and 'crime', as many respondents in their victimisation study felt that 'hate' did not reflect their experience and were also unsure as to whether the incident was a 'crime' worthy of being reported to police (2014). As will become apparent when we analyse the data drawn from our Victorian study, these divergences between the victimisation experienced, how it is understood by victims, communities and police, and the legislative framework are of crucial importance in understanding policing responses and the overall effectiveness and value of such instruments. The current approach in the UK (Home Office 2014) clearly identifies the perception of the victim as the crucial element in defining the hate crime, in line with Recommendation 12 of the Stephen Lawrence Inquiry report (Macpherson 1999) where the 'defining factor' in identifying a hate incident is the 'perception of the victim or any other person'. Operationally, the UK response does recognise that 'hate' itself may not be a necessary part of a hate crime and that the lack of evidence of a prejudicial motive is not relevant in recording or responding to the incident as a hate crime or incident (Home Office Police Standards Unit 2005). Moreover, as the ODIHR (2014) also points out, the prejudiced assumption by a perpetrator does not need to be based in fact: i.e. a mistake about the ethnic origin of a selected victim will not exculpate the offender. In such definitions, where perception is central, the importance of shared meanings is therefore embedded in policy and has significant impact.

The requirement to record hate incidents as well as hate crimes, and the centrality of the perception of the victim in assigning meaning and effect, are clearly reflected in the London Metropolitan Police Service where a 'hate incident' is defined as '[a]ny incident that is perceived by the victim, or any other person, to be racist, homophobic, transphobic or due to a person's religion, belief, gender identity or disability' (MPS 2013). Although this definition is not confined to incidents or crimes *motivated* by prejudice, the policy does encourage staff to identify underlying motives related to elements, such as race and religion, that may not be initially apparent. In our view, such requirements point simultaneously to the importance of compatible perspectives about the commission of 'hate' offences and the numerous different viewpoints and stakeholders that are necessarily involved in experiencing, recording, investigating and prosecuting such offences in the UK. These complexities are evident in other jurisdictions, too.

The centralised European approach uses hate crime terminology: at this level, the term has gained acceptance and understanding (ODIHR 2009, 2014). The

ODHIR defines hate crimes as having two key elements: the commission of a criminal offence and the deliberate targeting of a person belonging to a group against which the perpetrator feels bias or prejudice (ODHIR 2010). Garland and Chakraborti (2012) identify this as a progressive definition since it offers a broader platform than a requirement for a clear manifestation of 'hate'. However, they contend that, generally, the EU responses are characterised by the 'absence of a shared transnational understanding of what it actually is' (2012). This absence of shared perspective contributes to a failure to develop legislation that reflects or embeds the wider framework of hate crime. They outline very significant divergences in how different EU member states understand hate crime, what types of hate crime they police, and the priority assigned to hate crime enforcement, with some states requiring hate to be a primary motivation. They suggest in the main that the term hate crime lacks currency and clarity in the EU and that extant variations in data, definition of offences and policing create a confusing and complex context. In particular, they identify the different requirements for 'hate' as a central element of offences in some member nations as contributing to this confusion and to the lack of an effective 'hate crime umbrella' in the EU.

This observation about the diversity in how 'hate' is mobilised in many EU countries is reflected in academic disagreements about this term. As noted earlier, many consider 'hate' a misleading word – hate crimes may be motivated by anger, resentment, jealousy, peer group conformity, or hostility to 'others' or to ideas such as immigration. Perry (2003a) powerfully argues that these crimes are driven by the desire to maintain hierarchical relations of domination between groups based on bias and prejudice. It is for this reason that the ODIHR emphasises the value of the broader word 'bias' (2009), following the lead of many scholars who have observed that hate crime is less about hate and more about bias or prejudice (Jacobs and Potter 1998; Mason 2001; Perry 2003a). For example, McDevitt and his colleagues (2010) argue that hate is absent from the majority of so-called hate crime incidents. Brudholm considers that 'hate crime' is a misnomer, as 'hate' fails to 'capture something common to *all* conceptions of the crimes in question' (2015). In this approach, such incidents are best understood to stem from prejudices, or 'negative feelings held by the offender towards a social group that, in their eyes, have an "outsider status"' (Garland and Chakraborti 2012). The term 'hate' can therefore diminish rather than enhance understanding and the compatibility of frameworks.

Beyond the UK and Europe, hate crime terminology is used by the Toronto Police Service, the FBI, the US Department of Justice and the New Zealand Police. In Canada, the Criminal Code refers to hate, bias and prejudice as grounds for aggravated sentencing (s. 718). The concurrent use of all these terms is yet another indication of the variability and complexity of terms and meanings in the hate crimes field. In Australia, 'hate' is used by the South Australian Police and is referred to briefly in the Queensland Police Service Multicultural Action Plan (2011a) and by the Victorian Department of Justice (2010) in their Review of Identity Motivated Hate Crime in Victoria.

In the following section, we discuss the concept of bias crime and how it links to the hate crime definitional questions that we have already raised, as well as points of difference between the two.

'Bias crime'

The preceding discussion makes it clear that extant discussions, definitions and legislative schemas of 'hate' crime rely on concepts of both bias and prejudice, implicitly and explicitly. The terms 'bias crime' and 'hate crime' share similar histories, having both been coined in the United States during the 1980s, largely in response to a perceived emergence of violence directed specifically at homosexual, African American and Jewish populations (Green *et al.* 2001). As Green *et al.* (2001) note, this term emerged in conjunction with 'hate crime', indicating the common antecedents of the terms, and some argue that, within the US, bias crime is used interchangeably with 'hate crime' (Perry 2010b). In the US, where the term 'bias' is most prevalent, the FBI emphasises the need to objectively ascertain evidence that a bias crime is 'a committed criminal offense that is motivated, in whole or in part, by the offender's bias(es) against a race, religion, disability, sexual orientation, ethnicity, gender, or gender identity' (2015).

Those commentators utilising 'bias' as the preferred term argue that it promotes significant focus on the perpetrator's bias towards the victim (Iganski 2008; Lawrence 1999; Perry 2010b), which distinguishes it from the victim perspective that is emphasised in UK hate crimes frameworks. As Lawrence (1999) puts it, 'the key factor in a bias crime is not the perpetrator's hatred of the victim … but rather his [or her] bias or prejudice toward that victim'. This distinction is apparent in many of the statutory models in the US, which focus on prohibiting and punishing the offender's biased *conduct* in selecting victims from a particular group (commonly referred to as a group or discriminatory selection test), rather than his or her hateful *expressions* or *thoughts* (commonly referred to as a group animus test). Phillips and Grattet (2000) observe that 'bias' can both extend and expand the reach and meaning of hate crimes laws, since hate does not need to be present, thus bringing into view a wider range of actions. Perry agrees, suggesting that 'bias crime' is clearly preferable to the term 'hate crime' (2003a). The term 'hate crime' has a 'dramatic ring to it': it tends to suggest that these crimes are committed by 'pathological individuals', thus diverting social and enforcement attention from the extent to which the individuals who commit 'hate crimes' are influenced by dominant social attitudes (Perry 2003a). Yet, as Ignaski observes, while 'bias' appears to be a less emotive term than 'hate', its meaning is arguably equally ambiguous (2008). He makes the same criticism about the term 'prejudice', to which we will return when we discuss the Victorian legislation.

Jurisdictional use of 'bias crime'

The term 'bias crime' is predominantly used in the United States, where there are a range of legislative schemas encompassing both penalty enhancements and substantive offences (Mason 2015). The FBI's Hate Crime Data Collection Guidelines and Training Manual provides detailed definitions of various biases (2015); the associated Uniform Crime Reporting Program collects data regarding offences motivated by a bias against 'race, religion, disability, sexual orientation, ethnicity, gender, or gender identity' (FBI 2015). These definitions include non-violent offences such as the destruction of property, harassment of persons and trespassing, as well as violent criminal acts motivated by bias (FBI 1996; Green *et al.* 2001; Lawrence 1999). Despite the limited use of the term 'bias crime' outside the US, it is notable that the abstract concept of hate does not actually appear much in 'hate crime' legislation: generally, less extreme terminology is favoured, such as 'prejudice', 'hostility', or 'because of' attestation (i.e. the crime is committed 'because of' the victim's race, ethnicity or so on) (Mason 2013).

In Australia, the NSW Police Force has a Bias Motivated Crime Unit and defines bias crime as

> a criminal offence motivated against persons, associates of persons, property or society that is motivated, in whole or in part, by an offender's bias against an individual's or group's actual or perceived; race, religion, ethnic/national origin, sex/gender, gender identity, age, disability status, sexual orientation or homeless status.
>
> (2014)

Hate crime and bias crime are the most recognisable terms applied to crimes in which victims are targeted because of their attributes. Yet many scholars and activists (see in particular Hall 2005; Ignaski 2008; Perry 2005) recognise that both these terms, and the variability of associated meanings, import ambiguity and complexity into the field. For this reason there have been a number of other suggested terms that we canvass below, with 'targeted violence' emerging as one key option.

'Targeted violence'

As an alternative to London Metropolitan Police's use of the term 'hate crime', and reflecting on her experiences of the limitations and problems associated with policing hate crimes, Stanko prefers the term 'targeted violence'. She poses that targeted violence

> ... implies that an assailant *chooses* to hurt a particular individual in the way that assailant *can* do (1) because of who the victim 'is'; (2) because the assailant can rely on the available resources ... to do so; and (3)

because the assailant retries popular discourses that assist in justifying that such actions are legitimate in the eyes of some portion of the population.

(2001)

Stanko argues that in contrast to other terms that are in wide circulation such as hate and bias, targeted violence recognises both the vulnerability of the victim and the significance of the perpetrator's choice of that victim because of their perceived vulnerability. This attention to both the victim and the perpetrator has the potential to widen the scope and definition of hate crime as it allows for a more nuanced and meaningful account of relationships between parties. As Mason (2005) has noted there are often assumptions about hate crime as a form of 'stranger danger', whereas many racist and homophobic incidents reveal an existing community or social connection in the commission of the offence. Perry too supports this term:

> targeted violence ... allows us to recognise that racial or gendered or anti-immigrant violence ... are nested in a structural complex of relations of power ... [They are] ... embedded in the norms, practices and institutions that characterise our daily realities.

(2010b)

Garland and Chakraborti (2012) also stress the utility of this notion of targeting, suggesting that 'targeted victimization' is helpful in focusing on individuals and their perceived 'outsider' status, rather than on group identities. In the notion of targeting, meaning is developed in the context of the social relationships between individuals and the communities in which they live. This issue of individual and group identities is crucial, as we shall later see, to how communities and police services interact around the notion of hate crime, prejudice and effective enforcement.

Jurisdictional use of 'targeted crime'

In some cases, the term 'targeted crime' is used by UK police services. It has been mobilised in relation to the victimisation of people with disabilities (Sin *et al.* 2009), as well as in relation to the victimisation of members of subcultures identified as 'alternative', such as 'goths' (Garland 2010). However, in comparison to other terms, there is very limited use of 'targeted violence' and 'targeted crime' by academics, in policing or in legislation.

Prejudice Motivated Crime (PMC) Strategy

The final term we examine is 'prejudice'. Although prejudice is almost universally identified as central in understanding hate crime, Australian jurisdictions and policing services have been amongst the few who have taken up this term.

In particular, the VicPol strategy uses this term to define central elements of hate crime offences.

Prejudice motivated crime is defined by VicPol's PMC Strategy (2010) as a

> … criminal act which is motivated (wholly or partly) by hatred for or prejudice against a group of people with common characteristics with which the victim was associated or with which the offender believed the victim was associated. Characteristics include: religious affiliation, racial or cultural origin, sexual orientation, sex, gender identity, age, impairment (within the meaning of the *Equal Opportunity Act* 1995), or homelessness.

While prejudice is commonly recognised as a central element of hate crime and appears in many of the legislative schemas addressing hate crimes including some of those that we have cited above, the term attracts the same criticisms as do many of the terms in this field. Jacobs and Potter (1998) argue that prejudice is a 'complicated, broad and cloudy concept' (see also Hall 2005; Ignaski 2008); meanings attributed to such a term can be generic, either expansive or narrow, and are profoundly influenced by complex psychological and social debates. In highlighting these definitional problems, Jacobs and Potter (1998) argue thus:

> If prejudice is defined narrowly, to include only certain organized hate-based ideologies, there will be very little hate crime. If prejudice is defined broadly, a high percentage of intergroup crimes will qualify as hate crimes … in other words, we can make the hate crime problem as small or large as we desire by manipulating the definition.

Yet such a criticism is applicable to all terms that are used in defining and addressing hate crimes, as we have noted in our discussions of both hate and bias. Brudholm, by contrast, who suggests that the concept of hate is not useful, argues that the concept of prejudice may be preferable as it 'accommodates a range of group-directed antipathies' and is 'conceptually tied to … general antipathies that are irrational and morally unjustifiable' (2015). He observes:

> Sometimes, the violence is intended to send a hostile symbolic message to entire groups, but not always. Sometimes the acts are planned or systematic. Other times they take place in the heat of a moment, 'when the situational context provides the opportunity, or when it provides a trigger'. Victims are typically targeted on the basis of socially salient prejudices and thus belong primarily (not exclusively or necessarily) to minority groups.
>
> (Ibid.)

For Brudholm, the term 'prejudice' captures this wider and nuanced range of intents and contexts in the commission of hate crime offences and thus has greater descriptive and explanatory power. It offers a broad and inclusive platform for multiple meanings and may therefore enhance the likelihood of congruent understandings.

Jurisdictional use of 'prejudice motivated crime'

The term 'prejudice motivated crime' is used by VicPol, Tasmanian Police Force and, at times, the NSW Police Force, all of which are in Australia. VicPol is currently the only policing jurisdiction to consistently use the term to refer to offending within the hate crimes field. The reasons for this preference are unclear, although it seems the term was adopted because the relevant existing Victorian legislation used this term (including the *Racial and Religious Tolerance Act 2001* and a new provision of the *Sentencing Act 1991*, s. 5(2)(daaa) – both of which address hate crimes). In the other Australian policing jurisdictions using the term (Tasmania Police and the NSW Police Force), 'prejudice' is used interchangeably with other terms, including 'hate crime' and 'bias crime'. NSW Police define a prejudice motivated crime as 'a criminal act which is motivated, at least in part, because of someone's bias or hatred of a person's or group's perceived race, religion, ethnicity, sexual orientation or gender identity' (NSW Police 2012). The force does make reference to 'homophobic prejudice motivated crime' (ibid.) as well as homophobic violence, discrimination and vilification (NSW Police 2011a). However, as noted above, it has endorsed the term 'bias crime' to lead its policy and public-relations work in this area. The Tasmania Police (2011) refers to both 'prejudice motivated crime' and 'hate crime' as a 'criminal act carried out, at least in part, because of someone's bias or hatred of a person or group's perceived sexual orientation, gender identity, race, religion or ethnicity.' The Queensland Police Service investigates 'prejudice-motivated offences' and vilification (2011b), as well as 'hate crimes' and racially motivated incidences (2011a).

Two elements are worth noting about the definition of prejudice motivated crime offered in the VicPol PMC Strategy. First, it requires that a criminal offence has been committed. Second, it hinges on motivation that is driven by the offender's hatred or prejudice, whether wholly or partly. Evidence of the offender's motive does not lie at the heart of all policies designed to address comparable problems in other jurisdictions, as has been apparent in our exploration of other terms and other jurisdictions. The UK, as outlined above, emphasises the perception of the victim as central to identifying both hate crimes and hate incidents. Moreover, while legislative definitions in England and Wales do include a motive test, at a minimum it is only necessary for an offender to *demonstrate* hostility towards the victim on the grounds of one of the five protected attributes. Although US policies emphasise the element of bias, most legislative definitions do not, as noted above, come to rest on evidence of a biased motive but, rather, on a biased form of conduct on the part of the offender in selecting victims from protected groups. The ODIHR in Europe does refer to motive as a defining feature of hate crime but, in practice, it goes on to translate this to a group selection approach comparable to that found in many US states. Most EU member states operate with a diverse set of premises and perspectives that are not readily systematised (Garland 2012; Garland and Chakraborti 2012).

It is therefore clear that the terminology adopted to strategise against hate crime is not necessarily directly tied to the chosen legislative model or indeed to the ways in which victims and protected populations are included in different hate crimes approaches. The meanings in circulation further complicate the terrain. While the variation in terminology defining hate crimes is not optimal, in our view and emerging from our work with the VicPol Force, it is the convergence, or lack thereof, in shared or mutual understandings of how victims are identified, how they perceive and experience the incident, and how such events are recorded and investigated that is central in the value, validity and operational success of hate crimes frameworks. In the next section of this chapter, we look at the centrality of victim groups to the concept of hate crime and their significance in addressing the symbolic, expressive and community objectives of hate crimes legislation. The issues raised in relation to victim groups around the need for, and lack of, common meanings cut across all of the four concepts we have discussed above.

Identifying the victim: communities, relationships and hate crime provisions

A key defining aspect of all hate crimes is the victim, since it is the characteristics of the victim, and the potential inter-changeability of that victim for others belonging to the same social grouping, that are largely recognised as constituting the ground for the offence (ODIHR 2009). As such, it has been claimed that 'hate crime is generally directed towards a class of people; the individual victim is rarely significant to the offender' (Mason 1993). This is the key claim on which many hate crimes are identified as 'message crimes'. The victim's personal traits are subordinate to their membership of a community despised by the assailant (Garland 2012; Perry 2015) and this is ground on which it is said that the crime affects and threatens all members of that group. But, as Stanko observes, while 'vulnerability is thus collective, experienced by a group ... the spaces within these groups can be very wide indeed' (2001). These tensions between group and individual experiences, and how they relate to offender perceptions and behaviour, are part of the complexity of crafting and enforcing hate crime legislation that is meaningful for all stakeholders. Garland and Chakraborti raise the question of whether 'offenders target potential victims because of their membership of despised "outgroups", irrespective of who they are as individuals, or whether many offenders, at least to a degree, actually know their victims' (2012). They remind us that scholars and practitioners are divided on whether the legitimate victims of hate crime are only those minority groups who are the objects of historical and structural disadvantage, or whether a member of any community is deserving of the same legal protection (ibid.). Although there is much acceptance by police and advocate groups of the collective impact of targeted crime – 'any attack or threat against one is a violation against all' (Stanko 2001) – there is considerable and consistent debate and, in some cases, disagreement about what populations should be included as a 'vulnerable population' or a 'protected group'.

Indeed, as Stanko (ibid.) argues, the definition, identification and protection of particular victim groups has been one of the most contentious and complex aspects of hate crimes. Since its conceptualisation in the 1980s, there has been considerable variance in which groups are recognised as protected across jurisdictions and legislative instruments (Shaw 2002). While race and ethnicity were included in early hate crime instruments in most jurisdictions, sexuality, gender, age and disability have been more contentious (Gelber 2000; Maher *et al.* 2015; Mason-Bish 2013). Morgan (2002) argues that variances in the inclusion or exclusion of particular groups of people within hate crime legislation are often reflective of broader political influences and social movements at the time, including the likelihood that identified groups will attract policing and community support (see Morgan 2002 and Mason 2009a for discussion of groups such as sex workers and paedophiles). Chakraborti writes that the enumeration of protected groups is shaped by individual state histories, so that countries including Germany, Austria and Italy relate hate crime to right-wing elements and anti-Semitism, while hate crime responses in the UK grew from negative reactions to mass migration (2015). In most jurisdictions, characteristics to be protected are thus spelt out in legislative and policy documents, mirroring categories protected in pre-existing human rights statutes. In others, however, legislation or policy documents may leave these characteristics open-ended. For example, the VicPol PMC Strategy specifies only a non-exhaustive list of the attributes to be 'included' in the policy.

Despite the ambiguity inherent in defining racial and ethnic difference and identity (Alfieri 2013) and the complexities of translating these categories into law enforcement regimes, a review of existing law enforcement policies and procedures clearly shows that offences linked to racism, bigotry and xenophobia have been critical in driving contemporary hate crime discourses and enactments in many countries. In particular, offences relating to racism have been the most prominent and, some would argue, easiest to enforce. For example, England and Wales have had legislative measures against incitement to racial hatred for many decades (s. 18 of the Public Order Act 1986). Islamophobia has been of particular concern in recent years in the wake of the events of 9/11 and the rise of racial tensions within the UK, the US and the EU. In some instances, this has been joined by a renewed concern about anti-Semitism, as in the UK's College of Policing Manual, where anti-Semitism is specified in terms of race and religious hate crime (2014b). Anti-Sikh and anti-Muslim hate crime (ibid.) are also included. In Victoria, the site of our study, a review of cases where prejudice motivation had been established for sentencing purposes revealed that ethnicity and/or race were the attributes most commonly recognised by prosecutors and judiciary (Mason *et al.* 2014). This pattern was also apparent in other Australian states with hate crime sentencing legislation.

Other characteristics, where a 'group' identity may be harder to establish, such as sexual orientation and gender identity, have been more contentious. In early iterations of hate crimes in the US, for example, research found that less than half of the extant hate crime legislation recognised the sexual orientation of the victim as a motivator for this type of offending (Jacobs and Potter 1998). Sexual orientation, however, is now generally accepted as a characteristic that is protected, as is disability and transgender identity, although there are ongoing struggles in this area (Sherry 2010). There are also continuous debates over whether gender bias should be recognised as a ground for hate-motivated crime (Angelari 1994; Gelber 2000; Hodge 2011; Jenness 2003; Maher *et al.* 2015). Jacobs and Potter argue that violence motivated by gender bias should constitute a form of hate crime:

> There is every reason to believe that a high percentage of male violence against women is motivated, at least in part, by anti-female prejudice, especially if prejudice is broadly defined. Practically every act of male violence and intimidation against women is a potential hate crime.
>
> (1998: 20)

However, Stanko (2001) warns against considering violence against women as a form of hate crime, questioning whether such interpersonal violence is an abuse of an individual because of their membership of a particular group or population. Key concerns have been expressed over the floodgate potential of including women as a protected group, although advocates and commentators are clear that the inclusion of gender may not be applicable or useful in all forms of male violence against women (Gill and Mason-Bish 2013; Maher *et al.* 2015). Other recent discussions have identified elder abuse as a category of offending behaviour that may be defined as a form of hate crime (Mason-Bish 2012), given the centrality of victim characteristics and vulnerability to the offence.

Increasing attention has been paid to the importance of intersectionality in influencing the likelihood of victimisation and the intensification of vulnerability. Garland (2012), for example, examines the status of disablist victimisation, elder abuse and the victimisation of the homeless in relation to hate crime measures. He identifies the complexities of discussing these groups as if they are homogenous, and the complicating problems for enforcement and responses when victims share a number of attributes, such as the incidents of violent offences against people who are both disabled and elderly. Meyer (2010) explores the differential impacts of LGBTI violence when class and race are included in the analysis, following Mason's (2002) identification of the salience of these intersections in hate crime victimisation. A further complicating element, noted above, has been the recognition that victim and offender may be known to each other in some way, such as members of the same community (Mason 2015), which challenges a key element of common definitions of hate crime as a form of 'stranger danger' and the weighting assigned to group membership.

Such analyses have led some scholars to question whether group membership is the best way to identify and understand hate crime. Garland (2010) argues for thinking about hate crime in terms of violence and power, where vulnerability to hate crime is best defined by fluid concepts of difference rather than by structural conceptions of group attributes (Perry 2001). Garland and Chakraborti (2012) propose a way forward through the operation of a targeted victimisation framework that supports the human rights of individuals while simultaneously recognising the ways in which power functions in crimes of hatred and prejudice against targeted individuals (see also Perry 2003a; Stanko 2001). These questions of approach acquire more urgency when linked with the expanding reach of hate crimes legislation in Western countries over the last few decades and the broadening claims of minority groups for statutory protection and human rights (Mason 2014). Garland (2010), for example, argues that 'goths' should be accepted as legitimate victims of hate crimes, thereby extending protected identities and groups beyond existing parameters. As Mason (2014) observes, while claims for inclusion do need to be recognised, there are risks associated with widening and potentially watering down hate crimes instruments. This observation is important because in many jurisdictions, such as Victoria, effective enforcement of hate crimes legislation is already a challenging proposition. We turn now to an exploration of how these contests over definition, underlying frameworks and legitimate grounds for inclusion and/or protection in the domain of hate crimes are understood to impact on law enforcement practices. In particular, we consider the importance of shared meanings and frameworks for effective enforcement.

Terminology and the challenges of enforcement

It is not yet clear how the lack of a common definition and compatible understanding of hate crime generally and variations in local terminologies ('hate', 'bias' or 'prejudice', for example) translate into complexities in policing and law enforcement, both locally and globally. Giannasi considers that the prevention and prosecution of hate crimes present some of the most difficult operational challenges for contemporary police forces (2015b), but it is unclear how definitions, terms and meanings influence such difficulties. As police are first responders to criminal offences (ODIHR 2014), they are faced with the challenges of identifying, then gathering evidence about the commission of hate crimes (Mason *et al.* 2015). Policing agencies in many jurisdictions have committed to strategies aimed at preventing hate crimes, bringing offenders to justice, as well as recording and responding to hate crime incidents in an appropriate manner. This commitment is reflected in the attention to embedding hate crimes prevention and response strategies in policing approaches. But there appear to be common difficulties in many jurisdictions, which leaves open the question of how a lack of clarity in terms and a lack of shared perspectives impact policing and the communities these types of legislation are designed to serve.

UK Police recognise that hate crime is under-reported and understand the need to improve their data:

> This is one of the few categories of criminal activity where the police are actively seeking to increase the crime recording rate in order to reduce the gap between the actual incidence of hate crime and those that are recorded and treated as such.
>
> (College of Policing 2014a)

As Williams and Tregidga state, 'the policing of hate crimes has become a priority in most constabularies in the United Kingdom, as evidenced in its inclusion in many police and crime commissioners' actions plans' (2014). The UK has recently updated its national hate crime strategy via the College of Policing's Hate Crime Operational Guidance (College of Policing 2014a, 2014b). These guidelines seek to reduce the harm caused by hate crime while also increasing communities' and victims' trust and confidence in the police (College of Policing 2014a). Collaborative research focusing on improvements has also been commissioned in a range of UK services. For example, the All Wales Hate Crime project made several recommendations relevant to hate crime enforcement, including the need for: the continuing training of Welsh police forces; the development of multi-agency protocols; the training of judicial officers; the introduction of restorative justice approaches; and greater accountability amongst law enforcement personnel (Williams and Tregidga 2013). The under-reporting of hate crime to police was also investigated in the University of Leicester's Hate Crime Project: in order to encourage reporting, the researchers found that victims need a greater level of support from police (2014) to build trust and congruent understandings.

The complexities of hate crime under-reporting and the consequences for law enforcement are also evident in the US. As we noted in the Introduction, there is a considerable disparity between actual experiences of hate crime and the official data. For example, the US Victimization Survey found an average of 259,700 hate crimes, whereas the FBI recorded just 7,254 such offences (Giannasi 2015b). Such a gap suggests a significant divergence between victim experiences of hate or bias crimes and law enforcement definition of such events. Nevertheless, there is a clear and strong commitment to improving law enforcement agencies' identification and recording of hate or bias crime in the US (FBI 2015). Similarly in the EU, the ODIHR (2014) recently updated its 2009 'practical guide' for prosecutors with a focus on gathering evidence, working with witnesses and building successful cases.

The project on which we report in this book is similarly built on a commitment from VicPol to enhance reporting and build better responses around hate crime. As we will discuss in more detail in Chapter 4, VicPol introduced dedicated officer positions focused on social inclusion along with its PMC Strategy in 2011. In addressing multicultural and 'new and emerging' communities, these liaison positions seek to engage recently arrived communities from Africa, the

Middle East and India. VicPol's strategy was also accompanied by the increased prominence and resourcing of Gay and Lesbian Liaison Officers. In 2013, VicPol launched a community consultation process as a condition of the settlement of a race discrimination action brought on behalf of a group of Sudanese youth against them (Flemington Legal Service 2013). The consultation invited 'community members to provide feedback on cross cultural training and field contact policies and processes' (VicPol 2013). More recently, VicPol has developed a Priority Communities Division (PCD), which facilitates regular liaison with key community leaders about emerging issues. While the PMC Strategy is not the only tool or policy operating in this space, it has contributed to developing that communication and confidence. As we go on to explore, this nexus between community knowledge, shared expectations and meanings, and police understandings of hate crimes is a critical one.

Yet there is little direct evidence on how any particular term or framework influences policing practices or outcomes and whether there are terms that produce greater congruence of understanding than others, and thus serve law enforcement and their communities better. In all the jurisdictions discussed, problems of under-reporting and of mismatched expectations about the meanings of 'hate' (which also shape academic and policy discourses), and divergences in how individuals and communities experience hate or bias events, are commonly identified as the most significant challenges. It is well-recognised that the effectiveness of any policing policy is contingent upon the local law enforcement context, occupational culture and police discretion (Bowling 1999; Chakraborti 2009; Cronin *et al.* 2007; Grattet and Jenness 2005; Oakley 2005; Walker and Katz 1995). This point is even more salient in the context of hate crime policies, given the general difficulties of definition, mobilisation and meaning that we have discussed above (Bell 2002, Cronin *et al.* 2007, Grattet and Jenness 2008, Hall 2012). In our study with VicPol, shared languages and understandings were a key area of investigation. In following chapters, we examine in more detail how questions of language and terminology are more than conceptual issues in the field of hate crimes. Instead, shared language and common meaning are central to effective enforcement for the populations hate crime law and policy is designed to protect. We seek to extend current discussions about the variability and lack of cohesion in hate crimes discourses by examining how chosen terms work, or fail, in a specific policing context to meet the human rights of vulnerable groups of people.

Conclusion

This chapter has explored the terminology that populates the discourse, enactment and enforcement of hate crime regimes across Western developed countries. This review of academic literature and legislative frameworks indicates variable, contentious and inconsistent usage of terminology. Many jurisdictions have taken up and/or modified terms, in response to local pressures and sociopolitical contexts. Terms such as 'hate' are treated as interchangeable with others, such as 'bias', leading to confusion and ambiguity. While a range of terminologies may be necessary to reflect the broad spectrum of hate crime (Clement *et al.* 2011) and to encompass the diverse experiences of victims, the lack of common and consistent terminology has clearly influenced the development of the field, and contributes to discrepancies in criminal justice responses to and recording of hate crime. As Phillips and Grattet (2000) have demonstrated, the meaning of 'hate crime' is neither fixed in statute nor in police enforcement of such laws. Instead, the term is 'infused with meaning' through judicial opinion, which then returns to the field of policing to shape policy and operational responses. Confusion arises from multiple definitions, as well as a lack of uniformity and clarity (Brudholm 2015). Yet, the negotiation of shared frameworks, as a basis for confronting and combatting hate crimes, is central to legislative and enforcement programmes and aspirations. The direct effects of this confusion, variation and divergence in terminology and its impact on how meanings are made and shared have not yet been fully explored in the context of policing practices or police–community relations. Although under-reporting is recognised and strategies to improve recording are commonplace, there is little information on how specific terms and frameworks influence policing outcomes or community perceptions.

This chapter's analysis of hate crime terminology suggests hate crime is an area of definitional and semantic gymnastics. Language is key to this. Generally, it is well-recognised that language plays a central role in the operation of the criminal justice system, which expends considerable energy refining and debating statutory wording, police evidence, courtroom testimony, judicial doctrine and so on (Goodrich 1984). In the context of hate crime, language is significant in various ways. It may form part of the actual crime. The University of Leicester's Hate Crime Project, for example, reported that 87 per cent of respondents had experienced verbal abuse (2014). Yet, as we and others have found, the diversity of language and meanings attributed to hate crime has been identified as creating confusion and a barrier to reporting for victims. People with mental health and learning issues, for instance, may not necessarily relate to or identify with hate crime terminology (Clement *et al.* 2011). Williams and Tregidga (2013) found similar dissonance where everyday racial and other abuses were not always identified as such. In other words, concepts such as hate, bias and prejudice capture and construct such experiences in different ways for different audiences, which, in turn, steer law enforcement priorities and resources. The language used by law enforcement agencies is thus complicit in shaping public opinion, in expressing ideology, eliciting empathy, educating and informing society, and in framing police and criminal justice responses. This makes language and the negotiation of mutual perspectives critical to building trust, confidence and understanding between vulnerable communities and police (College of Policing 2014b). As we will explore in following chapters, procedural justice demands that such understandings collaborate with measures designed to bolster community confidence in law enforcement.

In effect, particular terminologies and labels shape the meaning of hate crime, carrying with them normative values about human rights mixed with 'mediums of class, ethnicity, gender, sexuality, and geography' (Alfieri 2013). In the field of hate crime, where identities, vulnerabilities and differential rights are central, confusion and contingency around meaning is likely to render the task of effective policing, including measures to combat the fear that affects vulnerable communities, much harder. This makes shared language and understanding between policing agencies and their communities vital to the success of hate crime policies. As Grattet and Jenness (2008) have observed, 'the more an agency is engaged in a symbiotic relationship with the community in which it resides, the more the policy affects reporting'. In the following chapters, we explore how these terminological dissonances, which inhibit shared or common meanings, impact on the case study of policing hate crime in the Australian state of Victoria.

3 Hate crime and policing

Police, community and social change

Introduction

This chapter focuses on the mobilisation of hate crime law and policy within the policing domain. As earlier outlined, the hate crime concept emerged in the 1980s in the United States on the heels of the Civil Rights Movement. Hate crime was originally confined primarily to racial prejudice. In the decades since, the concept has expanded to include crimes motivated by a broader range of prejudices. Hate crime laws and policies have proliferated over the past half century and are today commonplace in Western countries. These laws and policies typically aim to recognise the harms that such crimes inflict on individual victims and vulnerable and marginalised communities, to build trust between targeted communities and criminal justice organisations, and to punish offenders and promote human rights and social justice. Policing is critical in ensuring that the laws and policy are effectively implemented to achieve such objectives.

Police are the criminal justice system's front line, playing a critical part in people's experience of the law. Far from being neutral enforcers of the law, police are key in shaping the activities and people we come to recognise as crime problems, criminals and victims of crime. While legislators and policy makers set out the law in theory, the police are essential to the process of translating such laws into practice. In recognition of the significance of police decision-making and its impact on the operation of the law, Muir refers to police as 'street corner politicians' (1979). Police are effectively the law on the street, using their discretion in ways that uphold or undermine the values of non-discrimination that inform and underpin hate crime regimes. Along with prosecutors, police are recognised as the 'last phase of the formation of the policy domain' (Jenness and Grattet 2001).

Effective implementation of hate crime laws and policies requires that police identify, record, investigate and respond to such crimes in line with the provisions and intent of these initiatives. As the gatekeepers of the criminal justice system, police organisations and individual police have considerable influence and discretion in determining the seriousness with which different types and categories of crime are treated, the level and type of resources allocated to address different types of crime, and the nature of the treatment extended to victims and potential victims of different categories of crime. Even where police organisa-tions commit themselves to implementing the laws and policies that recognise hate crime as a serious crime and pressing social issue, the entrenched 'common-sense' views of front-line police may nevertheless conflict with such commit-ment and present a hurdle to effective implementation (Chakraborti and Garland 2015). The difficulties of implementing hate crime law and policy are well-documented (Bell 2002; Cronin *et al.* 2007; Grattet and Jenness 2008; Hall 2012). The challenges to effective implementation include interlinking issues related to the culture and structure of the policing organisation, the way policing is conceived, practical policing operational matters and, most crucially, the rela-tionship between the police and marginalised or vulnerable communities (Mason *et al.* 2015). As we have argued, the articulation and shared meanings that can be generated are a critical aspect of how hate crime schemas are implemented and the impact that they can have.

The chapter begins by setting out the genesis of hate crime law and policy internationally and the circumstances and context in which police organisations became implicated in implementing hate crime regimes and developing hate crime policies. It then considers the research on how police gain their knowledge of hate crime, how they translate legal requirements for prosecution and sentenc-ing into routine practices, and the ways in which they have responded to and developed hate crime policy and protocols. In particular, it focuses on the chal-lenges that frequently impede the effective police implementation of hate crime laws, policies and protocols and examines the policing strategies deployed or recommended to overcome these challenges. The chapter also considers the relevance and role of community policing and human rights frameworks in the hate crime domain. It critically evaluates the potential of these to support effective police implementation of hate crime laws and policy by ameliorating the long-standing trust deficit between police and marginalised and vulnerable communities. Specifically, it focuses on the utility and difficulty of developing shared meaning about the significance and nature of hate crime. We argue that the inevitable divergence in perspective surrounding hate or prejudice motivated crime and related terms, such as racism, that exist between police and marginal-ised or vulnerable communities, provides both a challenge and an opportunity to bridge this trust deficit and achieve hate crime-related goals.

Hate crime, social movements, law and policy

The genesis and spread of hate crime laws and policies are located within the history of social justice movements (Jenness 2007; Jenness and Grattet 2001). Hate crime was first recognised in the context of black civil rights in the United States and subsequently understood and advanced through activism tied to fem-inist, gay, lesbian, transgender, disability and victim movements. The human rights movement, which is seen as a highly influential social justice movement, has also been significant in the spread of the hate crime concept (Brudholm 2015). International human rights law enshrines a number of principles that require states to maintain standards that discourage hate crimes and sanction the discrimination that underpins the commission of hate crimes with impunity.

Not infrequently, hate crime legal and policy developments are linked to prejudice motivated murders that become the basis for, or part of, campaigns highlighting the frequency and history of such violence and/or the failure of police to adequately respond to and investigate such crimes. Contemporary hate crime regimes in the UK, for example, are inextricably tied to the 1993 racist murder of 18-year-old Stephen Lawrence in London. Lawrence was attacked and stabbed to death by five or six white men as he waited for the bus. The inquiry into the police response to Lawrence's murder found the investigation of his killing and the treatment of his family and that of his friend, who witnessed the killing, to have been 'institutionally racist' (Foster *et al.* 2005; Macpherson 1999). In the US, the 2009 Hate Crimes Prevention Act is prefaced by the names Matthew Shepard and James Byrd Jr. Matthew Shepard was a 21-year-old gay university student in 1998, when he was beaten and tortured to death by two men in Colorado. James Byrd Jr, an African American man, was lynched and killed in 1998 in Texas by three white supremacists, who beat and urinated on him before chaining him to the back of a pickup truck and dragging him for several miles before dumping his body (Chakraborti and Garland 2015; Petersen 2011).

The US has been at the forefront of hate crime legislation and policy, starting with the Civil Rights Act 1968. This act provided for the prosecution of offences targeting the victim's race, colour, religion or national origin (Chakraborti and Garland 2015; Turpin-Petrosino 2015). While crimes motivated by racism and religious difference are part the United States' history from the time of the first explorers (Jenness 2007), the history of slavery and subsequent segregation gave rise to the first hate crime laws (Aaronson 2013). The increased visibility of African Americans in public life and the demands for social change linked to the civil rights movement during the 1960s brought into sharp relief the history, extent and seriousness of racially motivated violence directed at former slaves and their descendants. The explication of the ongoing history of vigilantism, particularly lynching in the South, and the violence – sometimes lethal – directed against those taking part in civil rights activities put prejudice motivated crimes on the political agenda (Levin 2002).

During the 1980s, social movements in the United States successfully developed and pushed a hate crime agenda, generating recognition that violence motivated by prejudice or hatred differs from other violent crimes. The influence of the various social justice movements and resulting social change was gradually reflected in law reform, developments in case law and, eventually, law enforcement. As a consequence of these social and legal changes, criminal acts that were once indistinguishable from 'ordinary crime' were singled out as a separate category and subject to harsher punishment. In the second half of the 1990s, in the wake of this judicial and legislative activity, attention fell on the police and prosecutors whose role it was to implement novel hate-crime legal constructs (Jenness 2007; Jenness and Grattet 2001).

Hate crime, prejudice and policing

Beginning in the latter part of the twentieth century, United States enforcement agencies at federal, state and local levels sought to enforce hate crime legislation through new, specialised bias-crime units (Jenness and Grattet 2001). The literature concerning the development of hate crime enforcement focuses primarily on policing rather than prosecutorial practice. Though both law enforcement and prosecution work in tandem to concretise legal constructs, the police, as the front line of the criminal justice system, have a far broader interface with victims of prejudice motivated crimes and targeted communities. While hate crime prosecutions are important, there will be many incidents where, for various reasons, prosecution is not possible or practical. In these cases, which are likely to amount to a majority, the police are the victim's sole experience of the criminal justice system. Additionally if police do not recognise, record and investigate hate crimes effectively, then prosecutions become difficult or impossible. Finally the police have become a focus of particular attention because it has become clear that the entrenched beliefs of police about crime and justice may represent the foremost hurdle to the effective implementation of hate crime laws and policy (see, for example, Hall 2012). While hate crime laws and policy attempt to use the law to address an ongoing history of prejudice motivated violence, police organisations and individual police charged with implementing these laws sometimes share the prejudices that underpin such violence. Linked to this is a long history of police use of excessive force against minorities, particularly racialised minorities (Cunneen 2001; Skolnick and Fyfe 1993).

The exposure of the prejudice underpinning the failed police response to the racist murder of Stephen Lawrence in London in 1993 provided the backdrop to the development of hate crime laws and policy in the United Kingdom. The 1999 Macpherson Inquiry report into the police handling of that murder was undoubtedly a watershed in the growing focus on the police role in hate crime. The inquiry highlighted cultural and institutional racism in the policies and practices of the police and its impact on the quality and equality of service delivered to minority groups as victims of crime (Bowling 1999; Hall 2012). A deep-rooted experience of these groups was revealed by the inquiry – a feeling of being 'over-policed' and 'under-protected' (Hall 2012).

After the Macpherson Inquiry, strategies were developed to address the relationship between police and victimised communities (Chakraborti and Garland 2015). The UK Government responded to the inquiry's recommendations with an action plan and a raft of legislative measures. The Association of Chief Police Officers developed national standards for responding to hate crime (Giannasi 2015a). Nathan Hall's foreword to the College of Policing (2014) Hate Crime Operational Guidance document describes Stephen Lawrence's legacy in the 'developments in policing relating to critical incident management', as well as the improvements in law enforcement's community engagement (2014b). Various task forces and programmes were initiated, with a focus on establishing a common definition of hate crime in order to improve policing and data recording. By 2007, a shared definition of 'monitored hate crime' was agreed upon. Monitored hate crime in the UK focuses on 'five strands' (ibid.); race, ethnicity or nationality, religion, faith or belief, sexual orientation, gender identity and disability.

The hate crime concept emerged in continental Europe at the end of twentieth century (Chakraborti and Garland 2015). Hate crime responses in Europe have sought to address anti-Semitism, anti-immigrant prejudice, xenophobic or racially motivated incidents, right-wing extremism and anti-homosexual crimes (Turpin-Petrosino 2015). Human rights actors and institutions have been particularly influential in consolidating the spread of the hate crime concept in Europe (Brudholm 2015). As discussed in Chapter 2, the ODIHR developed a definition of hate crime applicable to all countries in the Organisation for Security and Co-operation in Europe. However, there are differences in emphasis throughout Europe arising from each country's specific history and culture. The multilingual context also gives rise to a range of different interpretations of the definition of 'hate crime'. This lack of uniformity amongst European nations generates a range of problems related to implementation of hate crime laws and policy.

In Australia, homophobic violence and the perceived need to address prejudice in law enforcement provided the impetus for developments in policing. Gay and Lesbian Liaison Officers were first appointed in 1990 to the New South Wales Police Service in response to a number of gay-hate murders and bashings (Thompson 1993). This policing policy initiative came a year after New South Wales became the first Australian jurisdiction to enshrine enforceable standards of tolerance in a multicultural society in legislation. This and similar legislation since enacted in other Australian jurisdictions aim to directly enhance the protection of marginalised and vulnerable communities while promoting broader objectives of tolerance and inclusion (see Mason 2009a). In subsequent years, government, inter-agency and community partnerships were developed in New South Wales, while police in that state developed a policy on sexuality and gender diversity in 1997. Such policies were not widely replicated in other jurisdictions, and to date Victoria is the only Australian jurisdiction in which police have developed a comprehensive, specific policy statement on hate crime (see Chapter 4 for further details).

Implementing hate crime policy – identification, recognition and reporting

There is a well-developed literature on the difficulties of mobilising hate crime statutes into policing policy and transmitting the meaning of these legal rules to front-line officers (Bell 2002; Cronin *et al.* 2007; Grattet and Jenness 2008; Hall 2012; Mason *et al.* 2015). There is wide variation between police forces in the way they translate hate crime law and policy into practice (see, for example, Grattett and Jenness 2005). International research indicates that one salient variable is the way that organisational resources are deployed (ACPO 2005; Bell 1996, 2002; Boyd *et al.* 1996; Cronin *et al.* 2007; Grattet and Jenness 2005;

Martin 1996; Oakley 2005). Issues of particular relevance include whether there is a dedicated police group addressing hate crimes, whether there is a systematic approach to recording elements of incidents, and what the nature of organisational leadership is. Yet, as Chakraborti (2009) argues, leadership and police organisational structure and initiatives supportive of the implementation of hate crime policies are not enough to guarantee effective enforcement. Individual officer response and broader occupational culture 'can retain a stubborn influence on police practice irrespective of changes to police policy' (Chakraborti 2009; see also Bowling 1999).

Policies are communicated from the top of the police organisation to frontline officers, and through this process the abstract concept of hate crime is institutionalised, normalised and brought into day-to-day practice as policies are transformed from 'law-on-the-books' to 'law-in-action' (Grattet and Jenness 2005; Jenness and Grattet 2001). However, even where the police organisation through the agency of senior management is committed to prioritising and effectively policing hate crime, the process of translating intention into on-the-ground action may be flawed. Hate crime policies that are prioritised at a corporate police level may not be similarly prioritised amongst those that are part of 'street cop culture' (Chakraborti and Garland 2015). Aspects of police culture tend to disincline operational police from focusing on prejudice as a source of social injustice and harm, with the result that hate crime has traditionally ranked low in the hierarchy of different types of crimes amongst front-line police (Bowling 1999; Chakraborti and Garland 2015). Some police feel that hate crime policies sensationalise hate crime, and others do not believe hate crime should be treated any differently than other crime (Nolan and Akiyama 1999).

The strategies for effective policing of hate crime are set out in various police policy documents. Such policies typically operate as the marshalling instruments for legislation, though in the Australian state of Victoria, as we detail in the next chapter, such policies have been implemented without a specific hate crime offence. The major hurdle in the way of effective implementation is the trust deficit between police and affected community. In line with this, a major goal of hate crime strategy is to build trust between affected communities and police. The recognition and accurate recording of hate crime is understood to be a key element of effective, inclusive policing, designed to meet the objectives of hate crime laws and policies. Linked to this, police hate crime policies typically seek an increase in the identification and recording of hate crime and hate incidents (see, for example, College of Policing 2014b). With a better understanding of hate crime and improvements in the recording of hate crimes, governments seek to encourage victims' confidence in reporting to address non- and under-reporting (Home Office 2014).

Increased reporting by the community and recording by police of hate incidents and crimes are sought as an indication of increased trust in police and an improved ability amongst police to recognise prejudice motivation and the negative impact of hate crimes and incidents on communities. Grattet and Jenness (2008) argue that symbolic hate crime law must be accompanied by instrumental action to avoid being seen as tokenistic or solely ceremonial. When hate crime policies are adopted, it communicates, symbolically, the significance of the issue to both police and communities. When hate crimes are actually identified and reported, this amounts to instrumental action. At one end of the spectrum are police agencies that have no hate crime policies and no reported incidents – they 'score low on symbolism and low on instrumentality when it comes to the politics and enforcement of hate crime'. At the other end, where there is a symbolic policy plus actual responses, the 'symbolic measure' has 'an instrumental impact', and the agency has enhanced legitimacy (Grattet and Jenness 2008).

The accurate classification and recording by police of hate crime, along with sympathetic treatment of victims, signals to impacted communities that police are operating in a non-discriminatory manner. Reporting and recognition are interlinked strategies that rely on victims trusting that police will treat hate crime seriously and respond appropriately. Willingness to report and ready recognition of hate crime thus form a virtuous circle that provide meaningful measures of the extent to which the relationship between police and community is facilitating the goals of hate crime laws and policies. Consistent with this, police policy goals typically include minimum standards for response and investigation and positive support for victims (Chakraborti and Garland 2015). The minimum standards in police response and investigation of hate crime in the UK, for example, aim to 'recognise the crime and undertake a quality investigation that supports an outcome which satisfies the victim and the community', as well as reduce repeat victimisation. Specifically, police are directed to be 'aware of the unique needs and vulnerability that result from being a victim of hate crime' and, where appropriate, police must engage with specialist support agencies (College of Policing 2014b). The virtuous circle of recognition and reporting, however, is difficult to achieve. For example, the 2013 Gay British Crime Survey found that more than three-quarters of victims of hate crimes did not report the experience to police. Those that did report to police found the process unsatisfactory, and half of the victims who reported found that no further action was taken (Stonewall 2014).

Apart from the relational issues between police and targeted communities and victims from minority groups, there are a number of other operational, conceptual and cultural challenges to achieving the goals of increased reporting and recognition. Effective policing requires that police pay attention to perpetrators' motives and the victims' or community's perception of prejudice motivation. This requires a shift in operational perspective because evidence of crime is typically based on the nature of the offender's intention and the character of their act(s). Motive is generally only relevant to the question of sentencing after conviction, not an element of an offence which police need to establish in order to lay charges and build a foundation for successful prosecution. At a deeper level, effective policing of hate crime also requires a shift in how policing is conceptualised. Hate crime frameworks challenge police to be 'active agents of social justice and inclusion' (Mason *et al.* 2015). Chakraborti and Garland (2015) maintain that hate crime should be conceived 'as an ongoing social process' that implicates patterns of prejudice, the lived experience of targeted communities and societal discourse. Conceived of in this manner, the harmful, cumulative effects of everyday, 'low-level' incidents are more readily perceived. However, in line with their self-perception as crime fighters, police tend not to respond to 'ongoing social process', but look instead to tightly defined individual incidents (Bowling 1999). This individual incident approach ignores the specific nature of the harms victims of hate crimes and targeted communities experience and runs counter to the recognition of specific types of harms that led to prejudice motiv-ated crimes being designated as a discrete category of crime.

Law enforcement agencies that participate in hate crime reporting pro-grammes are often accused by advocacy groups of under-reporting (Nolan and Akiyama 1999). Police officers have identified various reasons for misidentify-ing or refusing to identify hate crimes. For example, some law enforcement agencies have attributed lack of participation in hate crime reporting to lack of resources (ibid.). Police organisations employ various tactics to overcome the hurdles that stand in the way of effective implementation of hate crime policies and move it up the hierarchy of crimes dealt with by police. International research suggests that it may be possible to overcome some of these issues via implementation of procedures and protocols that inform and influence the discre-tion of individual police officers, by guiding and overseeing decisions about the classification of hate crime. Many police departments have created standard operating procedures, protocols or checklists to ensure accurate or consistent recording of hate crimes (Cronin *et al.* 2007). When combined with the creation of specialist hate crime units charged with oversight of initial classification deci-sions, these provide a basis for systematic internal review prior to formal record-ing (Bell 1997, 2000). Walker and Katz (1995) suggest that specialist units and procedures can provide a clear message for street level officers of the force's commitment to the effective policing of hate or prejudice motivated crimes.

These systems, however, are built around determinations about the types of offences and incidents that are defined and recorded as hate crime. As Jacobs and Potter (1998) argue, hate crime is a 'complicated, broad and cloudy concept'. As a result of limited practical experience linked to the relative newness of hate crime frameworks, myriad operational issue and aspects of police culture, police organisations tend to apply a restrictive definition of hate crime. A narrower, more legalistic definition of hate crime has the advantage of anchoring police response to prosecution requirements. This approach tends to be under-inclusive because it relies upon shortcuts to identify typical non-hate crime scenarios that allow officers to quickly rule out incidents, such as those where there is a pre-existing relationship between the victim and the offender, those with mixed motives, or those that would still have been committed if the victim were of another background. Such an approach risks alienating com-munities and victims that may perceive incidents to be prejudice motivated, even in the absence of compelling evidence of such motivation.

The UK system for classifying hate crimes is at the other end of the spectrum in that it classifies cases as hate crime based largely on perception. In 2007, the

UK Association of Chief Police Officers agreed on a common definition of hate crime as 'any criminal offence which is perceived, by the victim or any other person, to be motivated by a hostility or prejudice' based on a person's race, religion, sexual orientation, disability or transgender (ACPO 2010). This broad operational definition is more inclusive of community expectations than any of the statutory definitions used to prosecute hate crime in the UK, most obviously because it is sufficient if *the victim or any other person perceived* the offence to be motivated by hostility or prejudice. This has had a significant impact on recording practices.[1] In 2011–2012, UK police recorded 43,748 hate crimes (Home Office 2012). Only a proportion of these comes close to possessing the elements necessary for prosecution: in 2011–2012, the CPS prosecuted 14,196 hate crimes (CPS 2012). Although this definition is responsive to public perceptions and associated harms, it risks creating an inflated image of the problem. For example, the ODIHR demonstrates that England and Wales have the highest recorded rates of hate crime across Europe and North America, far higher than any other nation (ODIHR 2010). Such a large gap between recording and prosecution might sap public confidence by implying that policy statements have little practical impact when it comes to prosecuting and punishing offenders. (Over-)inclusive policy definitions and recording practices can obfuscate the signs that prompt investigating officers to gather evidence capable of convincing a court beyond reasonable doubt that the crime was motivated by hostility or prejudice. Such definitions may also affect police morale, where successful outcomes are conceived in terms of criminal charges and successful prosecutions, as well as undermine the legitimacy of any policy or strategy by severing the connection between the operation of the policy and any legal standard.

As outlined, hate crime introduces multiple forms of ambiguity and complexity – in the term 'hate crime' itself, the novelty of the inclusion of such specific forms of motivation as an element of the offence, the gap between what might legally count as a hate crime, and what might be perceived as an incident motivated by prejudice by a community or individual victim. Yet, although these aspects clearly are recognised as significant challenges in the implementation of hate crime policy and law, they can also provide the foundation for dialogue and the building of mutual understanding between police and vulnerable or marginalised communities. Ensuring that hate crime policies are implemented effectively requires the development of mutual understanding between police and targeted communities about what hate crime is and what is considered appropriate when responding to those who consider themselves victims of such crimes. It also requires that police demonstrate and that vulnerable and marginalised communities perceive that they take hate crime seriously. Cultivating the ground for mutual recognition of hate crime as a social and legal problem of significance is the basis on which the effective implementation of hate crime policies stand.

Human rights, community policing and hate crime

The relationship between the police and targeted communities has been identified as a key ingredient in the effective translation of hate crime policy into policing action. The policing hate crime agenda has been shaped by the widely recognised sensitivities surrounding this relationship (Chakraborti and Garland 2015). Building shared understandings between police and targeted communities of the extent, impacts and definition of hate crime and/or incidents is key to the implementation of social justice and inclusion agendas, and the strategies of reporting, identifying and recording such crimes. It is widely acknowledged that policing hate crime must first and foremost centre on improving community perceptions of law enforcement (see, for example, Perry 2010a). Positive police engagement with targeted communities is seen as part of the process of improving these perceptions. Recent national guidelines published by the UK College of Policing, for example, emphasise the role of community engagement in addressing hate crime (College of Policing 2014b; Home Office 2014). It is understood that 'the more an agency is engaged in a symbiotic relationship with the community in which it resides, the more the policy affects reporting' (Grattet and Jenness 2008).

One significant component of building symbiotic relationships between police and hate crime targeted communities is overcoming police prejudice and community perceptions of police prejudice. The engrained tendency amongst police to see marginal and vulnerable communities as suspect and to under-police these communities as victims has been resistant to reform in many jurisdictions. Human rights principles support the development and operationalisation of prejudice-sensitive policing that runs counter to the entrenched prejudice that makes it difficult for police to see vulnerable and marginalised communities as potential and actual victims. The International Covenant on Civil and Political Rights, for example, includes the right 'to be treated with humanity and respect for the inherent dignity of the human person', prohibits discrimination and requires that all people be considered equal before the law (ICCPR 1966). The United Nations' Code of Conduct for Law Enforcement Officials states that 'in the performance of their duty, law enforcement officials shall respect and protect human dignity and maintain and uphold the human rights of all persons' (Weber *et al.* 2014). 'Prejudice-sensitive policing' is thus alive to any indifference to or misunderstanding of hate crime as unimportant, recognises the history of vexed relations between police and marginalised and vulnerable communities and is aware of the need for dialogue with impacted communities to develop congruent understanding and mutual trust.

From the late 1990s onwards, unprecedented attention has been focused on the global expansion of human rights ideals, particularly as they relate to policing. More than any other time in history, police organisations today are likely to promote themselves as organisations devoted to achieving human rights. Discussing this focus on policing and human rights, Crawshaw *et al.* (2007) argue that:

Police agencies and police officials are uniquely placed to prevent the barbarity of gross abuse of power; to protect the mental and physical integrity of vulnerable people; to alleviate the suffering of victims of human rights violations; and to bring to justice those responsible for such violations.

(2007)

Hate crime laws and policies aim to promote human rights through the recognition, condemnation and sanctioning of prejudice motivated crime, the enhanced protection of marginalised and vulnerable groups, and supporting and promoting non-discrimination. Human rights principles around non-discrimination may provide a point of connection and shared language about hate crime between police and targeted communities. However, research suggests that the rhetoric of human rights policing does not necessarily coincide with the actions of police and police organisations. The more frequent reference to human rights in policing documents and policies has not readily translated into action. As Bradley puts it, 'there has been an enormous change in human rights consciousness [over the past twenty-five years] as it applies to police but considerably less in practice' (2015). Criminological research has found that an increased focus on human rights in policing does not embed a human rights culture in policing. Considering the impact of the Human Rights Act on British police, for example, Bullock and Johnson argue that '[i]nstead of shaping police work to make it more responsive to human rights, bureaucratic processes are used by officers to legitimise and justify their existing practices' (2011).

Community policing is another axis on which attempts to build trust, dialogue and mutual understanding might be built through symbiotic relationships with targeted communities. Community policing has become a staple of policing approaches since the 1970s (Lee and McGovern 2014). Although there is no one single definition, it can broadly be defined as '[a] philosophy of Policing which emphasises the working partnership between police officers and citizens in creative ways in order to solve community problems relating to crime' (Trojanowicz and Bucqueroux 1990). This notion of partnership between police and vulnerable or marginalised communities is critical to achieving strategic hate crime goals and implementing policy. The emergence of bias-crime units and prejudice-sensitive police policies are compatible with the development of community policing philosophy 'to the extent that they assume that jurisdiction-wide standards exist, [and] embrace values of tolerance rather than prejudice' (Jenness and Grattet 2001). Although the ideology of community policing has become the almost-unchallenged definition of good and democratic policing (Wisler and Onwudiwe 2009), for community policing to create effective partnerships that help bridge the historical and continuing trust deficit between marginalised and vulnerable communities, engagement needs to be substantive rather than tokenistic, sincere and open rather than cynical, and covert and consensual rather than coercive. Overarching this and going against the grain of history, such policing engagement, as it links to hate crime frameworks, needs to approach vulnerable and marginalised communities primarily as potential victims of crime rather than as potential offenders.

Murphy and Cherney's (2011) research on police engagement with ethnic communities in Australia is instructive. They emphasise the need for the 'voice' of the community to be accorded high status in police decision-making processes. The concept of 'instrumental voice' alludes to the community's ability to articulate localised concerns and be enabled to shape policies that impact its members (2011). Voice acknowledges the need for mutuality between police and communities, thereby promoting police–community collaborations and a perception of procedural justice. Such voice must be interactive and reciprocal, necessarily involving both the holders of power (police) and their audience (targeted communities) (Bottoms and Tankebe 2012). Conversely, if the community's voice is not instrumental – that is, their suggestions are ignored or sought only after decisions are made – engagement will be perceived as superficial, 'tokenistic and insincere' and undemocratic (Murphy and Cherney 2011). In that instance, Murphy and Cherney conclude that any engagement by police with that community will be fleeting only, co-operation will be compromised, and the community's low status will be reinforced. In some circumstances, vulnerable and marginalised communities may experience 'engagement' as a veiled extension of surveillance, coercion and over-policing, rather than as an experience that addresses negative perceptions about police prejudice. Thus, the practical outcome is that police must be 'open and receptive' to genuine dialogue with communities if they wish to increase police legitimacy (ibid.).

Police–community engagement with Muslims post 9/11 attests to some of the critical issues around community policing as a strategy to build trust between targeted communities and police. Since the attacks on the United States and the declaration of the 'war on terror' in 2001, there have been increased violent crimes targeted at Muslims or those perceived to be Muslim in Western countries (Zempi 2014). Many Western nations have invested heavily in community policing models premised on building mutual trust between authorities and Muslim communities (Pickering *et al.* 2008). However, it is clear that this 'consensual' community engagement is often intertwined with policing and intelligence-agency powers aimed at countering terrorism. There is research that suggests that engagement is often experienced as intrusive or intimidating. In addition to this, there are numerous documented case studies which suggest that engagement can take the form of invitations to inform and that refusing 'requests' to engage or inform can lead to serious negative consequences for Muslim people (Human Rights Watch 2014; Sentas 2014). In the US post 9/11, it has been suggested that 'community outreach programs [with Muslim communities] now serve as Trojan horses for intelligence-gathering agents' (Aaronson 2013). It appears, then, that although Muslim people are frequent targets of hate crime, community engagement is based on the premise of identifying suspects within that group. The sense of distrust amongst Muslim communities in the States has been compounded by false police assurances that no covert monitoring would occur without the knowledge of community leaders (Bartosiewicz

2012). Scepticism about the feasibility of establishing genuine symbiotic relationships between marginalised groups and police has grown with revelations in the UK in 2011 that a police officer working in the Metropolitan Police Muslim Contact Unit, purportedly in partnership with Muslims, spent many years working undercover amongst activist groups. As an undercover agent, he engaged in deception and was allegedly involved in criminal activity (Lewis and Evans 2013; Spalek and O'Rawe 2014).

It has been argued that there is 'residual mistrust affecting the policing of hate crime [that] has left its mark not just upon minority group perceptions of the police but also upon police perceptions of minority groups and other vulnerable targets of hate and prejudice' (Chakraborti and Garland 2015). While this mistrust is 'residual', in the sense that it is left over from the past, we must also recognise that it continues to be relevant in the present. Creating a genuine dialogue between targeted communities and police that facilitates a mutually negotiated understanding of hate crime requires a process and engagement that genuinely acknowledges that there is much room for improvement in ensuring that hate crime policy and law effectively translates into police action and community co-operation.

Conclusion

The hate crime agenda had its genesis in the social justice movements that emerged in the 1960s, particularly the Civil Rights Movement in the United States. Today, most Western countries have hate crime frameworks that recognise the particular harms to individual victims and targeted communities that arise from these crimes. Translating hate crime law and policy into everyday policing, however, has proved a challenge. There remains an implementation gap between law and policy on the books and the policing of hate crime. Even where police organisations commit to pursuing the objectives of hate crime frameworks with vigour, translating such commitment into day-to-day law enforcement is difficult. Police occupational culture, the way crimes are typically understood and investigated, the ambiguity that surrounds the definition of hate crime, police prejudice, and community perceptions about police all stand in the way of effective hate-crime law enforcement.

It is difficult to confirm categorically that the prioritising of hate crime 'has fundamentally altered the way in which police officers relate to the process of victimisation or recognise the wider harms of hate crime' (Chakraborti and Garland 2015). While human rights-consistent policing provides an opportunity to develop prejudice-sensitive practices, and community policing may provide a space to engage in dialogue with impacted communities, neither provide a panacea against the trust deficit that continues to exist.

4   Victoria Police and the Prejudice Motivated Crime Strategy

Introduction

This chapter introduces the case study that is the focus of this volume, detailing a local policing response to the pressures raised by minority group experiences of crime and violence. It traces the legal, socio-economic, and political drivers for the development of the Prejudice Motivated Crime Strategy by Victoria Police (VicPol) in 2010. The chapter then details the aims and objectives of the strategy, the significance and implications of the adoption of the term 'prejudice motivated crime', and the nature and genesis of the research partnership between the authors and VicPol. It then locates the strategy within the context of VicPol's history of and avowed commitment to community policing and human rights, as well as ongoing controversy over police racism, prejudice and excessive use of force against minority communities.

The approach in the PMC Strategy adopted by VicPol to deal with hate crime issues is distinctive, and thus instructive, in two ways. First, most hate crime policies require police to interpret existing law into everyday practice. As discussed in the previous chapter, much hate crime research examines how the meaning of hate crime legislation is distilled and transmitted through police organisations to front-line officers and communities. It examines the challenges of operationalising hate crime law and realising the intent of hate crime policy through policing. Also, as the previous chapters make clear, policing is critical to the effective implementation of hate crime policies, but police organisations and aspects of police culture are often resistant to the values that underpin the hate crime agenda. In Victoria, by way of contrast, police leadership did not respond to an externally imposed legislative and policy agenda in developing a policing approach; questions, therefore, about the implementation of hate crime policy are different from the typical questions about how police succeed or fail in implementing externally imposed policy and laws. In Victoria, there is effectively no offence that police can rely upon to charge hate crime offenders. VicPol then, in developing a strategy to address hate crime, proactively sought to advance human rights and social justice-related values such as inclusiveness, non-discrimination and social harmony tied to hate crime agendas. The policing of hate crime in Victoria provides an opportunity to examine the possibilities, contradictions and challenges that arise when police organisations take on the role of leading social change.

The second feature that sets the Victorian policing context apart, underlining its value as a case study in the field of hate crime and policing, is that VicPol adopted the distinctive terminology of 'prejudice motivated crime' in its strategy. The term 'prejudice motivated crime', which is not used by police in other jurisdictions, opens up opportunities for innovative and sensitive engagement with communities impacted by hate crimes. These opportunities arise because the meaning of the term is not widely understood and, as such, there is space for police and communities to work together to create shared understanding. Simultaneously, use of this term also raises the possibility that, similar to the term 'hate crime', it assumes divergent meanings for different minority groups and police, and these gaps in understanding are not easily addressed. Ambiguities surrounding terminology potentially undermine the PMC Strategy's utility and give rise to misunderstandings and thwarted expectations for both impacted communities and police.

Drivers of the Victoria Police Prejudice Motivated Crime Strategy

Prior to introduction of the VicPol PMC Strategy in 2010, a body of evidence existed suggesting that hate crime was a problem in Victoria. VicPol's Prejudice Motivated Crime Strategy diagnosis paper notes that prejudice motivated crime is a global social problem before indicating that '[r]esearch also shows that Prejudice Motivated Crime is a problem in Victoria' (2010). The paper points to evidence of this problem, including complaints made to the Victorian Human Rights Commission about racial and religious vilification and complaints about discrimination based on impairment (Victoria Police 2010). The paper also refers to research suggesting high levels of homophobic violence and harassment (Gray *et al.* 2006). In addition, it points to research that indicates that international students in Victoria perceived threats to their safety to have a racial, religious or cultural dimension (Babacan *et al.* 2010). Before the PMC Strategy was introduced, VicPol statistics indicated 1,891 recorded prejudice motivated crimes between 2001 and 2002, and 2009 and 2010, with the majority (52.4 per cent) related to race or ethnicity. Yet, most of the PMC crimes categorised under race or ethnicity were recorded as 'other', providing little detail on the kinds of racial or ethnic prejudice behind these incidents. Based on this, the paper concluded that recorded race/ethnicity categories on the police data-based 'are restricted and limit our ability to understand and analyse Prejudice Motivated Crime' (Victoria Police 2010). Other categories of prejudice recorded by police included religion (22.3 per cent), sexual or gender identity (11.9 per cent), political beliefs or status (7.2 per cent), and physical and mental illness (4.3 per cent) (ibid.). The paper notes that there were 1,725 victims of prejudice motivated crime recorded in police databases between 2001–2002 and 2009–2010, with the main type of offence being assault, and other categories of crime including property damage, robbery, harassment and theft (ibid.).

While the VicPol diagnosis paper makes it clear that statistics on prejudice motivated crime were being gathered prior to the introduction of the strategy, it also found that approximately one-third of PMC incidents were inaccurately recorded, and this, combined with under-reporting, meant that VicPol was prepared to conclude that 'we do not fully understand the true extent and nature of Prejudice Motivated Crime in Victoria' (ibid.). The statistics and other evidence set out in the diagnosis paper make it clear that Victoria, along with many other jurisdictions, had an issue with hate crime, and that police recognised they were inadequately equipped to understand and respond to it. Beyond this there were legal, social and political drivers that underpinned the development of the PMC Strategy. We turn to these now.

Legal drivers

The legal context for the development of the PMC Strategy can be traced back to the *Racial and Religious Tolerance Act 2001* (Vic) (RRTA). This legislation was introduced well after similar legislation in other jurisdictions across Australia. NSW, for example, introduced this type of legislation in 1989 (Mason *et al.* 2012). The RRTA aligns with legislation across Australia and other Western countries that aim to create enforceable standards of civil conduct in multicultural societies. Despite this, the introduction of the RRTA produced considerable controversy and encountered substantial resistance (ibid.). The Victorian Act provides civil remedies for vilification or 'hate speech'. A particularly controversial aspect of the RRTA was the creation of criminal offences for serious racial (s. 24) and religious (s. 25) vilification, which involve the incitement of hatred through threats of physical harm. Although the VicPol PMC Strategy identifies the RRTA as a platform for its approach, the legislation is only rarely used as the basis for criminal charges, due to its narrow definition of vilification, high standard of proof and complex procedures (Meagher 2006). Very few RRTA offences are recorded in police databases (VicPol 2010). Statistics provided by VicPol indicate that in the 12 years since the introduction of the legislation until mid-2013, only 25 incidents were recorded as RRTA offences, and no convictions were recorded. No successful criminal prosecutions have occurred in the period since. It appears, then, that while the RRTA has shaped the policy context and may be symbolically significant, it is of very little practical relevance to police when dealing with hate crime (Chapman and Kelly 2004; Cowdery 2009; Gray *et al.* 2006; Meyerson 2009). As outlined above, police in Victoria, unlike police in many Western countries, do not have a hate crime offence that they can rely upon to charge suspects.

Sentencing legislation provides another strand to the legal context for the development of the PMC Strategy. Typical of many of the significant developments in relation to hate crime law and policy internationally (see Chapter 3), Victoria's sentencing legislation was amended in the wake of the controversy over violent attacks on minority group members and dissatisfaction and controversy over the official response to these attacks (see discussion below). In 2009, a section was added to the Victorian *Sentencing Act 1991* to address hate crime and its impacts on victims and targeted communities. The amendment provides that, if a court finds beyond reasonable doubt that a criminal offence is motivated by prejudice or hatred, this will be an aggravating factor in sentencing. In relation to this provision, the court must have regard to s. 5(2)(daaa) of the Act, specifically:

> whether the offence was motivated (wholly or partly) by hatred for or prejudice against a group of people with common characteristics with which the victim was associated or with which the offender believed the victim was associated.

Although this new provision did not create a hate crime offence, it did recognise the nature of the harms produced by hate crime through the provision of harsher penalties for offences motivated by prejudice. A report by the Organisation for Security and Co-operation in Europe suggests that unless hate crime motivation is 'explicitly recognised and punished' in legislation (OSCE 2009), the potential to achieve a deterrent effect and a wider inclusionary impact is lost. By providing the opportunity for courts to punish more harshly offences motivated by prejudice or group hatred, the sentencing legislation aims to meet the hate crime policy goals of deterrence and, linked to this, social inclusion through recognising and supporting the human rights of minority groups. Though the aggravated sentencing provision does not provide police with an avenue for charging an offender, it does place an onus upon police to identify and collect evidence capable of convincing a sentencing court beyond reasonable doubt that an offence was motivated by prejudice or group hatred. Unless hate crimes are effectively identified and investigated by police, sentencing provisions become irrelevant. The PMC Strategy aligns policing practices directly with the aims of the sentencing legislation, implemented a year previously, so it is not surprising that it explicitly draws on the Act's definition of such crimes.

Social drivers

The amendments to the sentencing legislation and the subsequent strategy were initiated after violent attacks on minority group members and dissatisfaction and controversy over the official response, including that of police, to these attacks. The immediate precursor was a number of attacks on Indian students, typically by gangs of young men in metropolitan Melbourne. These violent crimes initially came to public attention in early 2009. The attack on Shravan Kumar Theerthala on 23 May 2009 was one of the first such incidents to trigger public outrage and a broader debate about racism, violence and the role of the police. Shravan was at a birthday party when gate-crashers attacked him with a screwdriver, leaving him with life threatening injuries and resulting in long-term, severe disabilities (Forbes-Mewett *et al.* 2015). In January 2010, 21-year-old Indian accounting graduate Nitin Garg was fatally stabbed by a teenage boy as he walked through a park at night on his way to work. The epicentre of these and other attacks on Indian students was Melbourne's western suburbs. At the time of these attacks, there were approximately 120,000 Indian students in Australia, a large increase over previous years, with Melbourne host to the largest concentration of such students (Joudo Larsen *et al.* 2011; Smith 2010).

These violent crimes against Indian students attracted national as well as international media attention, impacting on Australia's diplomatic relations with India, an increasingly important economic partner. The attacks and consequent dissatisfaction with the police and political response also impacted on Australia's lucrative and volatile tertiary-education export market. Higher education is one of Australia's largest export markets, generating billions of dollars annually. This sector is substantially reliant on international student fees to subsidise local students and remain financially viable (Davis 2006; Mason 2012b) and Australia's place in this increasingly competitive sector is thus heavily dependant on its image as a tolerant, safe, multicultural country (Forbes-Mewett *et al.* 2015). Yet, its reputation as a safe host country for Indian students was tarnished by the attacks and by what was seen as an inadequate official response, which failed to fully recognise the motivation for the attacks and the impact of these on the targeted community. As a result, the number of Indian students choosing to study in Australia fell markedly between 2010 and 2012 (Baas 2015). At the heart of the controversy over the attacks was fierce debate about whether the attacks were racist in nature, exposing significant disagreement between community-oriented and police understandings of racist violence, as well as the criteria through which racist and other forms of hate crime were to be categorised and defined (Baas 2015; Mason 2012b). The perceived failures in police response and understanding led to accusations that VicPol harboured racist attitudes. After the fatal stabbing of Nitin Garg, one Indian newspaper published a cartoon depicting a police officer wearing a Ku Klux Klan style hood and a text bubble which read 'we are yet to ascertain the nature of the crime', with the caption 'Indian killed in Australia' (Wilson 2010).

While this series of violent attacks were understood by many in the Indian community, particularly recent arrivals, as part of a broader culture of prejudice and discrimination, Australian politicians made a point of arguing that theirs was not a racist country (Mason 2012b; Smith 2010; Van Dijk 1992). Police maintained a somewhat contradictory stance, stating at times that the attacks were not racially motivated, while at other times conceding Indian students may have been targeted because of their ethnic or racial identity.

VicPol's initial response was to portray the attacks as 'opportunist' crimes motivated by financial gain (Baas 2015; Mason 2012b). Although acknowledging that people of Indian origin were over-represented as victims of robbery in Melbourne's western suburbs, police rejected the claim that the victims were primarily or typically targeted because of their race or ethnicity. They did, however, concede this could sometimes be the case (VicPol 2009a, 2009b). According to media reports, in early 2009, robberies in Melbourne's western suburbs had increased 27 per cent, and police estimated that a third of the victims were of Indian appearance. It was reported that '[a] special police group has been formed to combat the robberies amid fears that some are racially motivated and that Indian international students are soft targets because they carry iPods and laptops on trains late at night.' The police recommended Indian students use well-lit routes and not display iPods and phones or use their first language in public (Topsfield 2009). In June 2009, however, after protests by Indian nationals attracting thousands of demonstrators, VicPol's then chief commissioner, Simon Overland, publicly admitted that some of the attacks were 'clearly racist in motivation' (Rennie 2009).

In a study of international student safety, Babacan *et al.* (2010) interviewed members of VicPol and concluded from this that '[m]ost police could think of incidents in which both opportunism and racism were combined' and that some police officers felt racism was 'sometimes a clear secondary element used to further humiliate or weaken the resistance of victims during the course of a robbery or an assault' (ibid.).

While it is clear that police did acknowledge that racism could be an element in some attacks on Indian students, the rejection of the racism tag and statements that focused on the behaviour of the Indian victims angered those who felt unsafe and provoked those who felt that racism was an element that was being downplayed. The police characterisation of the attacks as opportunistic, rather than racist, in some statements, along with the advice to potential targets to modify their behaviour while in public, was 'mocked and criticised' by sections of the public and in the media (Baas 2015). Subsequent research found dissatisfaction with police for not publicly characterising the attacks as racist, responding slowly and not recognising the serious impact of the violence on the Indian community (Babacan *et al.* 2010; Graycar 2010). A study on perceptions of community safety amongst international students in Melbourne found that 50 per cent of international students who reported perceived threats to their safety believed that these threats had a racial, religious or cultural dimension, compared with only 17 per cent of domestic students (Babacan *et al.* 2010). While racism may have only been only one motive amongst several, or have had more or less salience, depending on the particular incident and offender, the failure of police to recognise or clearly condemn racism repeated the typical law enforcement mistake of examining incidents in isolation, rather than within the broader social processes that render it meaningful and particularly harmful for the targeted community (Bowling 1999). As one of the authors has argued elsewhere about the response to the attacks on Indian students: 'While the label of "racism" risks over-determining the multiplicity of drivers behind this victimisation, in the absence of more accurate descriptors, it is an important way of signalling the prejudicial element' (Mason 2012b). While a broad victim-oriented definition of hate crime would help to classify those incidents or crimes, where the victim perceived the motive to be one of prejudice, as hate incidents or crimes (see Chapter 2), such definitions bring with them their own challenges (see Chapter 7). The history of the drivers behind the PMC Strategy exposes the important public-relations role that terminology plays in the field of crime, at the same time as it reveals that real advancement in this field requires more than the will to use a particular vocabulary to publicly identify and record such offences. It also requires a commitment from police to work with vulnerable communities to develop a shared understanding of the rights violations that are implicit to hate crime.

Political drivers

Australia, and Victoria in particular, attracted substantial criticism in the international media and reputational damage over the handling of the attacks on Indian students. The United Nations rebuked the Victorian government and police for ignoring racial motives behind the assaults and criticised the lack of police statistics on migrant victims of crime. It stated that '[i]t regrets the failure by the government and police (both at a state and federal level) to address the racial motivation of these acts' (Flitton 2010). The perceived failures of police response to the attacks on Indian students, combined with the damage to Australia's international reputation as a tolerant, safe multicultural society, and the negative impact on economic interests that flowed from this, crystalised concerns about hate crimes and incidents and highlighted the absence of specific policing policies and structures.

Although the attacks on Indian students and the fall-out from these was the most immediate driver for the PMC Strategy, there was another high-profile case in 2006 involving an off-duty police officer, the verbal abuse of members of the Jewish community, and the harassment and assault of a Jewish male, Menachem Vorchheimer. The police response to this incident, and the failure of individual officers to be held responsible for their involvement in the crime, continued to attract critical attention over a number of years, as the assault victim pursued the issue through official channels and the media. Public criticism of an alleged cover-up brought into question the police commitment to the impartial and professional investigation of violent crimes against members of minority communities (see, for example, Rule and Silvester 2010). These perceptions of VicPol as insensitive or hostile towards minority communities, and unable or unwilling to respond with vigour and commitment to hate crimes, were also part of the impetus behind the introduction of the PMC Strategy.

Victoria Police's research partnership with the authors

It was in the context of the furore over attacks on Indian students, the above high-profile case involving the Jewish community, and other sources of evidence of hate crime, that in 2009 the authors were approached by VicPol to develop a research project, subsequently titled Targeted Crime: Policing and Social Inclusion. As discussions progressed, the aim of the collaboration became to submit a proposal for funding to the Australian Research Council's Linkage Grants scheme on policing and hate crime. This funding scheme is designed to foster research partnerships between academics and industry partners. The industry partners, in this case VicPol, are typically required to commit cash, resources and personnel time to proposed projects, and members of the partner organisation are listed as collaborators on funding applications. VicPol, particularly under the leadership of Chief Commissioner Christine Nixon (2001–2009), who herself has a master's degree from Harvard University, had initiated a number of research partnerships with academics aimed at generating new knowledge to deal with sensitive policing issues, particularly those involving minority communities (see, for example, Pickering *et al.* 2008). Bringing together six criminologists with expertise in policing and hate crime from three Australian universities, the project, as it developed through discussions between the researchers and police, aimed to improve understanding amongst police of hate crimes and the impacts of these crimes on targeted communities using qualitative and quantitative research methods.

Initially, the research project's primary objective was to produce a best-practice policing framework to deal with hate crime. However, after the initial project was submitted to the Australian Research Council in the first half of 2010 and before it was awarded funding in 2011, VicPol, in response to the perceived urgency of the issue, developed its PMC Strategy. The initiation of the strategy, ahead of the research project commencing, required a re-orientation of the research project towards supporting the policies and practices mandated in the strategy. It aimed to build knowledge about minority community experiences and understanding of the nature and extent of hate crime, and their expectation and accounts of the policing of these crimes. Fundamentally, the research project shifted to focus on considering the precursors for the effective implementation of the strategy. The methods were subsequently refined in order to provide insight and guidance to police on the challenges of implementing the strategy, while achieving the original objectives of analysing the incidence of hate crime in Victoria. The research project that went forward employed a range of objectives and methods, both qualitative and quantitative. Major activities included: mapping comparable policies in other jurisdictions to ensure that VicPol was well-informed about a range of different policing approaches; conducting focus groups with affected communities in order to enhance police knowledge of incidences of PMC as experienced by communities, and to garner knowledge about the community's responses to the strategy and experiences of policing; evaluating the effectiveness of new PMC training through surveys directed at recruits; analysing sentencing case law to understand how the Australian courts are applying and interpreting the concept of prejudice motivated crime; undertaking a quantitative analysis of VicPol data to assess changes in reporting practices since the introduction of the strategy; and conducting interviews with key personnel in VicPol to gather perspectives on the impact of the strategy and the greatest challenges of implementation in the five years since its launch.

PMC Strategy

In early 2010, Chief Commissioner Simon Overland requested that the Crime Strategy Group of VicPol develop a plan to address the problem of prejudice motivated crime (VicPol Diagnosis Paper 2010). In 2011, the PMC Strategy was launched. Australia has a diversity of policy and legislative initiatives that promote human rights, equality, multiculturalism and principles of anti-discrimination (for example, the Australian Human Rights Commission's 2012 National Anti-Racism Strategy). There are, however, few specific hate crime policies. Particular forms of hate crime, such as violence against LGBTI communities, have been tackled convincingly in some jurisdictions through government, inter-agency and community partnerships (for example, the NSW Government's Strategic Framework 2007–2012 – Working Together: Preventing Violence against Gay, Lesbian, Bisexual and Transgender People). Some of these policing policies have been in place for a number of years (for example, the NSW Police Force Policy on Sexuality and Gender Diversity was originally issued in 1997). Such policies have not been widely replicated in other Australian jurisdictions. Specific policies addressing the rights and needs of other hate crime target groups have also been slow to emerge. Although the promotion of effective hate crime policing is often identified as a priority in police policy documents in other Australian police forces, for example, through systems for recording hate crime, Victoria is the only jurisdiction in Australia to have introduced a comprehensive, specific policy statement on hate crime (Mason *et al.* 2012).

The PMC Strategy seeks to increase reporting and build better relationships with targeted communities, in the hope of sending explicit messages around social cohesion and the unacceptability of hate crime. The vision of the strategy is to develop a 'whole of organisation' response that enables the organisation to tackle the problem of PMC through sustained, integrated and coordinated capacity building (VicPol 2010). The strategy is concerned with addressing low reporting rates, harm to individuals and communities, and gaps in organisational responses (ibid.). Specifically, the strategy aims to increase VicPol's understanding of PMC, reduce the incidence of PMC in Victoria, and increase community confidence to report PMC (ibid.). To address these concerns, the plan focuses on key gaps and issues in VicPol's extant response. These gaps are set out to include: internal education and training; data collection and recording; analytical capability and intelligence; investigative responses; accountability and governance frameworks for monitoring progress and outcomes; policy formulation; and community engagement (ibid.). The overall performance measure of the strategy is to increase the number of PMC reports to police (ibid.). This approach is consistent with good practice internationally and mirrors jurisdictions where the recognition and recording of hate crime is a key element of inclusive community policing (for example, UK Home Office Police Standards Unit 2005). A complication inherent in the aims of the strategy is that improvements in community confidence may lead to an increase in reported and recorded prejudice motivated crime that could *prima facie* be taken as evidence of an increase in the occurrence of PMC. VicPol recognises this and, as in reforms in the policing of sexual assault or family violence, perceives any increases in reporting to be a positive development. VicPol maintains that any initial increases in reporting are likely to stabilise over time, so that in the longer term a more precise picture of any decrease in PMC can be captured. However, it appears that the aim of increased reporting of PMC has not been achieved in the years since the introduction of the strategy. We discuss these issues in more detail in Chapter 8.

As a central feature of the strategy, VicPol adopted a definition of prejudice motivated crime consistent with the *Sentencing Act 1991* (Vic), cited above, yet flexible enough to incorporate 'new groups and issues' as they emerge:

> A prejudice motivated crime is a criminal act which is motivated (wholly or partly) by hatred for or prejudice against a group of people with common characteristics with which the victim was associated or with which the offender believed the victim was associated. Characteristics include: religious affiliation, racial or cultural origin, sexual orientation, sex, gender identity, age, impairment (within the meaning of the *Equal Opportunity Act 1995*), or homelessness.
>
> (VicPol 2010)

The definition has three noteworthy elements: first, a criminal act must have taken place; second, it hinges on motivation driven by the offender's hatred or prejudice, whether wholly or partly; third, it adopts a flexible approach to protected categories.

Under the VicPol strategy, PMC is recorded only if there is a criminal act. The recording of PMC is divided into six motivation categories: sexuality/gender identity (homophobia); physical/mental impairment; political beliefs or status; race/ethnicity; religion; and 'other', including homelessness, age and gender (see also Chapter 8).

While VicPol maintains that it recognises the impact of hate incidents on the target community, the strategy adopts a definition of PMC limited to criminal offences (VicPol Diagnostic Paper 2010). In the UK, by way of contrast, police are required to record 'hate incidents' as well as a 'hate crimes' (Home Office Police Standards Unit 2005). Hate incidents are any incidents that are perceived by the victim or any other person to be motivated by prejudice or hate towards specified groups, while hate crimes must be a breach of the criminal law (MPS 2010).

A key element of the Victorian definition hinges on motivation. By way of comparison, the NSW Police Force's 2011 policy statement on Sexuality and Gender Diversity defines homophobic/transgender crime more broadly, as 'hate and fear based on harassment, abuse or violence directed at someone *because* they are, or are perceived to be, gay, lesbian, bisexual or transgender. It includes physical and non-physical forms of abuse and the fear of violence' (NSW Police

Force 2011; our emphasis). The use of 'because' in the NSW definition is broader than the concept of PMC adopted by VicPol. Like comparable tests that are found in hate crime statutes in the US, the former includes crimes motivated by homophobia *and* situations where the victim is selected because of his or her presumed membership of the targeted group (Mason 2015). Under such definitions, it is not necessary to prove *why* the offender selected the victim, only that he or she did so because of a perception that the victim was a member of the group in question. In contrast, hate crime policies and statutes that rely upon motive in their definition require proof that the offender's prejudice or group hated is the *reason why* he or she committed the offence. The motive element in VicPol's definition also sets it apart from definitions, such as those that operate in the UK, that only require evidence that the offender *demonstrated* hostility towards the victim based on selected characteristics, such as race or religion (Chakraborti and Garland 2015). In effect, the strategy's reliance upon a motive test sets a comparatively high threshold for identifying and defining hate crime (Mason and Dyer 2013).

The strategy does, however, take a relatively flexible approach to the kinds of prejudice covered, including prejudice based on religious affiliation, racial or cultural origin, sexual orientation, sex, gender identity, age, impairment and homelessness. While race, religious affiliation, sexual orientation, impairment and, to a lesser extent, age are commonly protected in other policing policies through the use of the same or comparable terms (for example, the term 'disability' is used by the London MPS instead of 'impairment'), it is less common for sex and homelessness to be explicitly included (see Chapter 1). While this elasticity stands in stark contrast to the prescriptive approach taken by many international hate crime statutes when specifying the narrow range of group differences covered by the law, it is consistent with recent policing trends, most notably in the UK, to recognise, record and respond to an increasing array of human characteristics that make people vulnerable to violence and abuse (Chakraborti and Garland 2012; Mason 2014).

VicPol is currently the only policing jurisdiction to consistently use the term 'prejudice motivated crime' to refer to offending that occurs within this context. As we noted in Chapter 1, other Australian policing jurisdictions (including Tasmania Police and the NSW Police Force) have used this term, but do so interchangeably with other terms, including 'hate crime' and 'bias crime'. 'Prejudice' was selected because it aligns with other relevant Victorian legislation, particularly sentencing legislation (see above). However 'prejudice' has been critiqued as a 'complicated, broad and cloudy concept' that can be defined either narrowly or broadly, thereby undermining the ability to accurately measure the extent of such crimes and incidents (Jacobs and Potter 1998; see also Hall 2005; Iganski 2008). While the strategy's definition of prejudice motivated crime also makes reference to 'hatred', as we discussed in Chapter 2, the concept of hatred has attracted equal criticism for pathologising and over-dramatising behaviour that is often a manifestation of everyday inter-group conflict, rather than extreme personal emotion.

Since its launch in 2011, VicPol's PMC Strategy has been supported by a range of institutional and operational changes that we explore throughout this book. Notably, prejudice motivated crime and human rights have been integrated into in-service training for recruits, new systems of recording PMC have been introduced, a two-tiered process for confirming and investigating offences that are initially categorised as prejudice motivated is now in place and, importantly, a Priority Communities Division (PCD) has been established as a mechanism for engagement with vulnerable communities, with the capacity to seek feedback from those communities on the categorisation of individual hate crime incidents. Responsibility for the PMC Strategy sits within the PCD, whose goal is to bring about cultural change in the way that police 'think' and 'operate' in relation to vulnerable and marginalised communities (The Age 2014). The PCD operates as an external 'conduit' between police and different community groups, but also internally into 'the corporate level' (Senior Operational Officer, VicPol, interview 6 May 2016). In effect, the PMC Strategy itself has been embedded in larger victim-centred and community-tailored approaches to policing which, together, are said by VicPol to have engendered 'a huge shift for the organisation and one that you can definitely see on the front line' (Senior Operational Officer, VicPol, interview 6 May 2016).

Yet, implementation of the strategy presents challenges for VicPol at all levels, including the provision of effective corporate leadership, intelligence-gathering, integrated training, sensitive and informed investigation, victim liaison, the establishment of inter-agency partnerships, and accurate recording. As we suggested in the Introduction, perhaps the most fundamental challenge, however, is to define and identify the kinds of criminal conduct that amount to PMC and, in turn, the nature of the evidence or circumstances needed to establish that an offence is motivated by prejudice for reporting and sentencing purposes. The recognition of crimes or incidents as prejudice motivated is important when communicating with the public, affected communities and victims. The attacks against Indian students and the criticisms of police characterisation of those crimes underline the importance of police recognising and being clear about prejudice as *the* or *a* driver of offences against minority communities. They further emphasise that a minority community's perception that offences are prejudice motivated is also important to take into account in the investigation of and public response to such crimes.

Policing diverse communities: partnership and conflict

The Victoria PMC Strategy arose out of a contradiction at the heart of contemporary policing. Hate crime policies are consistent with an emphasis on human rights and non-discrimination in policing. Partnerships with minority communities, strategies that promote social inclusion and respect for diversity, such as the PMC Strategy, promote a community policing ethos and respect for human rights as part of a police mission. Hate crime policies, however, typically arise amid a perception, well-supported by evidence, that police are not sensitive to prejudice as a motivation for crime and, moreover, express prejudice through everyday policing. Australian research reveals that both minority and non-minority groups hold the perception that police both unfairly target ethnic groups as potential suspects *and* neglect or trivialise the victimisation of these same communities, undermining the perceived credibility and legitimacy of police (Joudo Larsen 2010; Murphy and Cherney 2011). The tension between police as champions of social justice and human rights, while at the same time reflecting, reinforcing and expressing prejudice, is evident in the relationship between police and minority communities in Victoria. Since the turn of the twenty-first century, VicPol has in many respects been a leader in community policing and human rights. At the same time, however, there is an ongoing history of police discrimination, prejudice, and excessive use of force against minority communities.

The strategic focus of VicPol at the time the plan was developed and implemented is set out in the Way Ahead 2008–2013. This maintains that 'Victoria Police recognises the diversity of our community and is committed to providing an equitable, accessible and responsive policing service to each individual community in Victoria' (VicPol 2007).

The genesis for this emphasis on diversity, equity and community was set in place when Christine Nixon was appointed chief commissioner in 2001, continuing in the role until 2009. Apart from being Australia's first, and one of the world's only, female chief commissioners, Nixon came to the role with a firm commitment to community policing (Nixon and Chandler 2011; Prenzler 2004). Nixon's commitment to police support for diversity and engagement with minority communities was exemplified when she controversially took part in Melbourne's Gay Pride Parade in 2002. She explains her rationale for taking part in the parade as being 'to reinforce Victoria Police as an agency with a focus on community safety, on social harmony, that was responsive to community needs and priorities' (Nixon and Chandler 2011).

One of the rationales for and objectives of the PMC Strategy is to work with minority communities. The need to work with and for communities has become integral to professional police services, merging with crime prevention objectives and problem-oriented approaches to produce a commitment to community engagement (Putt 2010). Similar to the stated objectives of most modern police forces in Western countries (Oliver 2001), community policing, particularly under Nixon, became a strongly articulated element of policing in Victoria (Nixon and Chandler 2011; Pickering *et al.* 2008). Rather than instituting significant organisational restructure, VicPol's version of community policing tended to engage directly with local communities to initiate community-focused practices and partnerships in order to reduce crime and promote higher levels of confidence and trust (Beyer 1993; Fleming 2010; Murphy *et al.* 2008).

Much contemporary operational effort made under the banner of community policing has focused on 'hard to reach' or 'at risk' communities, and the most successful initiatives, or those with the most visible impact, appear to be those that target particular groups, defined according to criteria such as age, ethnicity, gender, risk, familiarity and experience of crime (Bartkowiak-Theron and Corbo Crehan 2010; Fleming and McLaughlin 2010). This type of targeting is in line with the focus of the PMC Strategy. While community policing has the capacity to improve engagement with what are seen as vulnerable populations, these populations are, of course, classified as such because they are seen as at higher risk of becoming victims or offenders, or both. These classifications may themselves be problematic, particularly when skewed either in conception or practice towards the view that such communities primarily represent potential offenders. While the PMC Strategy is focused on minority communities as potential victims, the research on police culture, community policing, racial profiling and the like makes it clear that it may be difficult for police to shift their suspicion of certain categories of people or communities away from the 'suspect community' frame (Joudo Larsen 2010; Murphy and Cherney 2011). The continued tendency of police to see engagement with marginalised communities as an opportunity to gather intelligence, rather than to genuinely relate, underlines the resilience of police attitudes that are prone to seeing marginalised communities through a criminalising lens (see Chapter 3; also McKernan and Weber 2016).

When police focus solely on communities' criminogenic factors, policing is likely to be perceived as unfair, biased, disrespectful, uncaring and untrustworthy. This perception challenges the notion of procedural justice, the main elements of which are neutrality, respect, trustworthiness and voice (Murphy and Barkworth 2014; Tyler and Murphy 2011). Procedural justice is critical in legitimating the exercise of police power (Bottoms and Tankebe 2012; Tankebe 2013). Community engagement premised upon procedural justice fosters communities' self-worth and, as a consequence, champions a more cooperative and reciprocal relationship between law enforcement and the communities they police (Murphy and Barkworth 2014; Murphy and Cherney 2011). The importance of treating victims and targeted communities with dignity and respect cannot be overstated – there is a correlation between such positive treatment, community satisfaction with policing, and a willingness to report crimes, including prejudice motivated crimes (Murphy and Barkworth 2014). However, procedural justice is not a panacea, and McKernan and Weber (2016) raise doubts over its effectiveness in fostering collaboration between police and marginalised communities. For example, perceptions of police as 'a white Anglo force' may be the basis of claims of unfair treatment amongst minority communities (ibid.).

While community policing and engagement with vulnerable communities is generally understood as promoting social inclusion and the antithesis of harder styles of policing, it has been problematised as a way of continuing histories of oppression, including discriminatory policing. Russell, for example, in a recent analysis of Christine Nixon's participation in the Melbourne Gay Pride March, suggests that the involvement of police in such displays of inclusiveness 'contributes to the normalisation of queerness as a site to be continually policed and regulated' and that it also 'buttresses police reputation against the negative press associated with incidents of police brutality' (Russell 2016).

The continued over-policing of marginalised communities has led to criticism that VicPol's community policing initiatives have failed to deliver on the public rhetoric, operating essentially as a smoke screen for more hidden developments, such as a trend towards paramilitary policing, whereby certain communities or categories of individuals are approached as enemies rather than rights-bearing citizens (McCulloch 2001). Community legal centres working with marginalised and racialised young people have consistently challenged VicPol's commitment to community policing, arguing, for example, that police 'community liaison' often operates as intelligence-gathering in marginalised communities, deepening distrust of police (Fitzroy Legal Service 2010; see also Sentas 2014). Hopkins (2009) claims that the complaints system in Victoria does not adequately respond to reported incidents of police misconduct, including discrimination and brutality against ethnic minorities. A racial discrimination action against VicPol on behalf of a group of African youth (Flemington Legal Service 2013; VicPol 2013) exposed the concerns of many stakeholders, including Indigenous Victorians, for whom over-policing, racial profiling, prejudice and police excessive use of force are significant and long-standing problems (Cunneen 2001; Hopkins 2009).

In response to critiques such as those set out above, VicPol introduced the Equality Is Not the Same process in 2013. In adopting this process, it acknowledged that discriminatory approaches undermine community trust and respect for police. Non-discriminatory approaches are integral to perceptions of procedural justice (Murphy and Barkworth 2014). VicPol training now recognises that bias, whether conscious or unconscious, can impact on police exercise of discretion, such as when to stop a person or how much force to use when arresting someone. The VicPol manual now defines racial profiling as 'making policing decisions that are not based on objective or reasonable justification, but on stereotypical assumptions about race, colour, language, ethnicity, ancestry or religion'. This new policy requires officers to consider under what law or authorisation they are acting when they stop someone (Kelly 2016).

An examination of the critiques of VicPol exposes three primary concerns and demands (Babacan *et al.* 2010; Fitzroy Legal Service 2010; Flemington Legal Service 2013; Graycar 2010; Hopkins 2009; Mason 2012b; Sentas 2014). First is the need for police to *recognise* the racial or prejudiced nature of (at least some of) the hostility directed towards minority communities by the public and to engage in culturally appropriate practices of identification and investigation (the problem of under-policing). Second is the need to move away from practices of racial profiling and hostility at the operational level towards greater respect and *fair* treatment (the problem of over-policing). Third is the call for a public *commitment* from VicPol's leadership to challenge organisational values widely seen as insensitive to the needs of minority communities. Put simply, minority communities need open lines of communication that facilitate genuine engagement and negotiation with police. They want their experiences and perceptions of PMC to be taken seriously and to have input into policy and responses (Murphy and Cherney 2011). They also want to feel safe from prejudiced abuse – both from police and the public – and to trust that police will play an active and positive role in helping engender such safety. Securing this kind of trust is imperative if Victoria's minority communities are to gain the confidence to report hate crime (Hough *et al.* 2010), which comes down to the belief that police will treat their complaints fairly and effectively. The PMC Strategy, sitting alongside initiatives such as the Equality Is Not the Same process, and embedded within the PCD, is an attempt to respond to community demands and critiques and to move away from the police culture of the past, which expressed and entrenched prejudice by seeing minority communities as primarily in need of control rather than protection.

Despite the good will exemplified by the PMC Strategy, vigilance will be required to ensure that the prejudice-sensitive policing becomes a reality that contributes to social justice and the substantive realisation of human rights. To be effective, the strategy needs to function as a significant public-relations document that looks externally to facilitate dialogue and partnerships with vulnerable communities at the local level. This is not to ignore the importance of internal practices but simply to say that the strategy provides police with a unique avenue to build trust with minority communities by sending the message that their concerns are recognised, that their complaints will be treated fairly, and that VicPol is committed to working with them towards the development of a shared and negotiated understanding of prejudice motivated crime. The absence of an animating offence in Victoria opens up the opportunity to pursue these community policing objectives, without the usual prosecutorial restrictions on investigation – to take the harm of hate crime to victim communities, not just the legal liability of the offender, as a defining feature of PMC.

Conclusion

Just as the Stephen Lawrence Inquiry and its revelations of institutionalised policing racism had a major impact on community-oriented policies to tackle hate crime in the UK (HM Government 2012), VicPol's PMC Strategy is the product of some serious trust deficits in the relationship between police and marginalised communities. The immediate precursor to the development of the strategy was a number of serious attacks on Indian international students in the inner west of Melbourne that came to public attention in 2009, sparking a fierce debate about racism in the community and the commitment of police to protecting minority communities. While the attacks on Indian students and the ensuing fall-out was the most obvious trigger for the development of the strategy, there was much evidence to suggest that there was a more long-standing and widespread issue with hate crime in Victoria. Further, there was a trust deficit between police and minority communities, underpinned by a history of discriminatory policing in which such communities were typically under-serviced as victims and over-policed as suspects.

Victims and communities are more likely to report PMC to police if they feel confident they will be treated with procedural fairness (Murphy and Barkworth

2014; Tankebe 2013). Trust that this will happen is built on perceptions of police effectiveness, culturally appropriate and sensitive responses to crime, and police reputations within communities (McKernan and Weber 2016).

In developing a PMC strategy and seeking the assistance of the authors as academics with expertise in policing and hate crime, VicPol was attempting to respond to the immediate criticisms related to the attacks on Indian students and to put in place a systematic process to ensure professional and non-discriminatory policing. The PMC Strategy is both a product of the trust deficit between VicPol and minority communities and an attempt to deal with this.

The VicPol PMC Strategy offers an instance of the trend across Western societies towards 'particularizing protections against abuse' (Feenan 2006) for groups that are commonly perceived to be marginalised or especially vulnerable, with the broader objective of promoting values of tolerance and inclusion. The strategy is unique in that it was developed without an animating hate crime offence. The lack of a prosecutorial imperative flowing from this means that the criminal law provides an indicative but far from exhaustive framework for identifying the kind of criminal conduct that amounts to PMC in daily policing activity. This opens up the opportunity for police to pay closer attention to the needs of targeted communities in formulating the meaning of PMC, implementing the PMC Strategy and policing hate crime. In addition to their traditional role as gatekeepers of the criminal justice system, this places a responsibility upon police to become more active agents of social justice and human rights.

Part III

The research

5 Is it all in the name?

Changing terminologies, procedural justice and hate crime

Introduction

As we have discussed, hate crime is a culturally and historically situated social construct (Perry 2001). Understanding the prevalence of hate crime and the development of appropriate responses to its occurrence are dependant upon 'how hate crime is conceptualised and defined' (Jacobs and Potter 1998). However, what constitutes a hate crime is contested. As we demonstrated in Chapter 2, scholars tend to agree that hate crime encompasses unlawful activity (such as destruction of property, trespassing, harassment and violence) perpetrated against those with a particular racial, ethnic, religious, or sexual identity or those with a physical or mental disability (Barnes and Ephross 1994; Boyd *et al.* 1996; Green *et al.* 2001). Yet, not all such incidents are driven by hate. 'Hate', as determined by legislation, is evident in only a small number of hate crimes (McDevitt *et al.* 2010). Incidents may stem from prejudices, or 'negative feelings held by the offender towards a social group that, in their eyes, have an "outsider status"' (Garland and Chakraborti 2012). Official definitions of hate crime are generally highly restrictive (Chakraborti and Garland 2009; Garland 2012; Garland and Chakraborti 2012; Hall 2013) and studies find that only a small proportion of people can define a hate or bias motivated crime or know anything about hate crime laws (Chakraborti *et al.* 2014). In fact, the people most in need of legislative protection are often those who know the least about the laws and services available to protect them.

Jurisdictions across the US, Europe and Australia have sought to mobilise the criminal law in response to hate crime. Yet, the absence of an agreed-upon terminology capable of reflecting community perceptions and promoting human rights principles gets in the way of effective policing practice. Adopting inclusive terminology and definitions that leverage higher levels of criminal justice engagement and enable legal traction is increasingly the focus of key agencies internationally. 'Bias crime', for example emphasises the offender's bias, rather than hatred, towards a victim (Gerstenfeld 2013; Ignaski 2008; Lawrence 1999; Perry 2010b). Similarly, 'targeted violence' recognises both the vulnerability of the victim and the significance of the perpetrator's choice of that victim because of their perceived vulnerability (Stanko 2001). In employing the term 'prejudice motivated crime' to frame their strategy to tackle crime motivated by hate, bias or prejudice, Victoria Police have adopted a broad definition recognising that such crime may only be partly motived by hatred and including a wide range of characteristics which might be associated with prejudice motivated crime. VicPol considered this to be a more inclusive definition than other definitions that aligned effectively with existing legislative provisions and thus offered an important step in building greater trust with victims and potential victims of hate crime.

Regardless of the label and/or definition assigned to incidents motivated by bias, hate or prejudice, police–citizen relationships will remain fractured if perceptions, experiences and responses to crime across these two groups also remain misaligned (Shirlow *et al.* 2013). For hate crime policies to be effective, there must be an improvement in community perceptions of law enforcement (Perry 2010b). A growing body of literature demonstrates that the procedurally just treatment of victims and the validation of victimisation experiences by the police not only provide empowerment and a sense of closure to victims (Bradford *et al.* 2013) but predict future reporting behaviour (Bradford 2014; Sargeant *et al.* 2014; Sunshine and Tyler 2003). This is so even for victims that experienced a less than favourable outcome in their most recent encounter with the criminal justice system (Murphy and Barkworth 2014). Thus, in this chapter we argue that, as important as it is, a shared understanding of concepts alone is unlikely to improve police–citizen relationships, enhance reporting or facilitate the collection of evidence necessary for prosecution or sentencing.

Drawing on the accounts of victims and victim advocates from diverse community groups, we examine whether VicPol's PMC Strategy, and particularly the use of the more inclusive term 'prejudice motivated crime', has impacted reporting behaviour or willingness to report prejudice motivated incidents to police. Additionally, we consider the extent to which differences in terminology are associated with trust in the police and their response to prejudice motivated incidents.

Procedurally just policing and hate crime

A consistent theme in this book is the crucial role of police in the effective implementation of hate crime policies. In earlier chapters, we discussed the policy shift in policing hate crime towards 'prejudice-sensitive policing'. This approach recognises the historical and deep-rooted experience of hate crime victims as over-policed and under-protected (Hall 2013). Police are often the first responders to an incident motivated by bias or prejudice, and entrenched beliefs relating to hate crime laws and policies may strongly influence both how police assess hate crime evidence and interaction with victims. Considering the difficult history police have with many of the groups likely to experience hate crime victimisation, enhanced trust and increased reporting can only occur when police are viewed by victims as legitimate and procedurally just in the execution of their duties. Part of this process is agreeing on terminology that best represents incidents motivated by hate and/or bias and the meaning of these incidents for targeted communities. Having a shared language is central to starting a meaningful conversation about the significance of hate crime between police and the community. But the utility of mutual language and understanding can only be realised if police execute inclusive policies through inclusive practice (Chakraborti *et al.* 2014).

In criminological scholarship, the procedurally just treatment of citizens and the validation of citizen experiences is viewed as essential for building trust between police and the community and for increasing reporting behaviour. As we have already noted, there are four elements that characterise procedural justice: citizen participation, neutrality, respect and trustworthy motives (Mazerolle *et al.* 2013; Tyler and Murphy 2011). The procedural justice approach suggests that 'compliance with the law and willingness to cooperate with enforcement efforts are primarily shaped not by the threat of force or the fear of consequences, but rather by the strength of citizens' beliefs that law enforcement agencies are legitimate' (Schulhofer *et al.* 2011).

For most people, contacting the police occurs because the person is in need of help or they are calling to report a crime. The way in which police respond can have a significant impact on the outcome of the event, as perceived by the individual and can influence the willingness of that individual to contact the police in the future (Tyler 2003). When victims of crime perceive the police as acting in a procedurally just manner, they are more likely to report feelings of closure, empowerment and safety (Elliott *et al.* 2011). Tyler (2003) argues, 'people's reactions to legal authorities are based to a striking degree on their assessments of the fairness of the processes by which legal authorities make decisions and treat members of the public'. Studies demonstrate that this holds true for people from both minority and majority backgrounds. Tyler and Huo (2002) found that whites, Hispanics and African Americans are more likely to see the police as legitimate if interactions and procedures were perceived as procedurally just. It also holds true for minority group members who are increasingly the subject of counter-terrorism policing. A study of Muslims living in New York reveals individuals are more likely to cooperate with the police when they believed police are not unfairly targeting members of the Muslim community (Tyler *et al.* 2010). Moreover, members of the general population perceive the police as less legitimate when strategies target subgroups unfairly (Huq *et al.* 2011).

Perhaps as importantly, perceptions of procedural justice also influence the degree to which individuals respond to criminal justice decisions (Tyler *et al.* 1997). If individuals feel as though a criminal justice process has been procedurally just, they are more likely to accept a given outcome, even if that outcome is not in their favour. A survey of Australians revealed that, although victims reported they would cooperate with police in the future if they had experienced a favourable outcome with them, perceptions of procedural justice mediated this relationship (Murphy and Barkworth 2014). As Murphy and Barkworth (ibid.) suggest, victims of crime are 'less concerned about whether the outcome of their recent encounter with police was favourable. Instead, they are more concerned with police use of procedural justice and/or police effectiveness when deciding whether or not to report crime'.

This finding is particularly relevant when we consider police responses to hate crime victimisation. Internationally, crimes motivated by hate or bias are considerably less likely to result in a conviction (Lyons and Roberts 2014). In Australia, there are few incidents of hate crime formally sanctioned through penalty enforcements (Mason 2009). Additionally, in our analysis of racial and religious vilification complaints to VicPol up til June 2013, not one of the reported incidents resulted in a formal prosecution (see Chapter 4). Thus, for many victims, it is unlikely that convictions will acknowledge the bias motivation behind their victimisation. This lack of a favourable outcome may prevent people from coming forward if they experience future victimisation, or it may influence the extent to which they will cooperate with police on other matters. However, if victims of hate crime experience a procedurally just process, this may minimise the effect of this outcome on police perceptions or their future co-operation.

The focus groups

For VicPol, generating an understanding of the incidence of prejudice motivated crime is considered an important outcome of the PMC Strategy. Thus, a key goal for Victoria Police is to better understand what constitutes PMC, so as to influence the likelihood that victims of it will report these instances to the police. At present, the level of PMC that occurs in the community is not clear. As we noted in Chapter 4, VicPol statistics prior to the introduction of the strategy indicated a total of 1,891 recorded prejudice motivated crimes between 2001–2002 and 2009–2010, with the majority (52.4 per cent) related to race or ethnicity (we return to an analysis of reporting data in Chapter 7). Yet, despite the roll out of the strategy in 2010, under-reporting remains extremely common amongst victims. A study conducted by the Victorian Equal Opportunity and Human Rights Commission (2010), reveals that 57 per cent of respondents who had experienced a prejudice motivated crime did not formally report these incidents. Of those who did report, only 23 per cent reported the incident to VicPol. To this end, available data on PMC incidents are severely limited and do not illustrate (a) how high-priority groups make sense of what is classified as prejudice motivated crime or (b) whether or not the more inclusive sense of this new terminology facilitates the reporting of prejudice motivated crimes.

As part of our study, we conducted focus groups and interviews with high-priority victim groups in Victoria, Australia, including nine focus groups and five individual interviews ($N = 53$), undertaken across the following groups: migrant youth (first and second generation under 20 years old); the African community; homeless people; people with disabilities; Muslim women; the Jewish community; the Indian community; LGBTI people; and the Indigenous community. These groups represented communities with the core characteristics identified in the strategy and were identified by VicPol as key communities from their victimisation experiences (including recent high-profile events). Further, a number of these groups are representative of long-standing communities of concern in relation to PMC in legislation and academic literature. We contacted leaders of these groups and asked them to invite others who would be willing to meet with us to discuss VicPol's PMC Strategy.

We sought maximum variation sampling within and across the focus groups in relation to age and gender. Focus groups and interviews were all conducted in Melbourne. The interview schedule was thematically organised around: prejudice motivated crime terminology; nature, frequency and scale of incidents and issues; and the reporting of prejudice motivated crime (including to the police, third-party reporting and other reporting practices). The majority of participants were service providers who worked with various organisations representing particular groups. Some of our participants self-identified as previous victims of hate crime; however, we did not specifically classify participants as victim or non-victims as the actual victimisation experience was not the focus of our research. Instead, we were interested in: how our participants defined the types of incidents that were affecting members of their community; whether they believed a more inclusive terminology would influence greater trust in police; and what the barriers associated with reporting PMC incidents to the police were. Focus groups and interviews were transcribed and analysed using NVivo.

Understanding the term 'prejudice motivated crime': it's a mouthful ...

The literature and policy context in which the PMC Strategy was developed lays out the need for more inclusive and enabling language around hate crime to facilitate higher levels of reporting and, ultimately, a greater alignment of police and community understandings of hate crime. However, our sample of high-priority communities, i.e. those individuals and groups considered most likely to be the target of hate crime, reported varying responses to this more inclusive language.

Our participants were not strongly opposed to the term prejudice motivated crime, yet many perceived it to be 'a bit of a mouthful'. Indeed, our respondents differed in their views about the kind of terminology that best represented the incidents they experienced. Members of groups targeted because of their race preferred 'hate crime' or 'racially motivated' crime over 'prejudice motivated crime'. Participants from the African focus group noted that 'prejudice' failed to capture the distinct 'racial animosity' experienced by the African community. This sentiment was also reflected amongst participants in the Indigenous focus group. It was suggested that ' "hate crimes certainly simplifies it", but "racially motived crimes roll more easily off the tongue" '. The need to emphasise race in the conceptualisation of hate crime for some of our participants is likely due to the politicisation of race and the history of over-policing for particular minority groups in Australia (see Chapters 3 and 4). Recognising the racial animus of hate crimes goes hand in hand with the desire to be recognised as legitimate victims with the same rights as other members of society.

Groups targeted for reasons other than race and ethnicity believed that hate crime definitions needed to be more inclusive. For example, members of the disability focus group called for more terms that reflected crimes against vulnerable groups. For them, 'targeted crime' was the most appropriate label:

> PARTICIPANT 1: I think 'targeted crimes'.
> PARTICIPANT 2: What's that?
> PARTICIPANT 1: 'Targeted crime' 's not a bad actual name for it.… Easy laymen's terms people understand. It's like you can say that to anyone: 'Oh, you're targeting someone?'
> PARTICIPANT 2: Absolutely.
> PARTICIPANT 1: And you don't have to think, 'Oh, what's that actually mean?' … because the word actually reflects the meaning: targeted.

Importantly, for many, the problem was less about what hate or prejudice motivated incidents were called, but rather what the concept meant. This was particularly evident amongst members of the migrant youth group. One respondent asked 'Does it mean that those people who discriminate against but, like, ethnic group or something?' Others were uncertain whether it referred to 'people who are targeted racially' or representative of 'mostly … racially discrimination than prejudice'. As one member summed up: 'I think it's just a word that is only made for those people who can understand it, so the community wouldn't understand what it actually means'.

Concerns over the applicability of the term 'prejudice motivated crime' were also expressed in both the Indian and Indigenous groups. Although accounts from members of the Indian focus group suggested the term 'prejudice motivated crime' had merit, they felt it would only be of use to the community 'as long as they know the word meaning for "prejudice"'. Members of the Indigenous group were equally uncertain:

> PARTICIPANT: … When I heard it the first time, I asked you again, remember? 'What is it again?' And I said, 'Oh, is it this and that?' It sounds like hate crime for me …

The participants from the Muslim focus groups were the most strongly opposed to the term 'prejudice motivated crime'. As one member stressed:

> For people coming from good education backgrounds, they can receive it straight away, but you are dealing with normal people, with no high qualification and not fully educated in their own language, so imagine in English. So English is a barrier already and to come to a very big terms like that, they won't understand what that mean at all. To me – even to me, I had to actually go and find out exactly what you mean because I was thinking to be in this interview, so I wanted to make sure what that really means.

None of our respondents felt that the term 'prejudice motivated crime', however inclusive it was intended to be, clearly articulated what kind of behaviour could constitute an actual crime. As one member of the Jewish community focus group stated, 'Everyone knows what anti-Semitism is, but understanding what is criminal is another thing entirely.' This was further articulated by another participant in the Jewish focus group:

> In terms of which incidents ... within that spectrum would be of a criminal nature and therefore defined as a crime, as opposed to others which are hateful but may not be criminal, that's a grey area ... I don't think there'd be anyone in the Jewish community who wouldn't be aware of what anti-Semitism is in some shape or form, or even probably most people would have experienced it themselves in some shape or form, I would imagine. So – but again, what's criminal and what is reportable and – that's a grey area, yep.

The question over what constitutes a prejudice motivated crime was also raised in the focus group with members of the LGBTI community. The continuum of anti-social behaviour through to criminal offending was obscured by the imprecision of the label 'prejudice motivated crime'. Speaking specifically about the experiences of sex workers:

> It's the verbal harassment that people yell out of the cars all the time towards the sex workers. Because we're talking about LGBTI – the transgender sex workers who work later at night on the street, in particular – [who] are really vulnerable to that sort of behaviour, that sort of yelling stuff out of cars and getting things thrown at them and stuff like that. And of course we see that as a prejudice against their sexual orientation and gender identity, but then also of their profession.

Low-level prejudice motivated incidents were repeatedly reported by our participants, however, as found in other research (Home Office 2013; Williams and Tregidga 2013); those perceived as less serious offences went unreported to police and, at times, even to the key organisations that represented the victim's group. Few saw the point of reporting these incidents to the police. Some felt this behaviour would simply continue. A participant in the African focus group reflected '... Most of the time they don't want to take it further. They just say, "Well, that's what happens" or "What am I going to do about it?"' Members of the Jewish focus group commented on the extensive low-level abuse, particularly verbal abuse, faced by the Jewish community. They stated that members of their community, and even people in their own organisation, do not report it informally anymore because it is 'not significant enough to report'. This was further echoed by a participant in the migrant youth focus group who stated, 'There is really no point of reporting that ... because it's not going anywhere ... There's no point, so then you have to step back and hopefully avoid that situation from happening'.

Thus, for the most part, when our respondents talked about the failures of language and the need to find a common tongue, they linked these failures to negative experiences in reporting PMC to the police. From the accounts of our participants, a lack of shared language was only part of the reason for lack of reporting and feelings of distrust towards the police. Certainly, it was important for a victim to be properly understood by police, and a shared language did have some impact on our participants' desire or willingness to report incidents to the police. Yet, the failure to agree on when to call something a prejudice motivated crime was compounded by a feeling that not much could be done for less serious PMC incidents. Additionally, as we discuss in the next section, our respondents identified other issues that influence reporting behaviour: police were not always aware of what constitutes a prejudice motivated crime and thus do not act accordingly and, perhaps more seriously, the perception of police as key perpetrators of PMC.

We speak to each of these in turn below.

We can define it, but unless the police understand it ...

Participants' own understanding of what constitutes a prejudice motivated crime was only part of the problem. Several reported that the police were no more *au fait* with what constituted a prejudice motivated incident than they were:

> INDIAN FOCUS GROUP PARTICIPANT: The one problem with all this is actually not the definition; it's the lack of a willingness to accept that anything could fall within that definition. If we say 'prejudice motivated crimes', 9 times out of 10, the police, well, probably all the time [laughter] the police will say, 'No, no, no, it's not prejudice motivated crime; this person is a criminal doing a criminal act'.

Even if participants could define prejudice motivated crime and convey this definition to their respective communities, many felt police were unable to properly identify when a crime motivated by prejudice was taking place. This perceived failure in the identification and response to a prejudice motivated incident was mentioned in every focus group. A member of the disability group described repeated instances of property damage that the police did not identify as a PMC:

> PARTICIPANT: So I've been working in the [disability] houses for about 10 years and in my time – the last house I worked at we used to get dead fish, smashed glasses on our front lawn. And we knew exactly who it was in the street and called the police: 'We can't help you.' And it was just like, 'But we know who's doing it. How hard is it for you to walk across the road and knock on the door so then they know it's taken seriously? Because we don't like dead fish on our door step.' In the house that I'm working at now, we've had two cars stolen, three cars smashed. The staff are scared to park their cars in the street.

The failure of police to acknowledge a PMC was also reflected in our discussion with the Muslim community group:

> There was one case where a group of white Anglo-Australian guys grabbed an Arab guy – and I hate stereotyping people, but of a Muslim faith – and they threw acid down his mouth. The police took on the report … but they didn't really follow it up.… In Noble Park there were young girls who had their scarves thrown off and thrown to the ground. Now to me this is bizarre: how you think something just as horrific and heinous came out of September 11. You're just basically doing exactly the same, maybe not the same calibre, but you're doing exactly the same. You're terrorising people … the police didn't know how to handle it because it was new. It was new to everybody. But they did not know how to handle it.

Participants from the Jewish community group expressed similar concerns over non-action for crime that was clearly prejudice motivated. After reporting property damage to a number of Jewish vehicles (the carving of swastikas into the side doors of the cars) in a particular street in Melbourne, the response from a junior police office to the complainant was 'If you're not happy living next door to this person, you should probably move'.

Police as perpetrators of prejudice

In some cases, not only did the police fail to engage with victims in a procedurally just manner, some of our participants felt police perpetuated prejudice in their response to victims. This was particularly the case for members of the LGBTI community. They reported that while PMCs were occurring at high levels in their community, the failure of police to address their own prejudices against the community was a serious concern: 'The prejudice comes from the police … and so it's the internal homophobia/transphobia from the police that actually gets played out more'.

Police were therefore viewed as perpetuating prejudice by non-response (or indeed by procedurally unjust responses). For some, police were also perceived as the main perpetrators of prejudice motivated crime, as evidenced by the accounts of two participants in the migrant youth focus group:

> PARTICIPANT 1: It's more the police who are racially profiling our clients and also policing in an inappropriate fashion, so the use of infringements to control behaviour, for example, which I think is inappropriate. So that's from our point of view. So then we've got to seek advice and assist our clients on those lines.
> PARTICIPANT 2: It's actually more to do with the police. I always believe that police officers are in a better position to look at things differently and to rectify things because they are well-trained, have knowledge of the law and everything, so they are in a better position. They have to

>look at the young boys. They're young boys, all right, no matter where they came from. So it's more to do from the police side. Of course, we are not saying that the young people are innocent. They are not all angels, of course.

Members of the Indigenous group also noted the problems with prejudice motivated crime perpetrated by police:

>But one of the things that gets me, it's really hard to report, sort of, like a racially motivated crime, to perpetrators of racially motivated crime [laughs]. So, in our communities, numerous assaults have occurred by Victorian Police on Aboriginal people, so it's very hard to go and think that they're going to have any particular interest – answering to, or taking seriously, any sort of charge like that.

Although participants of the Jewish community reported police inaction for some prejudice motivated incidents, for the most part, they did not experience further prejudice when reporting incidents. As one respondent reported:

>We, in the Jewish community, have a very different relationship with the police to what most other communities have, in that I think by and large the vast majority of people in the community believe that the police are there to help and that's a pretty good starting point compared to most others [groups].

The labelling and reporting of prejudice motivated crime is fundamentally shaped by questions of police legitimacy for our participants. PMC cannot be separated from recent events or historical relations between communities and the police. For some of our participants, a history of poor police–community relations prevented police from recognising and responding to victimisation claims. This 'residual mistrust' (Charkraborti and Garland 2015) undermined police legitimacy and increased the likelihood of non-reporting. On the one hand, this presents serious challenges in advancing agendas to increase reporting of PMC, should communities continue to harbour suspicion and distrust towards the police. On the other hand, if police mobilise effectively to support and respond to reports of prejudice motivated crime, this may contribute to some amelioration of historical distrust and alienation. Therefore, enacting procedurally just processes in response to victimisation motivated by prejudice, bias or hate is critical.

Third-party reports as a way forward?

From the accounts of our participants, and in line with other research (Chakraborti *et al.* 2014; Clement *et al.* 2011; Home Office 2013; Ignaski 2007; Sailsbury and Upson 2004; Sin *et al.* 2009, 2010; Wells and Polders 2006; Williams and Tregidga 2013; Wong and Christmann 2008), there were several reasons proffered for non-reporting of prejudice motivated crime. Fear of retribution or prior criminal histories were identified by members of the homeless focus group as reasons for non-reporting:

> The victim can't report it because he'll be known as a dog, et cetera. So you've got that stigmatising thing. But also if there's a complaint against the offender, the offender might be looking at eviction and a whole lot of stuff as well. They might be on parole.

Also, as mentioned earlier, the perceived seriousness of the incident was another factor for non-reporting amongst the Jewish participants:

> The Jewish person on the street, when something may be a bit more serious happens, they think, 'Oh well, this isn't serious enough to report to a community organisation, let alone the police'.

Yet the main reasons for non-reporting, as we argued previously, were linked to a lack of trust in effective responses from the police and procedurally unjust treatment from the police. That is, they were linked to the extent to which police treat victims and communities with respect for their human rights. The label or the term used to identity a prejudice motivated incident was not strongly associated with our participants' past reporting behaviour or their willingness to report future behaviour. Drawing on their previous experiences with the police, many of our participants shared the view that reporting PMCs to the police was a waste of time:

> DISABILITIES GROUP PARTICIPANT: We interview people who have disabilities who have been victims of crimes and those who haven't, and all of them said that they would go to the police if they wanted to report a crime or that's where they would go to talk about crime. But those who were victims would say, after they had reported it once, they wouldn't go back again.
> LGBTI GROUP PARTICIPANT: So I think for our community, the LGBTI community, they're not used to reporting. It's not part of our culture because they've [the police] always been the bad guys, the people that entrap you in public toilets, or they're going to pull you over for no reason, and they just think we're all drug addicts and having sex all the time. And negative experiences ... it's not in our collective cultural consciousness that the cops are the good guys that are on our side.... It's normally – unfortunately – they're still the bad guys.

Others felt reporting the incident to the police subjected the victim to further re-victimisation:

> I don't even go the police at the station. I don't have confidence and I don't want my clients to be re-traumatised again. I think also there has

been a history of inappropriate behaviour on the police side as well, and that most have heard stories of inappropriate responses and reactions from the police, which undermines any confidence that there might be that they're going to get a fair hearing and not suffer further abuse and prejudice.

Yet, a hesitancy to report prejudice motivated victimisation to the police stood in contrast to a strong desire for reporting processes that could be used by police to increase the identification of PMC perpetrators and protect victims experiencing low-level and more serious forms of PMC. Many of our participants were service workers or key representatives of high-priority groups and could see the importance of accurate and reliable prevalence rates of prejudice motivated crime:

> LGBTI PARTICIPANT: So I'm always encouraging them to report, report, report, because if I don't and then they do it to the next person, the police won't know to look for a white Commodore with four guys in it, that tends to be there on Saturday nights, yelling out abuse.

The service workers in our focus groups had various mechanisms for reporting prejudice motivated incidents. Service providers in our disability group were legislatively bound to report incidents affecting their clients; however, others relied on the police liaison officers to act as a 'go between' the victim and the police or developed their own reporting systems. In lieu of reporting data to the police, service providers took it upon themselves to record reports of PMC occurring in their community. The level of organisation of these reporting systems differed across the groups. Some reports were informal and ad hoc. Some organisations, like those in the LGBTI community, were highly organised and disseminated their results to local police and other key organisations to aid in identifying offenders. For example:

> We have a program called Ugly Mugs where the sex workers can report violent and abusive, harassing clients, and we're always encouraging our street sex workers, but also our brothel and escorts, to report those sort of behaviours, exactly as you said, so people can look out for a white Commodore and harassing people, and then that can be shared amongst the sex worker community. We share those reports, the summarised reports, with the police, St. Kilda Police and SOCA and a few other groups.

In addition to identifying the mechanisms for informal reporting already underway in many of the high-priority communities we studied, some of our participants discussed possible advances to the reporting system. One of these advances was the development of a formalised third-party reporting system. Several participants discussed the benefits of such a system that did more than collect information for researchers, but instead provided police with enough information to allow for targeted interventions and prosecutions. Members of the LGBTI community were strong advocates of this approach, as many of their clients are unable to identify themselves as victims:

> I have been trying to get third-party reporting, which would be excellent, particularly with the LGBTI community. Sometimes they can't go to the police and say, 'Hi, I was in a park and this guy – I was there for sex – and some guy tried to bash me or rob me or take my wallet.' Or particularly for young people, you can't just go – they come home and they can't just say, 'Yeah, mum – people at the train platform called me a fag or dyke or whatever,' because they haven't told their parents they're gay. So there's not too many avenues for them, whereas if there was this electronic reporting form, you could just go and it could be anonymous. You don't have to leave your name. You can just go, 'This time, this place, Box Hill railway station, group of schoolkids called me a dyke' … and then when the police or the PSOs are down there walking the platform, they can go, 'Okay, there's big gangs of schoolboys or schoolkids', and if they hear anything they can say, 'Hey, that's not on'.

Having robust data that could speak to the types of incidents that were occurring (criminal or non-criminal), where incidents were occurring, and the perpetrators and the targets of prejudice motivated crime was a desired goal for most of the people we interviewed. Some suggested that accurate reporting would allow for an evidence-based preventative approach to incidents motivated by prejudice. Certainly, this would go some way in bridging the gap between the 'victim-centred reporting mechanisms and evidence driven criminal justice processes' (Williams and Tregidga 2013) that we discuss in Chapter 8. Yet, as we know from large-scale hate crime projects in the UK, although third-party reporting provides a valuable conduit between victims and police, the vast majority of victims do not report their victimisation to victim support groups or other organisations that could offer support. Indeed, victims are significantly more likely to report to police (Chakraborti *et al.* 2014). Considering the lack of awareness of hate crime legislation amongst victims (ibid.), it is possible that they are also unaware of alternative reporting organisations. Public campaigns bring attention to third-party reporting strategies (see, for example, The Anti-Hate Campaign undertaken by VHREOC 2012). The extent to which they increase awareness of hate crime and improve reporting, however, is not well-established in the literature. Some suggest third-party reporting is not a preferred alternative for traditional reporting to the police (College of Policing 2014; Wong 2009). Thus, while third-party reporting may be perceived as a legitimate alternative to police reporting, it will not necessarily lead to increased reporting to the police or improved police–victim interactions.

Conclusion

Deciding upon the most appropriate term for hate crime and its subsequent definition continues to be hotly debated. While 'hate crime' remains the most widely accepted term, there is much contention over the utility of the word 'hate'. Further, it is unclear what point on the spectrum a 'prejudice' against a minority group becomes an act of 'hate' (Hall 2013). In addition, the success of hate crime legislation relies on the police actively enforcing it; however, this task is not always simple. A lack of confidence in the police has serious consequences for victim reporting (Chakraborti and Garland 2009; Gerstenfeld 2013; Wong and Christmann 2008). Even when victims do report to police, there appear to be problems with police identifying an offence as a hate crime and difficulties in finding evidence of the motivation for the offence (Hall 2013). Yet, not labelling incidents as hate has implications for those groups most likely to be vulnerable to incidents and most in need of effective interventions.

Our focus group discussions suggest that the inability of terminology to capture both definition of events and desired criminal justice responses has a small impact on efforts to engage communities in reporting prejudice motivated crime. While academic and practitioner attention has been paid to the political and legal attribution of terminology, and in particular what does and does not constitute hate crime, communities have not been sufficiently engaged at the development stage to find a shared meaningful vocabulary. Participants in our focus groups agreed that what we label crimes motivated by hate, bias or prejudice is important in assisting the public to understand the crime. Many also felt that a more inclusive label that represented experiences across victim groups was a step forward. Yet, they suggested that 'prejudice motivated crime' is a convoluted phrase, whereas terms such as 'hate crime', 'targeted violence', as well as more group-specific terms like 'anti-Semitism', are more easily conceptualised and understood. Despite various terms being used almost interchangeably, all participants agreed that targeting an individual due to their perceived minority group status should be against the law.

While there are important challenges associated with labelling and defining hate crime, the most pertinent issue emerging from our focus groups was the lack of trust between police and targeted communities. Indeed, there was limited evidence from the accounts of our participants that changing hate crime terminology alone would enhance trust in police and police responses to incidents motivated by hate, bias or prejudice. Beyond the terminology used, it is the broader matters of police–community trust and procedurally just practices that fundamentally shape the nature and extent of changing reporting practices. We argue that procedurally just practices can create awareness of hate crime legislation and prioritise congruent understanding of concepts such as prejudice motivated crime or hate crime. This, in turn, is likely to encourage a greater willingness to report PMC incidents to the police.

A recent randomised control trial of police legitimacy and procedural justice in Australia provides support for our argument. Mazerolle and colleagues (2013) found that procedurally just police interactions during random breath tests (RBT) significantly increased motorists' perceptions of police. In the experimental condition, officers incorporated key elements of procedural justice – citizen participation, dignity, respect and neutrality – into their dialogue with motorists. Motorists were informed of the importance of drink driving legislation and the degree of harm drink driving caused to the community; they were asked to assist the police but were told they were not singled out by the police for the RBT. They were also asked about other problems police should be aware of. In the control condition, it was business as usual. Participants who had a procedurally just encounter with police saw the police as more legitimate, which in turn significantly influenced their willingness to cooperate with the police when compared to those in the control condition. This trial provides strong evidence that even in a very short encounter, procedurally just practices can increase perceived police legitimacy and co-operation rates. As the authors note '[a] little bit of being nice goes a long way' (Mazerolle *et al.* 2013).

Our focus group participants did not view prejudice motivated crime terminology as a barrier to reporting or trusting police. But they did consider the unjust treatment of victims of PMC as a significant problem. Pursuing procedurally just treatment of PMC victims and promoting the human rights of marginalised and vulnerable groups would not only prioritise common understandings and meanings around PMC, it would demonstrate VicPol's support for non-discriminatory practices. This is absolutely critical, considering that many victims of hate crime have a history of fraught relationships with police. Although some of our participants experienced some success in overcoming historical alienation, particularly members of the Jewish and the LGBTI communities, for others, the historical mistrust was all-consuming, particularly in relation to issues of racism. For these groups in particular, moving to an inclusive terminology without making significant changes to police responses would do little to improve police–victim relationships or encourage reporting of prejudice motivated incidents.

It is unlikely that debates surrounding hate crime terminology will be easily resolved and, perhaps, as the results of our focus groups suggest, other areas require more immediate attention. While some terms are more easily recognised and understood by potential victims, our participants suggest the role of terminology in criminal justice responses is a lower priority when compared to the willingness to report such incidents to the police. Further, the perception that police are unwilling or unable to assist victims was one voiced by many participants across several of the high-priority groups. Until relations between police and these targeted groups are improved, changing the terminology will have limited impact on improving reporting behaviour. Moreover, changing the terminology might not influence policing practice. As others have argued, innovation in criminal law and organisation policy does not necessarily lead to confirming behaviours amongst officers (Brooks 2001; Jenness and Grattet 2005). Front-line officers who represent what Jenness and Grattet (2005) refer to as 'law-in-action' may not embrace the changes in legislation or, indeed, understand what constitutes a prejudice motivated incident (Bayley and Shearing 2001).

Despite the progressive steps made by VicPol to devise an inclusive strategy and terminology to increase reporting and confidence in police, the accounts of our participants suggest that there is still much to do to bridge the gap between policy innovation and policing practices. As is clear in recent large-scale hate crime studies (Chakraborti *et al.* 2014; Home Office 2013; Williams and Tregidga 2013), a substantial number of victims perceive the police as unable or unwilling to address hate crime. Further, a common theme amongst victims is that the reporting process itself can leave them feeling vulnerable (Chakraborti *et al.* 2014). In line with an increasing human rights approach to policing hate crime, we argue there is a need to develop procedurally just practices that acknowledge the significant harm experienced by victims of incidents motivated by hate, prejudice or bias. As growing evidence demonstrates, even when victims fail to achieve a satisfactory criminal justice outcome, trust in the police can remain strong if procedurally just processes have occurred (Elliott *et al.* 2011; Murphy and Barkworth 2014; Tankebe 2013). Certainly, how we label and define incidents that target members of particular communities will influence whether police can formally acknowledge the specific form of harm that communities want recognised. Further, these labels and definitions are non-trivial when it comes to the collection of evidence that can lead to arrest and prosecution of offenders. However, by themselves, they are not sufficient for encouraging reporting and building trust. Responding to victims with empathy and providing viable solutions to prevent re-offending are needed to build strong links between police and members of communities at risk for prejudice motivated crime. It also provides a space for police and communities to come together to mediate understandings of hate crime that incorporate victims' perspectives and essential human rights, a point we develop further in Chapter 8.

6 Training police on prejudice motivated crime

Introduction

Hate crime laws and strategies rely on police for effective implementation. In the case of Victoria, police leaders have communicated a commitment to policing hate crime by developing the Prejudice Motivated Crime Strategy. The legitimacy and effectiveness of the strategy depends largely on the willingness and ability of operational police to implement it and to buy into a set of shared understandings of PMC and how to respond. As we have already noted, the barriers to effective implementation of hate crime legislation and policy are well examined in the literature. These relate to the difficulty of recognising hate crime, the complexities of dealing with marginal or vulnerable communities and the low priority such crimes often receive amongst operational police (Hall 2012). One challenging aspect is that marginalised communities are often perceived by police as potential offenders rather than potential victims (Alpert *et al.* 2007; Dunham *et al.* 2005; Smith and Alpert 2007; also see Chapter 3). Previous research indicates that police officers generally categorise members of the public into groups based on the level of suspicion assigned to them (Stroshine *et al.* 2008; Van Maanen 2005). As such, police engagement with members of diverse communities can become multifarious situations, especially when officers are faced with diverse groups who require specific treatment or who expect to be handled or treated in a certain way.

Public demands on police are no longer straightforward and the various expectations of diverse community members are reflected in mission statements, targets and goals addressing the needs of multiracial and multicultural communities (Walker and Archbold 2013). Facing these demands increases the operational challenges for police organisations when policing diverse groups. Police training, then, is critical in overcoming entrenched prejudices and operational practices that would lead police to overlook or underplay prejudice as a serious policing issue. Most importantly, it is critical that this training contribute to shared understanding between the organisation and individual officers as to what constitutes PMC and what then is required of the officer. Often, the aim of such training is to reinforce the imperative for police to see hate crime as 'real crime' and respond effectively. The second critical element of training is to effectively communicate to operational police how to recognise, record and respond to hate crimes. In this chapter, we draw on the results of a survey conducted at the police academy with new police and protective service recruits as well as some exit interviews with senior Victoria Police personnel to make sense of the successes and challenges of training in arriving at a mutual understanding of PMC. It considers how police make sense of hate crime and charts how prejudice motivated crime has multiple meanings for operational officers. It examines how these meanings shift and conflict with their own prejudice, institutional values and professional conduct. It specifically focuses on the challenges for police in effectively identifying, responding and preventing prejudice and hate crime.

Training police for hate crime

Despite increased attention to prejudice motivated crime, otherwise referred to as hate crime, there has been little effort to evaluate the effectiveness of police training focused on it. While other areas within the criminal justice system have been subject to evaluation, training for police (and other criminal justice staff) has been largely neglected (Bradley and Connors 2013). Bradley and Connors argue that training evaluation that goes beyond the immediate participant's attitudes towards the training they have received is vital, and essential if criminal justice personnel are to perform their duties effectively. While there is a significant body of literature that highlights the importance of training (Kielinger and Paterson 2007; Mason *et al.* 2015; Wickes *et al.* 2015), evidence to support good practice and key elements for inclusion in training, specifically for PMC, is limited.

Where research does exist, it suggests that there needs to be consideration of both the skills and knowledge being disseminated (see, for example, Organization for Security and Co-operation in Europe in ODIHR 2012), as well as the way in which the training is delivered (Trickett 2015). A review of the literature for the National Hate Crimes Training Curricula by the United States Department of Justice identifies several training elements that are critical for officers to effectively respond to hate crime (or PMC). These include an improved understanding of diversity, improved data collection and documentation, community relations, greater outreach efforts for victims and targeted communities, and an overall better understanding of the law and the roles and responsibilities of law enforcement in preventing PMC. In later research, the US Department of Justice (2008) also indicated that operational skills and practices, and policy and procedures, should all be covered in PMC training to enhance deterrence and prevention efforts. It should also include the officer's ability to support victims and their community, and the effectiveness of investigation, reporting and prosecution. Similarly, Bishop (2007) argues that training needs to enable officers to quickly and effectively identify, report and record PMC. Within the skills proposed by Bishop, the Center for Problem-Oriented Policing (Freilich and Chermak 2013) identifies the ability to recognise and classify the offender/ perpetrator in a way that supports the overall investigation and prosecution as vital aspects of police PMC training. These skills are particularly important as PMC becomes increasingly complex with the influence of international hate groups, the Internet and social media. In the context of international and organised PMC, Bishop (2007) draws attention to the necessity of regional and international law enforcement co-operation in identifying and responding to hate crimes. She notes that 'increased knowledge and training is needed in order to read the intelligence, symbols and music of organised hate crime' (ibid.).

Given the diversity of PMC, the Center for Problem-Oriented Policing (Freilich and Chermak 2013) indicates that in addition to key investigative and reporting skills, there needs to be a focus on developing each officer's cultural awareness. Research by Miles-Johnson (2015, 2016) indicates that training which seeks to enhance police awareness of issues facing minority groups is vital in improving perceptions of police and policing services amongst these groups, since poor perceptions of police are a frequently cited barrier to self-reporting PMC victimisation (Trickett 2015). Given the criticism of police amongst members of minority groups for a lack of awareness regarding the different types of PMC victimisation (Freilich and Chermak 2013; Miles-Johnson 2015), training to enhance cross-cultural communication, particularly where victims are involved, is important. Research highlights how the ability to effectively communicate and engage with members of minority groups not only supports incident investigation, it also enhances community relations between the police and the public (Rowe and Garland, 2013), underlining the need for this type of training. Supported by a human rights framework, this engaged approach to training may be capable of mitigating the 'trust deficit' that shapes police–minority relations (Chakraborti and Garland 2015), thereby helping to build the legitimacy of hate crime strategies in the eyes of marginalised communities.

Rowe (2013) argues that the impact police training can have on police–community relations has been largely neglected by research and, as a result, there is little understanding about how officers actually adopt operational techniques for responding to PMC. This is arguably due to the fact that PMC-specific training is still in its infancy (Campbell 2014; Miles-Johnson 2015). Finally, Hunt and Martinez (2015) argue that this type of training will also help address any issues of personal bias amongst officers. However, because training in PMC is in its infancy, it has not been widely evaluated, so it is not possible to test these claims.

Research by Trickett (2015) into the utility of hate crime training in supporting officer responses to incidents found that police could generally describe and define what acts constitute both hate crimes and hate incidents; however, most could not recall the details of the training in which this information was provided. Our research also found that while officers generally agreed that hate crime was a useful category, there were issues with the nature and delivery methods of their training. Trickett argues that 'training needs to be much more skills based and there needs to be a great emphasis on "why" officers are doing the training and "how" these skills might benefit them in their daily policing' (2015). Based on this, Trickett identified police receptiveness, retention, value, applicability and context as key considerations in the delivery of PMC training for police.

In response to these issues, Trickett (2015) recommended that any training on PMC should focus more on the human element and include the experiences of other officers who have dealt with different types of hate crime. Involving colleagues in the training reportedly increases the legitimacy (and ultimately the receptiveness) of the training as a direct result of the more personalised approach. This is evident amongst other training programmes, with the OSCE/ODIHR indicating that their hate crime training is 'best implemented' through a 'training-of-the-trainer' approach (ODIHR 2012). Officers involved in this project noted that the current online approach to PMC or hate crime training was 'boring', and many officers joked amongst themselves about how to simply finish it more quickly. These examples were highlighted as a demonstration of the officers' lack of information retention and engagement with the training. Officers also cited that their lack of engagement with the training was partially the result of feeling 'patronised' or as though they were being lectured, which was often interpreted as criticism.

To build on previous emphasis on enhancing cultural awareness, Trickett (2015) recommends that training provide exposure to people from different backgrounds and with different types of disabilities. Further to this, exposure to external agencies would support enhanced victim referral and support. Addressing negative attitudes and preconceived ideas regarding diverse communities within police training sessions should reduce the likelihood that the aim of the training session will be undermined. Negative police attitudes invalidate objectives of training courses implemented by police organisations to create awareness of different groups (Miles-Johnson 2016). As such, exposure to external agencies and the presence and involvement of people from diverse groups within training programmes could raise interesting questions about potential police contact and future engagement. Educating police officers to make positive comparisons between themselves and diverse members of the public during training may later inspire sympathy or empathy while interacting in a professional capacity, particularly when responding to incidents of PMC. To foster a police officer's capacity to interact with all members of society, while tackling complex situations and addressing an assortment of social situations, is part of the intention of training programmes. Certainly, numerous police organisations around the world have recognised this requirement and have created policies specifically targeting police training in this way.

Evidence-based policy and operational responses require consistent and timely data collection and analysis, therefore ensuring that training covers the application of legislative definitions. In 2015, the FBI Criminal Justice Information Services released their updated Data Collection Guidelines and Training Manual, which covered legislative mandate information, criteria and definitions for data collection, data submission guidelines and procedures, as well as a range of learning modules developed to enhance data collection efforts. Further to this, although the training modules focus on data collection, the manual also helps in raising awareness amongst officers about hate crime. Finally, the literature examining the response to PMC suggests that there are several factors that require specific and recurring training, particularly when there is no special PMC (or equivalent) unit or officer, meaning that responding or investigating falls into the remit of general officers. Variety and ongoing training was thus identified by Trickett (2015) as a vital element of any effective hate crime training for police.

PMC training at the police academy

As part of its implementation of the PMC Strategy, VicPol undertook to train all new recruits in PMC at the police academy as of 2011. This training included police recruits (PRs), as well as protective service officers (PSOs), who primarily patrol train stations.[1] All police recruits undertake 18 weeks training at the Victoria Police Academy and two sessions across this period are now dedicated to PMC training. PSOs undertake 12 weeks of training and, similarly, two sessions are dedicated to PMC training.

The training that police and PSOs receive takes the form of two sessions of two hours each, in which the legislation and policy relating to PMC is delivered by an experienced senior police member. The content of the training, delivered in seminars, is based on cases of PMC that VicPol has dealt with and focuses on what kind of PMC may have taken place, as well as appropriate reporting strategies. There is also content delivered that explores why PMC is a serious concern, warranting policing attention. It is an interactive seminar format, based in large classrooms where information is presented both thematically in relation to different kinds of PMC and with a focus on the operational requirements for recording PMC.

Survey

Using a survey-based experimental method designed by Toby Miles-Johnson (Miles-Johnson *et al.* 2016), we collected data from a population of 1,609 police officers (comprising PRs and PSOs) to understand their perceptions of PMC, pre- and post-training. This was undertaken in 2013–2014. We examined the effects of pre- and post-PMC awareness training on the police officers' perceptions of five variables: PMC Recognition; PMC Handling; PMC Attendance; PMC Reporting; and PMC Arresting. Our survey also examined officers' perceptions of professional conduct and diversity in general. Those items that showed the most notable results will be the focus of our analysis in this chapter.

Instruction in PMC was offered to 60 classes, each containing approximately 25 police officers. Accordingly, a three-page pre-lecture survey (nine items) and a 43-page post-lecture survey (120 items) were administered to each participant. The pre- and post-lecture surveys were administered via Qualtrics Survey Online Software (on iPads). All the items included in the survey were adapted from previous studies: The Self Esteem Scale (Rosenberg 1979); The Group-Value Model (Smith *et al.* 1998); Legitimacy measures (Murphy *et al.* 2008; Sunshine and Tyler 2003); Respect from Police Scale (Tyler and Wakslak 2004); generalised Group Attitude Scale (Duckitt *et al.* 2005); Sexuality and Attitudes Towards the Police (Miles-Johnson 2013); and the Australian Community Capacity Study survey instrument (Mazerolle *et al.* 2012). Each of the items in the survey used a Likert scale. It was found that the adapted items used in the online survey all had good, acceptable or excellent internal consistency with Cronbach alphas, similar or close to the original alpha levels recorded in the original studies.

The final sample comprised 1609 recruits (n=1,609), which included 946 police recruits and 663 protective services officers. There were more male than female participants in the final sample, with 1,215 males and 370 females completing the pre- and post-training sessions. The ages of the participants ranged from 18 to 65 years of age. The average age of the total of participants was 30 years. In the final data set, only two PR participants identified as Aboriginal, with three PRs and one PSO identifying as both Aboriginal and Torres Strait Islander. The majority of the participants were born in Australia (n=1,172), while 148 participants were born in India, 44 in England, 34 in New Zealand and 13 in China.

Although over three-quarters of the participants speak English at home (n=1,506). A number of participants (n=136) chose 'other' to indicate their chosen language, alongside participants who speak languages commonly heard in Victoria, such as Hindi (n=103), Punjabi (n=98), Italian (n=29), Mandarin (n=15), Greek (n=13), Spanish (n=14) and French (n=14). The majority of the participants identified as heterosexual and were single at the time of the research. The majority identified as having no religion or religious affiliation (n=699), and almost a quarter of the participants identified as Catholic (n=387). A large number of participants selected 'other' when identifying their religion at the time of the research (n=227).

The goal of the survey was to ascertain the factors that facilitate or constrain the capacity of PRs and PSOs to appropriately classify and deal with prejudice motivated crime upon completion of PMC training at the Victoria Police Academy. Both stages of the survey were self-administered by the full class of PRs and PSOs, prior to PMC training and upon completion of it. All the PRs and PSOs were given identical training sessions regarding hate crime awareness and, although these were delivered by the same training team over the course of the data collection period, variations in the differences of outcomes of responses of PRs and PSOs to the items included in the survey were considered. We will first consider the general perceptions items and then the PMC items.

Survey results

Responses to the survey showed that the PRs and PSOs are aware of the importance of the choices they make when professionally working with members of diverse communities. However, the majority of officers (79 per cent) are only somewhat trusting of members of minority groups when meeting them for the first time. Yet, many of the participants expressed their acceptance of working alongside colleagues who belong to diverse minority groups and indicated that they did not care about the superordinate or subordinate identifiers of other police officers that are based on characteristics such as race, ethnicity, religion, sex, sexuality and gender differences.

The PRs and PSOs do recognise that, as members of VicPol, there are expectations placed on them regarding professional conduct; they consider retaliatory responses to specific acts, such as rudeness, different than emotional responses to situations, where unspecific acts of disrespect occur. Although there are small variations regarding the PRs' and PSOs' perceptions of the use of force in relation to different communities and contexts, the majority of the participants (84 per cent) disagree with the use of force as an educational tool for people from different races, ethnic groups and religions and for people whose gender and/or sexuality is considered different (85 per cent). This is important since it underpins the officers' awareness of the tough line that VicPol takes on improper behaviour amongst its officers in the form of unprofessional interactions with people from diverse backgrounds.

While almost all of the PRs and PSOs are aware of the importance their supervisors place on the detection of unprofessional conduct, some PRs and PSOs (3 per cent) question the professional conduct of fellow officers and superior officers in different contexts. However, it was clear that the majority of the participants (85 per cent) believe that the ethical training of members of VicPol regarding interaction with people from different races, ethnic groups and religions, and with people whose gender and/or sexuality is considered different, is effective. Almost all of the PRs and PSOs indicated in their responses that ethical training and professional conduct underpins their role as a member of VicPol. This was apparent in the number who believe that breaking the rules is unacceptable during professional engagement, and in the majority of the responses indicating a belief that members of VicPol are very respectful in their treatment of people from different races, ethnic groups and religions (76 per cent) and are also very respectful in their treatment of people whose gender and/ or sexuality is considered different (76 per cent). This suggests that VicPol's attempts to operationalise human rights principles into prejudice-sensitive attitudes to policing has gained some traction.

However, the results indicate that the training process has a *negative* effect on police officer identification of a range of different kinds of PMC victimisation, with many police officers failing to recognise and categorise an incident of PMC post-training. For example, post-training responses are only 61 per cent as likely to be 'Yes' as pre-training responses indicating that some police officers were able to recognise an incident of PMC before the training but not after, suggesting that the training may have confused their perceptions of PMC. This raises questions about the effectiveness of current PMC police awareness training and education strategies, especially since police are typically the first responders to a range of incidents, and when a PMC occurs they need to be able to identify the elements of victimisation that are unique to victims of prejudice motivated crime.

The results also indicate that post-training there were only small improvements in relation to whether or not the PRs and PSOs are able to respond to PMC incidents in an appropriate way once they have identified them as matters of PMC. There were also only small changes in relation to whether or not the PRs and PSOs will identify the incident and record the crime correctly as an incident of PMC, and consequently, take appropriate further action (such as arrest).

While changing the frequency (and content) of PMC awareness training may help improve the capacity of police to recognise and appropriately respond to PMC incidents, other factors may also influence the perceptions of officers' opinions of PMC and PMC victimisation. For example, previous research by Miles-Johnson (2015, 2016) suggests that training programmes implemented by police organisations regarding the needs of minority group members are often subject to negative police attitudes that are reinforced by police culture, and the attitudes of superior officers conducting the training programmes. Moreover, other research shows 'operational and professional' police attitudes are informed by police culture, police training and previous experiences with certain groups of people (see MacVean and Cox 2012). Thus, it may be reasonable to conclude that our survey results derive from personal prejudice or the influence of other police officers on police attitudes towards PMC. Certainly, this raises a question regarding how PMC training can improve or change police officer perceptions in these situations. In 2015, VicPol launched its victim-centred approach to policing. This all-encompassing policing framework is intended to reduce victimisation and improve service delivery (VicPol 2015). This framework is arguably the context in which the PMC Strategy, and specifically PMC police training, can most usefully be located moving into the future. Informed by the Segrave and Wilson (2011) police station report, the victim-centred framework is explicitly geared to the diverse needs of victims. Yet, it must be acknowledged that previous research by Myhill and Bradford (2013) and Reiner (2010) posit that many police officers are opposed to this service model of policing, which replaces traditional crime fighting strategies with victim-centred approaches and which are, accordingly, reticent to reform dimensions of policing.

Training in prejudice motivated crime: key challenges moving forward

Our survey work with police on PMC training highlights three key areas for future consideration.

First, prejudice motivated crime is sufficiently complex that training approaches need to be finely calibrated and considered in relation to a host of interconnecting issues and factors.

In short, prejudice motivated crime training needs to comprise more than segmented double sessions scheduled in the academy classroom. There is a range of reasons for suggesting this. Notably, recruits are able to more easily dismiss or diminish the importance and complexity of the issue when it is circumscribed to a relatively time-short component of their overall training. While police training curricula are often crammed with many and multiple demands, most critically for PMC, the approach has been to focus on PMC for a short period of time that is insufficiently linked to broader operational and organisational imperatives and understandings. It is reasonable to expect that, for some recruits, the training directly confronts what may be deeply held or unconscious prejudices. As a result, PMC training may develop greater traction if delivered in a way that embeds it within clearer understandings of police legitimacy in all communities – not only diverse communities or communities experiencing conflict. This is essential because past research has found that PMC not only has an enormous impact on the victims and other members of the targeted group, but it also has an effect across wider society in terms of striking at the core of societal values and offending the collective moral code (Iganski and Levin 2015). It also has an effect on public perceptions of confidence in the police as fighters of crime.

Enhancing the direct relevance of PMC for the specific communities and locations police serve is also likely to assist in overcoming superficial or con-fused responses to content, purpose and requirements. This is recognised by VicPol:

> I think there's more education – education and information – that needs to be delivered to our members about the "what". What it looks like, how it affects their community that they police. It's not what happens over there, it's what happens here. And it's not just in relation to – well, I think that's about that education awareness raising piece. And that's a reinforcement piece.
>
> (Commander, PCD, VicPol, interview 6 May 2016)

Moreover, for VicPol it would make sense for PMC training to be a core com-ponent of the victim-centric approach recently instituted by the organisation through their Priority Communities Command. PMC training needs to be seen as something other than managing expectations and experiences of vulnerable com-munities, that is, the welfare work that for decades police have railed against as being 'soft' or at least non-core police activity. Understanding the relationship between PMC, hate groups and emerging security risks is likely to elevate its status in the minds of recruits from a 'low policing' activity to one of greater utility. However, this is more likely to be systematically achieved if there is a more robust understanding of how PMC impacts communities directly. This will require broader kinds of education and training across the organisation, includ-ing that which draws on human rights principles and prejudice-sensitive approaches to communicate and engage with communities. As one senior member of VicPol relayed:

> So, the communication strategies that were developed were from those very generic pieces such as gazette articles and hot issues, and on the back of some of the incidents that we had, being able to remind members of what

opportunities exist and what vulnerabilities might exist for a broader range of community participants. But also, then, reinforcing through those other training forums around member options and raising member awareness. Media and communications are really an important part for our organisation.

(Commander, PCD, VicPol, interview 6 May 2016)

But, importantly, the way recruits are trained in PMC needs to mitigate the sense that this is another strategy or priority that overlays existing police needs and approaches. Contextualising the training through greater integration with broader approaches can reasonably be expected to enhance outcomes. For example:

We have a victim-centric strategy that is about focusing on the intent, that – you know – the experience of the victim. So, that is – that's a really – bringing it back to the victim's experience, is really important, and making sure that it connects across a range of activities, so, rather than doing things just in silos, rather than just having a community engagement strategy or a PMI strategy or PMC strategy or family violence strategy or whatever it is, it's about making sure that we weave through our education, our information, our capability building pieces, those clear messages.

(Commander, PCD, VicPol, interview 6 May 2016)

Or, as another senior member of VicPol reiterated, there is a need for consistent and routine messaging across the organisation about both *why* and *how* police should be active in developing a mutually reinforced understanding and response to PMC:

I would say I think there's still work [to be done]. I don't think it [the training] was a failure by any means at all. I think it moved forward but I think further work could have been done getting the message out in a way where it was, you know, reiterated over time, maybe chunked up little bits of – so instead of a big launch and then, you know, certain aspects through certain programs that they do at the academy for example, having some sort of consistent messaging or training options more broadly across the organisation may have assisted in just that awareness of front-line members a bit more.

(Senior Operational Officer, VicPol, interview 6 May 2016)

In short, there is clear recognition that police need to engage with victim and community experiences of PMC if they are to develop a complex appreciation of what hate crime means to those subjected to it directly, as well as those who experience it indirectly as part of vulnerable communities. This kind of messaging would arguably assist police in understanding community perspectives and reduce the dissonance between recruit, organisational and community perspectives.

Second, where there is dissonance between the trainee world-view and the specific key underpinnings of a prejudice motivated strategy, training is likely to fall short of expectations.

It is crucial for effective police training on PMC that organisational understandings of the specific drivers, context and impact of PMC resonates with the world-view of the police trainee. Our research suggests that where there is dissonance, sooner or later, the world-view of the trainee undermines the aims and objectives of policing PMC. This idea is supported by Blumberg *et al.* (2015) who argue that the majority of PRs are highly service-oriented and extremely ethical at the start of training and ensuing placement. However, many police officers will revise their moral standards and values at different moments in their careers. This may occur particularly when faced with an ethical dilemma or when responding to a complex situation (such as PMC), which may cause an officer to break rules and regulations when the rule breaking or action taken is perceived as honourable and in line with other values (Caldero and Crank 2011; Reiner 2010). Certainly, this raises questions about how ongoing police training can continue to uphold competent performance in the field after PMC training.

Third, where there is dissonance between the trainee world-view and the broader organisational view, training is likely to fall short of expectations.

The crux of this is that the failure to understand, identify and respond to PMC by action or omission has a close relationship with unprofessional conduct (which in the past has been called out as racist, sexist, homophobic and otherwise discriminatory policing) which, in turn, has far-reaching implications. This message is brought home by VicPol Command:

> I think we've done engagement well – and in different areas of the organisation do it better than others, but I think we finally have lifted the arrogance, and understand what absolute value community can have in us testing our tools, our strategies, our policies, our education programs, whatever it is, in a much more beneficial way. So, for argument's sake, when you invite people in to help you problem solve for a problem for the organisation, the outcome of that is often a much more common sense, clearly understood – so, the difference between community expectations and organisation expectations are minimised and the product is much more substantial and adds value to the organisation and to the community.
>
> (Commander, PCD, VicPol, interview 6 May 2016)

Increasing the gravitas of the organisational context, victim-centred policing and the clear execution of consistent and systematic messaging depends on a centring of community expectations and community engagement in mapping ways forward for PMC policing. It not only advances the capacity of police to arrive at a stronger shared understanding of PMC and increased effectiveness in their responses, it has the capacity to positively change policing more broadly.

Conclusion

PMC police training has the greatest potential to impact when it can clearly answer the question as to why it is being undertaken, how it informs every aspect of prejudice-sensitive policing and where it directly contributes to organisational values and institutional legitimacy. When these elements are in place, only then can the 'How is it done?' be comprehensively supported. Police training is a serious issue, especially when police officers are challenged by increasingly complex public demands, reflected in modified and updated policy documents, changing mission statements, shifting targets and varying operational goals, frequently adjusted to meet the needs of diverse communities. Public expectations of service delivery challenge police organisations to effectively train officers to identify, respond to and prevent crime. For certain groups in society, this also means identifying, responding to and preventing hate crime in ways that are attuned to the larger social processes of prejudice and the violation of human rights. Facing this task increases the operational tests police organisations face in their daily operational duties and amplifies the challenge of effectively engaging with diverse groups. Enhancing police–public relations with diverse communities is therefore critical in overcoming entrenched prejudices, histories of mistrust and operational practices that would lead police to overlook or underplay prejudice as a serious policing issue.

This begins with police awareness training, which not only supports officers in delivering good practice but also informs officers about the complexity of PMC in local, national and international contexts. PMC training must enhance operational skills, confidence and practices, such as being able to quickly and effectively identify, report and record PMC, as well as develop knowledge about deterrence and prevention, victim and community support, and appropriate skills for PMC investigation, reporting and prosecution. Without doubt many police organisations around the world have recognised this requirement and have created policies specifically targeting police training in this way, particularly when there is no special PMC (or equivalent) unit or officer, meaning that responding to or investigating PMC falls under the responsibility of general duties officers. PMC is a multifarious matter and training must be carefully attuned and constructed in relation to numerous interconnecting issues and factors, presented by both officers and members of diverse communities over numerous training sessions. Since PMC training is likely to fall short of officer expectations over time, and while officers may be highly service-oriented at the start of training and subsequent appointment, dissonance between the recruits' world-view and the key underpinnings of PMC may change throughout their careers. As such, conflicting perceptions and opinion of PMC between the recruits and the police organisation have a high likelihood of creating moral discord between the high ethical standards recruits have at the start of their careers and the failure to understand, identify and respond to PMC by action or omission over time.

Note

1 Protective Service Officers (PSOs) are part of the transit safety division of the police. They are employed to monitor peak-hour train services and have the same power as an operational police officer.

7 The Prejudice Motivated Crime Strategy and hate crime reporting

Introduction

Determining the nature and extent of hate crime is central to preventing and reducing its occurrence, yet official hate crime data represents only a fraction of total incidents occurring in society (Levin *et al.* 2007). Studies consistently find that most hate crime victims do not notify the police, with estimates suggesting that hate crime is reported less than 30 per cent of the time (Levin 1999; Perry 2001). For example, in England and Wales, there were 44,480 hate crimes officially recorded in 2013–2014, yet victimisation data revealed a much higher prevalence (Home Office 2013; Office for National Statistics 2014). This is also the case in the United States. Hate crime statistics from the FBI for 2013 report 5,928 hate crime offences involving 6,933 incidents, 7,230 victims and 5,808 known offenders (FBI 2014b), whereas the National Crime Victimization Survey revealed that 275,590 hate offences were reported in the same year (Wilson 2014). Even when offences are reported to the police, there appears to be a significant gap between what is reported and what is recorded (ibid.).

Under-reporting is both a function of poor police–minority relations (Perry 2003b; Zaykowski 2010) and definitional challenges as to what legally constitutes a hate crime (Cronin *et al.* 2007; Nolan *et al.* 2002; Rubenstein 2003). Nolan and Akiyama (1999) identify several, predominantly sequential, steps to reporting a hate crime. A breakdown at any stage of the process diminishes the likelihood that an incident will be officially reported as a hate crime. First the victim (or a witness) must be aware that a crime has been committed and must be able to identify the hate motivation. Next, a victim (or a witness) must report the crime to police and, in so doing, effectively communicate the bias motivation to the police. The police must then recognise this bias motivation and then decide whether or not to record the incident as a hate crime offence. As McDevitt and colleagues (2003) argue, the steps associated with hate crime reporting demonstrate the importance of trust between the victim and the police.

As is the case internationally, under-reporting is extremely common amongst victims of hate crime in Australia. Studies find that victims are hesitant to report hate crime as they are fearful of retributive attacks and lack confidence in the criminal justice system (Harlow 2005; Martin 1996; VEOHR 2010). In our focus group interviews (see Chapter 5), participants reported that it was difficult to distinguish a prejudice motivated incident from one that would legally qualify as a prejudice motivated crime. As a consequence, victims only reported serious crimes, like violence, to the police. Another barrier to reporting, as indicated by our participants, was the often difficult relationship between victims of hate crime and police. Thus, broader matters relating to trust and procedurally just practices were fundamental to both the nature and extent of hate crime reporting.

The level of under-reporting makes it exceedingly difficult to effectively target where and when hate crime is occurring, to determine the most likely victims of hate crime and to identify the perpetrators of such acts. As we have discussed in earlier chapters, a key initiative of VicPol's PMC Strategy was to remove the barriers to hate crime reporting by increasing trust and engagement between key priority groups and police. As specified in the strategy, an increase in reporting in the period following the plan's implementation would be an indication that it was successful in removing barriers to reporting. As importantly, increased reporting would enhance the likelihood of obtaining usable evidence, would allow for more effective targeting of areas where hate crime is a problem and, eventually, reinforce the trust between police and victims from vulnerable and marginalised communities.

In this chapter, we examine the types of hate crime reported to VicPol leading up to and following the strategy rollout that occurred in July 2011. Using offence incident data from VicPol recorded on the Law Enforcement Assistance Program (LEAP) database, we employ time series analyses to assess whether or not the introduction of the strategy had a noticeable influence on reporting behaviour. We find that the PMC Strategy, for the most part, did not result in an increase in reported hate crimes. Indeed, reported hate crime offences have declined overall following the introduction of the strategy. However, for some groups, in particular those targeted on the basis of their sexual orientation, there is a small, but significant, increase in reporting. In our conclusion, we revisit our interviews with our focus group members and with VicPol Command, and we consider the limitations of the PMC Strategy to increase reporting. Despite the efforts of the strategy, from the accounts of all participants, there is continued confusion around what constitutes a hate crime. The lack of common or shared understanding concerning hate crime offences is a major barrier to reporting. Further, ongoing issues with how front-line officers respond to hate crime, coupled with the process of hate crime reporting itself, can leave victims doubting that a complaint of hate crime will be taken seriously by members of the police and acted on accordingly.

Hate crime reporting in Australia

In Australia, empirical studies of prejudice motivated crime rely almost exclusively on case studies and non-probability samples of victimisation experiences. From this scholarship, there is some evidence that ethnically motivated offences have increased in Australia since the 9/11 attacks in the US and the 2002 Bali bombings. The Australian Arabic Council reported a twentyfold increase in the numbers of reports of vilification of Arab Australians following the September 11 terrorist attacks (Poynting 2002). This report led to the development of the IsmaU project conducted by the Human Rights and Equal Opportunity Commission in 2003. This three-part mixed-methods project involved 69 national consultations with 1,423 Arab and Muslim Australians, a survey completed by 186 Arab Australians, with 34 follow-up semi-structured interviews, and an audit of current initiatives and strategies designed to deal with anti-Arab prejudice, discrimination, vilification and victimisation. The majority of participants involved in the group discussions, surveys and interviews noted an increase in discrimination and vilification targeted towards themselves and the wider Arab/Muslim community since September 11, 2001. Two-thirds of respondents reported having personally experienced an increase in racism since that date, and women were more likely than men to report higher levels of racism, abuse or violence due to their visibility in the community (HREOC 2004).

As we noted in the Introduction to this book, to date only two studies have used official statistics or a population-based sample to examine prejudice motivated offences in Australia. The first considers gay hate-related homicides in New South Wales between 1989 and 1999. Drawing on data from the National Homicide Monitoring Program, Mouzos and Thompson (2000) compared male gay hate-related homicide with male non-gay hate-related homicides. They found that victims of gay hate-related homicide were more likely to be killed in a private residence, have multiple attackers and to be beaten to death (ibid.). The second study concerned differences in ethnically motivated victimisation. Johnson (2005b) employed International Crime Victimisation Survey data and found that compared to the general population sample, the level of victimisation believed to be racially motivated was higher in the Middle Eastern and Vietnamese migrant samples. Respondents from these backgrounds reported that 42 per cent of the experienced assaults were perceived as racially motivated (ibid.), compared to 10 per cent of assaults thought to be racially motivated in the general population sample. Moreover, respondents in the general sample who perceived their victimisation to be racially motivated were born in Asia or Africa (14 per cent), elsewhere overseas (30 per cent) or were non-English speaking (20 per cent) (ibid.).

PMC in Victoria

Over the last decade, hate crime has been a significant problem for VicPol. As we discussed particularly in Chapter 4, two years prior to the introduction of the PMC Strategy, a large number of Indian students living in Melbourne experienced victimisation that was perceived as hate crime. Federal politicians did not acknowledge these events as hate crimes, which brought on a wave of negative media attention from Indian journalists and news outlets (Mason 2012b). It also led to a sharp decline in Indian tertiary-student visas immediately following the attacks (ABC News 2014). In May 2009, thousands of people in Melbourne protested the targeted property and violence victimisation experienced by Indian students. These protests received international media attention and threatened India–Australia relationships.

In the months following the attacks, there were several efforts to assess whether or not the motivation behind the offences was driven by prejudice and/ or hate. An extensive report from the Australian Institute of Criminology found that Indian students were more likely to be victimised than students from other countries but concluded that this was more to do with the clustering of Indian students in particular types of employment at particular times of the day (e.g. service stations and convenience stores that operate 24 hours per day) (Larsen *et al.* 2011). In other words, these crimes were motivated by opportunity, not racial animus. Yet, others found sufficient evidence of hate crime motivation. For example, Mason's (2012) analysis of publicly available documents during the time of the victimisation demonstrates that at least some of these attacks were motivated by race or anti-Indian sentiment. Drawing on court data, Mason (2012) revealed several successful convictions in which perpetrators were acknowledged as carrying out targeted attacks on individuals from an Indian background. Details of targeted attacks reported in media outlets also strongly indicated that many offences were motivated by race and/or ethnicity.

Official data does indicate a peak in hate crime recording at around the same time as the targeted attacks were carried out in Victoria. In 2000, VicPol began systematically collecting information on offences that could possibly be motivated by hate or prejudice. As we have outlined, while hate crimes are not prosecuted as such in Victoria, as there are no specific hate crime laws, serious racial and religious hate speech can be criminalised under the *Racial and Religious Tolerance Act 2001*. Yet, burdensome definitions and procedural requirements make it difficult to prosecute these offences. Thus, the only hate crime laws in Victoria are sentencing provisions, which require police to gather such evidence for sentencing purposes. As a consequence, information pertaining to offences motivated by hate crime is formally recorded in VicPol's LEAP database. This information indicates the motivation (in whole or part) for the crime. There are several closed-ended response options relating to motivation and officers may choose one or more of these responses. These include: sexuality/gender identity (homophobia); physical or mental impairment; political beliefs or status; race and ethnicity (Aboriginal/Torres Strait Islander; Asian; Caucasian; Indian sub-continent; Middle Eastern; black; and other) and religion (Muslim; Jewish; Sikh; and other). There is also an 'other' PMC category to indicate offences motivated by age, homelessness and/or gender. The LEAP form also includes information on the victim relevant for understanding crimes motivated by hate and/or prejudice, for example, the victim's gender, ethnic appearance and whether the victim was of Aboriginal and/or Torres Strait Islander origin. In what follows, we provide a breakdown of reported hate crime incidents using the LEAP data.[1]

Figure 7.1 shows that, in Victoria, the number of reported prejudice motivated offences by crime type (as recorded in the LEAP database) have increased steadily since 2002, peaking in 2009 following the attacks on Indian students, and then declining thereafter. Without concomitant self-report data, we cannot state whether or not this increase in reporting is a consequence of the attacks. Thus, it is possible that these increases are associated with an increase in actual hate crime offences. Alternatively, the publicity surrounding the events in Melbourne may have encouraged greater reporting of hate crime in this period.

In examining these reporting trends, we also see they demonstrated a strong increase from 2000 to 2002. Again, this increase may not reflect an increase in prejudice motivated crime, but may be due to the introduction of the Victorian *Racial and Religious Tolerance Act (2001)* (see Chapter 4) and to increasing awareness of both police and victims of a legislative move to enforce tolerance in multicultural societies (Feenan 2006). Notwithstanding the limits of using reported hate crime offence data, Figure 7.1 is revealing in that there was also a sharp decline in reporting in offences against the person and, to a lesser extent, property crimes, in the periods following the attacks against Indian students.

Looking further into the 3,919 offences reported between January 2000 and June 2014, the majority of prejudice motivated offences reported to police occurred in the suburbs of Greater Melbourne.[3] Of the offences reported to police, 65.3 per cent of offences took place in the suburbs of the city, suggesting that victimisation may be more likely in residential communities, compared to the Central Business District (CBD), where 13.1 per cent of offences are reported. In contrast, prejudice motivated offences in regional Victoria comprise 21.6 per cent of all reported offences. PMC offences were also more likely to occur in public. The

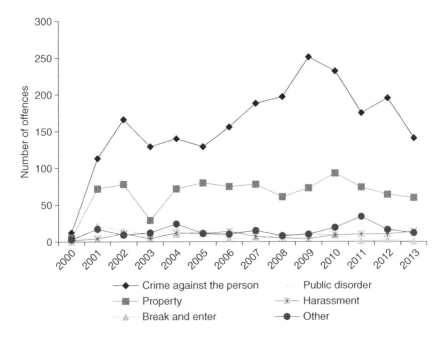

Figure 7.1 Prejudice motivated offences reported to Victoria Police by year, 2000–2013.[2]

most common places for hate crime offences were the street, a lane or a footpath (29.7 per cent). This was particularly true of crimes against the person, including assault, rape and abductions/kidnappings (see Table 7.1). These offences against the person also occurred on public transport, including buses, trains and trams, their stops/stations and associated car parks. Nevertheless, a large proportion of reported offences occurred in private residences (23.6 per cent), particularly crimes against the person and property crime such as arson, property damage and theft. Reported harassment was highest in private residences.

Overwhelmingly, prejudice motivated assaults were the offences most frequently reported to police (see Figure 7.2), constituting 49.7 per cent of the reports between January 2000 and June 2014. For non-hate crimes, rates of reported assaults are relatively rare when compared to rates of theft, property damage and public nuisance offences. Yet, for hate crime offences in Victoria, and elsewhere, assaults are reported at much higher numbers. An extensive study on hate crime in Leicester suggests higher rates of reported assaults reflect the confusion in the general population regarding what legally constitutes a hate crime (Chakraborti *et al.* 2014). Scholars suggest that victims may only recognise those acts that are particularly severe, like assault, as a reportable prejudice motivated offence (see also Williams and Tregidga 2013). Alternatively, victims may feel that violent assaults are more likely to be taken seriously by the police, with less serious offences going unreported (Home Office 2013; Williams and Tregidga 2013).

Property damage is also frequently reported, with 20.3 per cent of the offences reported fitting this category. Other offences such as robbery, theft and burglary are less common. Harassment only constitutes 3.2 per cent of reported

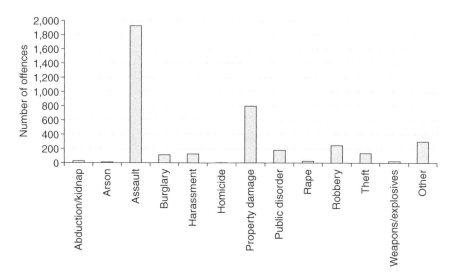

Figure 7.2 Prejudice motivated offences reported to Victoria Police, January 2000–June 2014.

Table 7.1 Count (and percentages) of offences by offence type and location of offence, January 2000–June 2014

Offence location	Offence type						
	Break and enter	Crime against the person	Harassment	Other	Property	Public disorder	Total
Business	6 (5.3)	143 (6.9)	12 (9.6)	15 (6.1)	79 (6.7)	10 (5.6)	265 (6.8)
Entertainment venue	1 (0.9)	3 (0.1)	0 (0.0)	0 (0.0)	4 (0.3)	5 (2.8)	13 (0.3)
Industry	1 (0.9)	10 (0.5)	0 (0.0)	0 (0.0)	9 (0.8)	0 (0.0)	20 (0.5)
Street, lane or footpath	0 (0.0)	728 (35.4)	5 (4.0)	35 (14.3)	311 (26.2)	80 (45.2)	1,159 (29.7)
Other	3 (2.7)	71 (3.4)	15 (12.0)	18 (7.3)	42 (3.5)	7 (4.0)	156 (4.0)
Private residence, including front or back yard	50 (44.2)	349 (17.0)	82 (65.6)	89 (36.3)	344 (29.0)	6 (3.4)	920 (23.6)
Public open area	3 (2.7)	200 (9.7)	1 (0.8)	13 (5.3)	121 (10.2)	21 (11.9)	359 (9.2)
Public transport	1 (0.9)	282 (13.7)	0 (0.0)	15 (6.1)	53 (4.5)	13 (7.3)	364 (9.3)
Religious area	26 (23.0)	5 (0.2)	1 (0.8)	8 (3.3)	73 (6.2)	3 (1.7)	116 (3.0)
Retail	15 (13.3)	153 (7.4)	4 (3.2)	38 (15.5)	100 (8.4)	23 (13.0)	333 (8.5)
Service	7 (6.2)	113 (5.5)	5 (4.0)	14 (5.7)	49 (4.1)	9 (5.1)	197 (5.0)
Total	113 (100.0)	2,057 (100.0)	125 (100.0)	245 (100.0)	1,185 (100.0)	177 (100.0)	3,902 (100.0)

offences, despite others suggesting it is the most common prejudice motivated offence (Moss 1991). However, the under-reporting of harassment to police may be due to confusion as to whether or not it constitutes a criminal act or, in some circumstances, because complainants choose to deal with it under civil anti-discrimination laws.

Of the 3,919 offences recorded in the data, 1,887 (47.2 per cent) occurred between the hours of 3 p.m. and 11 p.m. Increased offences reported during this time are consistent across all offence categories, with the exception of harassment, which most frequently occurred between midnight and 7 a.m. Certain PMC offences demonstrate a weekend effect. Crimes against the person and property crimes are more likely to occur on a Friday, Saturday or Sunday. Further, a cross-tabulation of the day and time at which all offences occur suggests that a large number of offences occur on Friday and Saturday nights in the geographical areas across Victoria.

Perpetrators and victims of prejudice motivated crime

In the LEAP database, approximately 45 per cent of offence reports involve an unknown offender and thus approximately 1,761 of cases do not contain offender demographic information. Of the offences where demographic information is available, the majority of the 1,840 offences (85.3 per cent) involve a male perpetrator (see Table 7.2). Further, offenders are likely to be either between 18 and 24 or 30 and 59 years of age.

Only 51.6 per cent of offence reports record the offender's country of birth. The overwhelming majority of offenders (79.7 per cent) were born in Australia, though there is no indication of parents' place of birth or ancestry. A further 3.4 per cent of offenders were born in other Oceania (including New Zealand and Samoa), and 4.0 per cent were born in Asia, mainly China and India. Of the offences between 2000 and 2014 that were reported to police, 1,044 offences (26.6 per cent) were committed by a repeat offender. This data indicates that repeat offenders are more likely to be responsible for public disorder offences or other offences (as categorised in LEAP data). Property crime and break and enter appears less likely to be committed by repeat offenders. LEAP data from 2000–2014 also suggests that repeat offenders are more likely to offend against Caucasians (33.0 per cent), followed by offences towards individuals based on their race, ethnicity and/or religion (see Figure 7.3).

Table 7.2 Breakdown of offender age and gender for offences where both demographics are known, January 2000–June 2014

	<18 years	*18–24 years*	*25–29 years*	*30–59 years*	*60+ years*	*Total*
Male	443	578	213	567	39	1,840
Female	85	64	50	115	4	318
Total	528	642	263	682	43	2,158

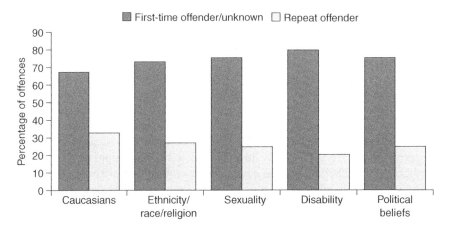

Figure 7.3 Motivations of offences committed by repeat offenders, January 2000–June 2014.

Offence information from the LEAP database indicates that victims[4] of prejudice motivated crime are also likely to be male (63.4 per cent). Victims are most likely to be in the 30–59 year age bracket (see Table 7.3). Only 66.5 per cent of victims have recorded information on their race, place of birth or religion. From the available LEAP data, 60.8 per cent of victims were born in Australia, 16.6 per cent were born in Asia. A further 5.7 per cent were born in the Middle East and 3.6 per cent in Eastern Europe. Again, as with offenders, this does not tell us anything about their parents' country of birth or ancestry.

Of the 3,919 offences reported, 1,014 (25.9 per cent) victims were previous victims of a prejudice motivated offence. Victims of public disorder and other offences were overwhelmingly more likely to have previously been victimised (94.4 per cent and 86.2 per cent respectively) than victims of other offences. Property offences and crimes against the person were least likely to have previously reported their victimisation to the police. Repeat victimisation was more likely to occur in a public open area (32.3 per cent) or other area (37.6 per cent) or in a private residence (31.2 per cent). The prejudice motivations for repeat victims, as indicated in the VicPol offence data, were political beliefs, (37.8 per cent; see Figure 7.4) or offences against victims identified as Caucasian

Table 7.3 Breakdown of victim age and gender for offences where both demographics are known, January 2000–June 2014

	<18 years	*18–24 years*	*25–29 years*	*30–59 years*	*60+ years*	*Total*
Male	181	630	393	859	86	2,149
Female	83	161	117	339	41	741
Total	264	791	510	1,198	127	2,890

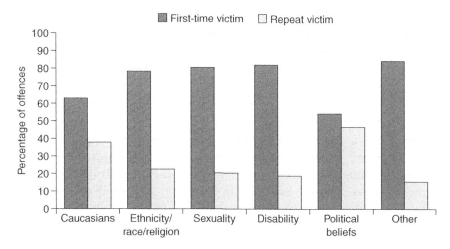

Figure 7.4 Motivations of offences involving individuals who have and have not been victimised in a previous prejudice motivated offence, 2000–2014.

(30.2 per cent). They were least likely to be based on physical or mental disability (24.7 per cent) or ethnicity, race and/or religion (24.2 per cent).

Examining the effectiveness of the PMC Strategy

The data discussed in the previous section reveal interesting patterns of offending and victimisation. However, they also reveal significant shortcomings in reporting and recording PMC offences. We see this in the types of offences reported. Serious crime offences are reported at greater frequency than other PMC offences. We also see the shortcomings in the significant absence of victim and offender data.

Improving the reporting and recording of PMC offences in Victoria are two key foci of the VicPol PMC Strategy. As we have discussed in greater detail in earlier chapters, to achieve these objectives VicPol identified five strategies that would enhance community confidence and lead to a greater willingness to report prejudice motivated crime to police. These included working in partnership with the community, treating victims with dignity and respect, responding to offences in a timely and professional manner, supporting victims and facilitating referrals to support services, and thoroughly investigating all reports of prejudice motivated crime (Victoria Police 2011). On its website, VicPol provides information on what a hate crime is and what to do if someone experiences or witnesses a hate crime. It also includes examples of offences that would constitute a hate crime and provides links to Crime Stoppers, third-party reporting agents (e.g. the Victorian Equal Opportunity and Human Rights Commission) and police liaison officers who can address the needs of particular groups (e.g. Indigenous non-English speaking and LGBTI liaison officers). As we saw in Chapter 6, VicPol also engaged in specific training with PRs to better train new officers to more accurately identify an offence motivated by hate or prejudice and to better record information into the LEAP system, although our research suggests that there are enhancements to ensure training is more effective that could be usefully developed.

It is difficult to assess the extent to which a hate crime strategy has been successful. One way to determine strategy success is to see an increase in recorded prejudice motivated offences. Indeed, VicPol notes that improvements in community confidence and reporting will, by necessity, lead to an increase in recorded prejudice motivated offences. Thus, the overall performance measure of the strategy is to increase the number of PMC reports to police (as recorded on LEAP) (PMC Strategy 2010). We therefore analysed the monthly counts of offences officially recorded in LEAP as PMC offences ($n=3,919$) that occurred between January 2000 and June 2014. In each month, the overall count of PMC offences ranged from 0 to 68, with a mean of 22.5 reports per month. This data provided us with a sufficient time period leading up to the strategy and following the launch of the strategy to assess whether or not any meaningful change in reporting occurred after the July 2011 rollout of the strategy.

As we discussed in earlier chapters, and as revealed in our focus group interviews, there is significant distrust of the police in many of the identified priority victim groups, though the degree of distrust varied across the groups. We therefore considered the effect of the strategy on hate crime reporting with differing motivations. Further, as officers could choose multiple motivation response categories when entering PMC information into the LEAP database, we collated the offences into five meaningful categories. The first includes specific ethnically and racially motivated offences, for example, where the victim was reported as Asian, Caucasian, or Aboriginal or Torres Strait Islander, and the motivation for the attack was reported solely due to race. These offences accounted for 2,101 of the 3,919 offences. The second category includes offences where multiple ethnic and/or other cultural beliefs were noted as the motivation. We label this category 'cultural' motivation, and offence incidents in this category represent those where the victim was targeted because of their political beliefs, their religion or their minority status. Examples include offences against Jewish, Hindu or Muslim victims and those motivated by political beliefs held by Asian victims. These events constituted 868 of the 3,919 total offences recorded. The third category represents offences solely motivated by political beliefs (258 offences). The fourth category includes offences solely motivated by sexual orientation and/or gender identity (497 offences) and category five includes offences solely motivated by physical or mental disabilities (171 offences).

Data were analysed, using an interrupted time series model (using Stata statistical software). An interrupted time series model evaluates the extent to which an intervention affects the immediate level and ongoing trend of the outcome variable (Linden 2014). Underlying this model are ordinary least-squares regressions designed to adjust for autocorrelation, which provide more flexibility in a time series context than the standard autoregressive integrated moving-average models (Linden 2015). In all models, the lag specifications were obtained using

Table 7.4 Monthly information for offences by PMC categories for months recorded between January 2000–June 2014

Variable	Number of observational months	Mean	Standard deviation	Minimum	Maximum
Race/Ethnicity	174	12.040	8.787	0	59
Cultural	174	4.954	3.913	0	28
Political	174	1.482	2.705	0	20
Sexuality/Gender identity	174	0.971	2.837	0	17
Physical disabilities	174	0.247	1.375	0	7

selection statistics for Vector Autoregressions. The statistics were calculated for a maximum of six lags in all models. In models where the statistics suggested different numbers of significant lags, the value for Akaike's information criterion (AIC) was selected as it is argued in the literature to be the most accurate with monthly data (Ivanov and Kilian 2001; Torres-Reyna n.d.). After calculating the number of lags for which the autocorrelation is present, an interrupted time series model was run for each of the motivation categories commencing with an overall count. Summary statistics and coefficients for the time series models are provided in Tables 7.4 and 7.5 respectively.

Overall hate crime trends

Selection statistics on the overall hate crime variable showed two significant lags. In terms of the number of hate crimes reported to police, the starting level in January 2000 was estimated to be 12 hate crimes reported per month. Hate crimes significantly increased between January 2000 and June 2011 at a rate of one per six-month period ($t=3.54$, $p<0.001$). During July 2011, when the strategy was implemented, there was no immediate effect of the policy on hate crimes reported to police in this time ($t=-0.52$, ns). After this time, monthly counts of hate crime significantly decreased at a rate of one per two months ($t=-3.89$, $p<0.001$). This trend is displayed in Figure 7.5.

Race and ethnicity trends

Autocorrelation of the race and ethnicity counts was present for four lags. In January 2000, the estimated number of hate crimes based on race or ethnicity was three per month. This figure significantly increased between January 2000 and June 2011 at a rate of one per six-month period ($t=5.04$, $p<0.001$). When the strategy was implemented in July 2011, there was again no immediate effect of the policy on hate crimes reported to police in this time ($t=-0.06$, ns). However, monthly counts of racial and ethnically motivated hate crime significantly decreased after the strategy at a rate of one per two months ($t=-4.20$, $p<0.001$) (see Figure 7.6).

Table 7.5 Coefficients for time series analyses by category

	Overall		Race/Ethnicity		Cultural		Political		Sex and gender		Disability	
	Coeff	Std Error	Coeff	Std Error	Coeff	Std Error	Coeff	Std Error	Coeff	Std Error	Coeff	Std Error
Pre-trend	0.139***	0.039	0.124***	0.024	0.006	0.013	0.005	0.006	0.002	0.007	0.003	0.003
Intervention	−1.935	3.740	−0.216	3.756	−0.388	1.153	0.247	1.301	−2.146	1.194	0.356	0.532
Post-trend	−0.477***	0.122	0.552***	0.131	−0.041	0.035	−0.021	0.062	0.143**	0.054	0.001	0.022
Constant	12.434	3.436	3.210	1.613	4.639***	1.261	1.011*	0.441	2.524***	0.712	0.639*	0.313
$F_{(3, 170)}$=	7.15***		11.54***		1.44		0.51		2.95*		1.77	

Notes
ITSA model uses Newey-West standard errors.
Significance levels:
* $p < 0.05$;
** $p < 0.01$;
*** $p < 0.001$.

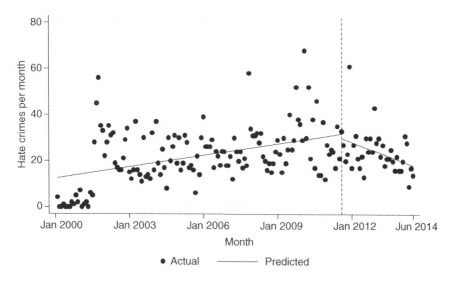

Figure 7.5 The pre-post intervention trends of overall hate crime rates reported to Victoria Police.

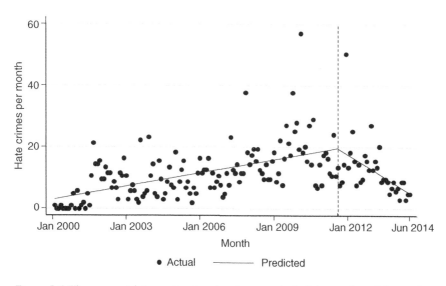

Figure 7.6 The pre-post intervention trends of race and ethnicity motivated hate crime rates reported to Victoria Police.

Cultural motivation trends

Analysis of the hate crimes based on cultural motivations demonstrates that the number of crimes with this motivation has remained stable from 2000 to 2014, with approximately five offences reported per month. However, autocorrelation of the culturally motivated counts was present for two lags. While the trend shows a slight decrease in offences reported after the strategy was implemented, this difference is statistically non-significant.

Political belief trends

As with cultural motivations, analysis of the hate crimes based on political beliefs demonstrates that the number of crimes with this motivation has remained stable from 2000 to 2014, with approximately two to three offences reported per month. Autocorrelation of politically motivated counts was present for one lag. Results indicate a slight increase in hate crimes associated with cultural motivations until the launch of the strategy and a slight decrease in offences reported after the strategy was implemented; however, these slopes were statistically non-significant.

Sexual orientation and gender identity trends

Analysis of the hate crimes based on sexual orientation and gender identity demonstrates that the number of crimes with this motivation remained stable from 2000 to 2011, with approximately three offences reported per month. Auto-correlation of the sexual orientation and gender identity counts was present for three lags. Although there was a sharp decrease in crimes reported to police in July 2011, this number is non-significant ($t = -1.80$, ns). However, monthly counts of sexual orientation or gender identity motivated hate crime significantly increased after the strategy at a rate of one per six months ($t = 2.66$, $p < 0.01$). This trend is displayed in Figure 7.7.

Physical and mental disability trends

Analysis of the hate crimes based on disability demonstrates that the number of crimes with this motivation has remained stable from 2000 to 2014, with approximately one to two offences reported per month. However, autocorrelation of the culturally motivated counts was present for two lags. Results indicated a slight increase until the strategy was implemented and a slight increase in offences reported afterwards; however, these slopes are statistically non-significant.

Did the PMC Strategy work?

Our examination of VicPol prejudice motivated offence data reveals a number of key findings. First, assaults are overwhelmingly the most frequent offences

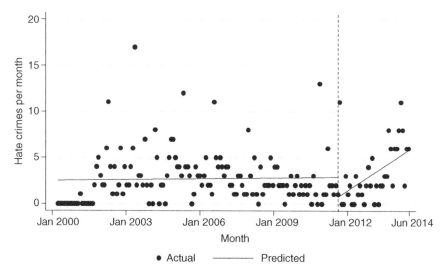

Figure 7.7 The pre-post intervention trends of hate crimes motivated by sexual orienta-
     tion or gender identity as reported to Victoria Police.

reported to police, and victims are more likely to report prejudice based on race
or ethnicity than other forms of biases. Yet, we do not know if the more frequent
reporting by racial/ethnic minority members represents their higher rate of victimisation compared to other victim groups. Second, there are more reports of
assaults against the person than all other offence categories combined. This may
simply reflect higher levels of police awareness and, thus, inclination to record
these reports over other forms of prejudice. As revealed in our focus group interviews, and evidenced in the broader hate crime literature, many victims of
lower-level hate crime offences do not believe that much can be done for less
serious offences and, as a consequence, do not report them to the police. Third,
our in-depth examination of the offence data reveals clear patterns concerning
the timing and location of prejudice motivated offences. A large proportion of
offences occur on weekend evenings either in the street, a lane or a footpath and
are committed by male offenders. That so many hate crime offences occur in
public suggests that ongoing campaigns targeted to the wider public may be
useful in developing prevention and response initiatives. However, as Wickes
and colleagues (2016) argue, in particular communities, especially those with
large numbers of ethnic minorities, witnesses may find it difficult to distinguish
a hate crime from a non-hate motivated offence. Thus, prevention campaigns targeted towards the broader community must clearly convey what constitutes hate
crime. Fourth, these data reveal significant limitations in the recording of
information relating to the motivation of the PMC and the racial/ethnic background of the victim. Nearly one-third of the racial and/or ethnic background
information is missing for PMC victims. This makes developing relevant

prevention programmes for specific victim groups extremely difficult. Officer training associated with recording relevant and complete data for PMC victims would greatly assist our ability to understand and appropriately respond to reported PMC offences.

Finally, and perhaps more importantly, this data reveals that the PMC Strategy had little influence on reporting behaviour. Our analyses of prejudice motivated crime trends before and after the rollout of the strategy provide limited evidence that the plan resulted in an increase in reporting overall. Of course, this could reflect a downturn in offences motivated by prejudice and hate. It is possible that publicity surrounding attacks on Indian students brought about a greater awareness of hate crime and greater intolerance for racist slurs or harassment of anyone because of their race, ethnicity or religious orientation. Yet, without frequent victim surveys to identify levels of non-reported hate crime in the broader community, we simply cannot validate this possible explanation for the overall decrease in official reporting in the period post 2011.

Revisiting our interviews with focus group participants and members of VicPol Command, however, does shed some light on why official reports of offences motivated by hate or prejudice have declined. Despite the progress made with particular community groups across Victoria, there remains a significant distrust of police amongst members of minority groups. This was particularly true of ethnic minority groups and our migrant youth group. As we discussed in Chapter 5, even after the rollout, there was a lack of trust that offences, when reported, would be taken seriously. As importantly, apart from a violent attack, our focus groups demonstrated that there was general uncertainty as to what legally constitutes a hate crime in general and VicPol's label of 'prejudice motivated crime' more specifically. It is possible that the introduction of a new, albeit more inclusive, label for hate crime further confused victims, which in turn reduced reporting. We argue that if there were greater common ground around the meaning of 'prejudice motivated crime', community members might be more certain about what constitutes an offence. Yet, as noted throughout this book, a shared understanding will only result in increased reporting when there is greater trust in the police and a confidence that police will accurately record events and take the complaints and experiences of PMC victims seriously.

Our work with focus groups, interviews with senior officers at VicPol and surveys of new recruits suggest that another significant barrier to reporting lies with front-line policing efforts. Our new-recruits survey, detailed in the previous chapter, reveals that specific training on PMC identification does not necessarily lead to greater clarity about what constitutes a prejudice motivated offence or what cues are most relevant for distinguishing a PMC incident from one not motivated by hate or prejudice. Participants from our focus groups readily acknowledged the lack of awareness of what formally constitutes a prejudice motivated offence. As a member of our Indian focus group stated, 'If we say prejudice motivated crimes, nine times out of ten, the police, well, probably all the time, the police will say, "No, no, no, it's not prejudice motivated crime; this person is a criminal doing a criminal act"'. This quote epitomises the gap in police–community understanding and underscores the importance of a shared language to describe and respond to PMC offences.

Interviews with members of VicPol Command and senior officers reveal the difficulties in translating the key principles of the strategy into front-line policing. There are clearly struggles with front-line officers in their attempt to understand the nuances of PMC. A senior officer notes that there is still 'a fair bit of work we need to do with our own membership in relation to the taking of the action … concerns about action or inaction by members is the ongoing problem for us' (Commander, PCD, VicPol, interview 6 May 2016). Thus, while there is a recognition from the top that building trust will take time, there is also an awareness that there is much more work to do at the operational level to build that trust. This is clearly evidenced in the following interview with a senior officer:

> You can have a strategy for anything and everything.… But unless you have a workforce that understands the value of that connection, then it becomes a compliance regime rather than actually an engagement tool … you know, communities who are still saying, 'Well, we identify it; do you identify it?' And we really need to continue to develop a culture which is reinforcing 'Yes, we identify it and, yes, we will take action'.
>
> (Commander, PCD, VicPol, interview 6 May 2016)

The decline in reporting is not lost on VicPol. As a senior officer notes 'Well, I think if we use the numbers of reported incidents of PMC as only the benchmark of success, then you'd have to say – there's a question mark' (Commander, PCD, VicPol, interview 6 May 2016). Yet our interviews reveal that senior members of VicPol do not consider the drop in reporting as an indication of the PMC Strategy's failure. Rather, they see this as an indicator that more is to be done to assist victims in recognising a hate crime, to facilitate reporting and to encourage police to be sensitive to the difficulties surrounding prejudice motivated offences. Simply put, greater effort is needed to assist police and community members in negotiating and agreeing upon common language and understanding of PMC.

At the operational level, there is still optimism that things are changing and, while it may take time for these changes to manifest in marked increases in official reporting of offences motivated by hate or prejudice, VicPol remains committed to ensure greater trust and a mutual understanding between victims and police. Again, a senior officer in VicPol recognises that 'there's work to be done', but stresses that continued engagement with community leaders and 'building the confidence of community to understand that we will act' remains an important goal for police (Commander, PCD, VicPol, interview 6 May 2016). A member of VicPol Command echoes this view:

> We want to understand prejudice motivated crime. We want to understand vulnerable groups and victims but we don't want to racially profile or

religiously profile … so it's a really hard balance … the awareness of the balance of human rights and privacy and not profiling people based on certain characteristics or certain beliefs is really high but then also balancing that with the need to tailor our service to vulnerable communities and understand the differences.

(Senior Operational Officer, VicPol, interview 6 May 2016)

Despite the difficulties in building trust and enhancing relationships amongst victims and police, our analyses do reveal some positive results. The time series analyses provide some evidence that reporting has increased for hate crime offences motivated by the sexual orientation of the victim. The increase in hate crime reporting for offences motivated by sexual orientation is intriguing. On one hand, these increases might reflect actual increases in victimisation amongst members of the LGBTI community. On the other hand, they could suggest a greater willingness of LGBTI people to report offences to the police. Although many of our focus group members reported a difficult history between members of the LGBTI community and the police, the accounts of some of our respondents did indicate some success in overcoming historical alienation. This could be, in part, due to the work of the LGBTI liaison officers in the police force. But, more broadly, it could be the consequence of a significant shift in public opinion regarding the gay and lesbian community. In the last few years in particular, the support for gay rights has increased substantially. For example, support for gay marriage has increased in Britain, the US, Canada, France, Sweden and Norway (Brewer 2014). Discrimination in employment practices for members of the gay and lesbian community is also decreasing (Becker 2014), and what has been referred to as an income penalty for people who identify as gay is significantly decreasing (Clarke and Sevak 2013). Twenge and colleagues (2016) argue that, in the Western world, we have moved beyond tolerance towards the gay community to a genuine acceptance of their civil rights and the 'freedom to engage in same-sex sexuality'. We can only hope this will extend beyond the LGBTI community to all minority groups currently experiencing prejudice and discrimination.

Conclusion

While the goals of the PMC Strategy are indeed progressive and inclusive, there remains a significant chasm between recognising the need for change and then ensuring these changes occur at the victim–police exchange. Certainly, police want to generate a common understanding of prejudice motivated crime, and there is a strong awareness, at least at the operational level, that it is important to understand the needs and complexities of dealing with crimes motivated by hate and prejudice experienced by vulnerable groups. As we have discussed in previous chapters, victims must be listened to, and procedurally just practices that not only encourage trust but provide victims with a legitimate voice are needed to increase reporting. As we further illustrate in the next chapter, a key challenge for Victoria Police is to effectively filter these messages down to front-line officers and reinforce these messages through victim–police interactions.

Notes

1 Due to small numbers for some categories, or in cases where officers reported more than one motivation, we collapse some categories (for example religion/race/ethnicity) where necessary.
2 Victoria Police only provided offence data from 2000 to June 2014. As our trend analysis relies on data for full calendar years, we examine the trends between 2000 and 2013 only.
3 For the purposes of giving a spatial overview of crime in Victoria, postcodes of the incident location were categorised into Melbourne CBD (all postcodes fully or partially encapsulated within the City of Melbourne municipal council), Greater Melbourne (postcodes located within the Melbourne Statistical Division excluding the city centre) or regional Victoria (postcodes located outside of the Greater Melbourne Division).
4 Here we refer only to individual victims. We do not analyse information on hate crime victimisation against businesses, churches, statues or other inanimate objects.

8 Identification

The markers of prejudice motivated crime

Introduction

> The key point is that the experience of violent racism is not reducible to an isolated incident, or even a collection of incidents. Victimization and racialization –the processes by which a person becomes a victim of this form of crime are cumulative, comprised of various encounters with racism, some of which may be physically violent, some lying only at the fringes of what most people would define as violent or aggressive. Some of these experiences are subtle and amount to no more than becoming aware that someone is annoyed or disgusted by the presence of black people or fleeting instances such as a half-hearted racist joke or epithet. At the other end of this continuum are the more easily remembered instances when racism is coupled with physical aggression or violence.
>
> (Bowling 1999)

Bowling's important identification of racial violence as a process in *Violent Racism: Victimization, Policing and Social Context* (1999) offers a valuable way to capture many of the divergences that we have identified in the field of hate crime enforcement between Victoria Police and the communities they serve. For Bowling, racism is cumulative and cannot be reduced to the incidents that meet the threshold of criminality. That is, hate crimes, like other violent crimes, harm individual victims but, in addition, they draw on a history of discrimination to attack the individual's sense of identity and may instil enduring fear on whole communities. As such, hate crimes are 'triply harmful' (California Commission 2008). Essentially, the experience of hate crime in vulnerable and marginalised communities, and the meanings in circulation around such concepts, need to be understood longitudinally and collectively, not just on a case-by-case basis or in relation to individual victims. Hate incidents are social issues that require long-term solutions.

In comparison, police tend to respond to discrete incidents that are more easily categorised and recorded as hate crime, rather than considering those incidents as part of a continuous social process of prejudice – the 'process-incident contradiction' (Chakraborti and Garland 2015; Williams and Tregidga 2014).

But hate crimes are constituted by surrounding communal attitudes and shared meanings, local events and social histories. While isolating incidents for record-ing, investigation and prosecution purposes, police may fail to appreciate these historical and collective impacts of prejudice in the context of recurrent human rights violations for victims and communities (Waddington 2000).

Our ambition in this chapter is to address these concerns by contributing to the literature on the mobilisation of hate crime policing policy that we examined in Chapters 3 and 4 and some of the dissonances we identified in Chapters 5, 6 and 7 in implementation. As we explained there, the Prejudice Motivated Crime Strategy adopted by VicPol is atypically proactive in responding to prejudice motivated crime outside any legal requirement to do so. Although the difficulties of operationalising hate crime legislation into policing policy and practice has been well-explored (Bell 2002; Grattet and Jenness 2008; Hall 2012), the lack of a prosecutorial imperative in Victoria means that police have an indicative, but far from exhaustive, framework for identifying what amounts to hate crime. Fur-thermore, as we saw in Chapter 2, the absence of a universal definition of preju-dice motivated crime, and of associated concepts such as hate or bias crime, both reflects and reveals enduring divisions between scholars, policy makers, police and targeted communities. These divisions are evident in multiple competing narratives and may operate to derail attempts to effectively and meaningfully consolidate policy and practice (Chakraborti and Garland 2014). In choosing to adopt the distinctive terminology of prejudice motivated crime, VicPol has taken a path less trodden with definition and precedent.

This move can produce uncertainty. Our discussions of community percep-tions in Chapter 5 and police training in Chapter 6 revealed significant differ-ences in how the meaning of prejudice motivated crime – as well as hate, bias or targeted crime – is understood by different stakeholders in Victoria. These dif-ferences in experience and interpretation crucially impact policing. Police are the first responders to any incident of hate or prejudice. It is the evidence gathered and recorded, the further questions asked regarding the surrounding social context, and the ensuing investigation that will determine whether the incident is recorded as a prejudice motivated offence for policing purposes. In the case of a successful conviction, early identification by police is essential to ensure that evidence of a prejudiced motive (aggravating the offence under s. 5 (2)(daaa) of the *Sentencing Act 1991* (Vic)) will ultimately be available to the sentencing court. As Chapter 7 explained, VicPol has specified categories for recording the relevant motive or category of hate crime (e.g. race/ethnicity, sexual orientation, disability). Yet, they acknowledge there are still considerable difficulties around how front-line police assess and record prejudice motivated incidents, most importantly whether they even identify an event as a motivated by prejudice to begin with (Commander, PCD, VicPol, interview 6 May 2016). The long-term change inaugurated by their PMC training will take time to be fully integrated across the force.

This model of policing hate crime hands considerable discretion to police to collect and weigh evidence in determining whether an offence is motivated by prejudice (VEOHR 2013). At the same time, this degree of discretion supports the needs of targeted communities, highlighted throughout this book, by allowing for the formulation of a more mutual understanding of prejudice motivated crime. Such an understanding facilitates implementation and operationalisation of the PMC Strategy, while acknowledging different perceptions of the problem in the eyes of law enforcement and targeted communities. Within these dialogues between police and communities, we have also stressed the importance of procedural justice, that is, perceptions of fairness generated through police neutrality, respect, trustworthiness and the empowering of community voice (Murphy and Barkworth 2014; Murphy and Cherney 2011). A common perspective on hate crime, in combination with fair police treatment and the development of good relationships, fosters an environment in which the exercise of police power is more likely to be perceived as legitimate (Bottoms and Tankebe 2012; Tankebe 2013) making victims more trusting and willing to report crimes (Murphy and Barkworth 2014). The impact of these wider police–community relations on the success of the PMC Strategy is recognised by VicPol:

> PMC gave us the springboard to it, but the underpinning relationship piece is key. Because confidence, if you don't have confidence in the individual, you don't necessarily have confidence in the organisation.
>
> (Commander, PCD, VicPol, interview 6 May 2016)

We suggested in Chapter 3 that hate-crime policing policies all too often fall into two camps: 'under-inclusive' and 'over-inclusive' approaches. The former tend to restrict the meaning of hate crime to its prosecutorial elements, excluding the cumulative processes of prejudice experienced by vulnerable communities. Driven by these community concerns of rights violations, the latter tend to rely upon an expanded understanding of hate crime that is difficult for front-line decision-makers to validate. Taking an evidence-based approach to policy implementation (Neyroud 2009), we propose a middle ground between these approaches and the means to address ambiguities in the meaning of prejudice motivated crime. In particular, we advance a series of flexible, rather than prescriptive, markers that provide operational police with a practical guide for identifying PMC.

The markers are the outcome of a two-tiered process of research and analysis (discussed further below). First, looking to the law, we identified and analysed judicial interpretations of prejudice motivated crime under Victorian sentencing legislation, as well as comparable legislation in other Australian jurisdictions. Extracting the core ingredients of these interpretations (based on evidence collected from initial investigations by police and prosecutors), we built a legal framework of prejudice motivated crime, into which we fed three key expectations, synthesised from the findings of earlier chapters, as necessary for minority communities to develop the confidence and trust needed to report hate crime: recognition, fairness and commitment. The result of this analysis is a set of legally grounded but community-oriented markers that provide a scaffold for negotiating compatible understandings between stakeholders about the nature and significance of prejudice motivated crime.

The chapter begins by briefly recapping the challenges for VicPol, identified in Chapters 3 and 4, in implementing hate crime policy in an environment where community policing has a vexed relationship with minority communities. This analysis reveals the limits of over- and under-inclusive approaches to policing hate crime. We then provide more detail on our socio-legal analysis of the case law on prejudice motivated crime. The third section of the chapter advances the flexible markers we have developed to minimise the pitfalls of both approaches.

Community expectations for the policing of prejudice motivated crime

VicPol's commitment to community engagement in the pursuit of crime reduction and community confidence is well-documented (Nixon and Chandler 2011). However, police efforts to focus on marginal communities can lead to perceptions amongst these communities that they are being over-policed as suspects, yet remain under-policed when it comes to victimisation. As we saw in earlier chapters, a history of police misconduct, racial profiling and brutality against ethnic minorities, including Indigenous and African youth, has been exposed as a consistent problem in Victoria (Fitzroy Legal Service 2010; Hopkins 2009). When police focus on communities as an amalgam of criminogenic factors, they are perceived as operating in a fashion that challenges human rights and procedural justice measures. At the same time, VicPol has been criticised for their resistance to label the victimisation of racial minority groups, such as students from India as driven, even partially, by racial bias (Mason 2012b). In so doing, VicPol has repeated the well-rehearsed mistake of examining each incident in isolation from the larger social processes that rendered it meaningful for the victim community (Bowling 1999).

In Chapter 4, we concluded that the current state of knowledge about the impact of policing on vulnerable minorities in Victoria could be crystallised into three key expectations – expectations that were confirmed by our focus group participants in Chapter 5. First, if police are to challenge the residual mistrust (Chakraborti and Garland 2015) that shapes their relations with many minority communities, cultural change is required at the organisational level. For example, the embrace of procedural justice approaches, especially providing communities with an instrumental voice, can assist in legitimating police practices and engendering trust (Murphy and Cherney 2011). Yet, distrust is difficult to dislodge. For example, Fathi (2013) describes how immigrant and refugee communities may project their prior negative experiences of corrupt law enforcement in their homeland onto the police force of their new country. Linguistic and cultural barriers, community marginalisation and fear of retribution or deportation all deter reporting (Johnson and Cuevas Ingram 2012; Singh *et al.* 2013). McKernan and Weber (2016) report that racial and ethnic minorities, in particular, suffer more negative experiences with police than other communities.

For instance, amongst Vietnamese Australians, they found that 'negative reputational effects' were amplified when any violence or corruption of Victorian Police mirrored similar behaviour of Vietnamese police (ibid.). But while prior negative experiences with police result in a reluctance of victims to report crimes, procedural justice strategies can build a 'stronger willingness from victims to report future victimization' (Murphy and Barkworth 2014). Therefore, the advancement of institutional values that champion, rather than belittle, the needs of such minority groups depends on the preparedness of organisational leaders to make a public *commitment* to such change. The recent introduction of the PCD, and the protocols of communication and liaison, signal VicPol's ongoing commitment to address and improve relationships with minority communities.

On its own, however, institutional change is not enough. Individual bias amongst police can also block reporting and appropriate investigation (Moran and Sharpe 2004). Although operational guidelines in England and Wales, for example, have sought to minimise police discretion in the categorisation of hate crime incidents, individual officers' preconceived attitudes continue to shape police responses (Chakraborti and Garland 2015). Second, then, vulnerable communities need police to address the problem of under-policing by adopting prejudice-sensitive practices, enabling the identification and investigation of hate crimes: this is a matter of *recognising* the prejudicial element of a crime. Hall (2012) suggests that the most influential element of police response to hate crimes is linked to 'operational common sense' and the actions of rank and file officers. Towards this end, VicPol's strategy is supported by training and 'social inclusion' programmes, including liaison positions dedicated to multicultural, gay/lesbian and new/emerging communities (VicPol 2011, 2013). The re-orientation of the force towards a victim-centred approach more broadly (VicPol 2016) has further supported this process of inclusion. This organisational investment is designed to send a clear message of commitment to the policing of PMC and to embed PMC in 'common sense' objectives of everyday policing activity (Walker and Katz 1995). This is vital if the strategy is not to be seen as a cynical method of managing criticism or a ploy for intelligence-gathering in presumed high-crime communities. As we discussed in Chapter 6, however, there are limitations in how such training is being taken up by police themselves, which will also have an impact on policing and reporting.

Third, to ameliorate the problem of over-policing in minority communities, there needs to be a shift in the perspective of front-line police towards impartiality and respect for human rights – a matter of neutrality or *fairness*. In addition to sitting within the general context of international and Australian human rights instruments (Chakraborti 2015; Crawshaw *et al.* 2007; Weber *et al.* 2014), VicPol's PMC Strategy must also reflect Victoria's *Charter of Human Rights and Responsibilities Act 2006,* which seeks to ensure that human rights are considered in the delivery of all government services. A fundamental challenge for VicPol is to maximise opportunities for investigating officers to meet these larger social and political objectives in ways that uphold the rights of targeted communities, particularly accurate data collection, effective training, enhanced community confidence and incidence reduction of PMC. This is a challenge of which they are well aware, as noted in Chapter 7. In effect, the quality of the relationship and communication between police and the community, and viable shared perspectives on key elements of hate and prejudice, are key ingredients in the effective translation of hate crime policy into policing action (Chakraborti and Garland 2015). This is well-recognised in jurisdictions, such as the UK, where a cross-government action plan 'frees' up police to work more closely with their communities (HM Government 2012), precipitating the importance of police–community engagement in national guidelines for law enforcement (College of Policing 2014).

The tension between operational and community concerns

The challenge for day-to-day officers in meeting these standards cannot, however, be underestimated (Grattet and Jenness 2005; Hall 2012). Even where police have a clear legislative definition of hate crime, implementing both law and policy into routine policing requires multi-layered strategies (Chakraborti and Garland 2015; Williams and Tregigda 2013). At the initial investigation stage, it is critical for front-line police to have the tools to identify hate crime or, alternatively, to resist such labelling if the evidence clearly does not warrant it (Turpin-Petrosino 2015). Initial identification is vital, as under-recording is one of the greatest operational dilemmas for police (Giannasi 2014, 2015b) and an ongoing problem for VicPol. As our focus groups with representatives from different stakeholder groups in Victoria revealed (see Chapter 5), community perceptions that they can trust police to work for and not against them are key to victim preparedness to seek police support. Yet, the sensitive task of sometimes deciding *not* to apply the hate crime label is also important, if police data is to represent reliable evidence on the nature and size of the reported problem. Certainly, as we have already seen, community feelings of vulnerability can be amplified if police are reluctant to acknowledge and record the prejudicial element of victimisation (Mason 2012b; Perry 2001). However, community anxiety may be unnecessarily heightened, if the official rate of recorded hate crime becomes inflated.

The public furore over attacks against Indian students in Melbourne in 2009, one of the drivers of VicPol's PMC Strategy that we discussed in Chapter 4, helps exemplify this tension. At the time, community groups representing the interests of Indian citizens or recent migrants studying in Australia, such as the Federation of Indian Students (FISA), were explicit about the racial victimisation of their constituency: 'How can they say that none of these attacks were racist when we hear criminals saying terms like "curry bashing?"' (Mason 2012a). FISA's claim was that individual incidents that were reported in the media and to the police during this period were part of a much larger problem of anti-Indian racial violence. In addition to extensive media coverage in Australia and India, these concerns were supported publicly by other student groups

(University of Melbourne Graduate Student Association 2009), as well as indirectly by universities (Babacan *et al.* 2010), and the Australian and New Zealand Human Rights Commission (Mason 2012b), leading to denunciation in the Indian parliament by the Indian prime minister (Hindustan Times 2009). As our earlier discussions about this issue indicated (see Chapter 4 in particular), there is complexity in assessing and responding to such incidents.

Establishing the extent of the violence against Indian students, however, has been difficult. A study of publicly available documentation surrounding approximately 20 incidents that received media coverage between 1 June 2009 and 31 May 2010 (Mason 2012b) concluded that some of the violence reported by Indian nationals certainly had a racist element. For example, in a case before the Victorian Supreme Court, the sentencing judge stated that he was 'satisfied beyond reasonable doubt that an element of racism was involved':

> [Y]ou focused on members of the Indian community as targets for physical assault. You wanted to cause them physical injury. You took the trouble to learn how to swear at Indians. So, having found your second victim, Bhinesh Mosaheb, you swore at him in Hindi. Not only that, but the language you used was designed to cause the maximum offence. That is unequivocally racist.
>
> (*DPP* v. *Caratozzolo* [2009] VSC 305)

However, this same study also concluded that in some media claims of racist violence, the evidence for a racial motive was weak (Mason 2012b). In a second study (discussed in more detail in Chapter 1), the Australian Institute of Criminology found a heightened vulnerability to robbery amongst Indian students, but the study was unable to provide a 'reliable' finding on the question of racial motivation (Joudo Larsen *et al.* 2011).

Arriving at the conclusion that an incident is motivated by racism or other forms of prejudice rests initially on how prejudice motivated crime is defined and understood. Crimes motivated purely by racism, such as the populist image of a random attack on a racial minority by a white supremacist, present little definitional difficulty. Crimes that are only partially motivated by racism are more difficult to categorise, such as an offender who selects robbery victims on the grounds of their Indian appearance. Much will hang on the legal and policy environment within which law enforcement agencies work. As our analysis in Chapter 4 made clear, VicPol did make sporadic attempts to acknowledge the racist element of victimisation patterns against Indian students. For example, then Chief Commissioner Simon Overland stated that 'undoubtedly some of these attacks have a racist motive' (Rennie 2009). However, when coupled with the many public denials of racism that were issued by police and parliamentarians at the time (Mason 2012b), this recognition came too little and too late to appease valid community concerns which, as this case demonstrates, can quickly escalate when law enforcement officers appear unwilling to acknowledge any prejudicial element to victimisation. On the other hand, the above research does suggest that some incidents were claimed as racial in nature in the absence of supporting evidence (ibid.). We should not be surprised by this. Communities that feel under siege will naturally see the spectre of discrimination when one of their members is victimised (Mason and Pulvirenti 2013). This is an inevitable consequence of the collective and longitudinal process through which prejudice and discrimination permeate the day-to-day lives of minority groups (Australian Human Rights Commission 2012; HREOC 1991) and through which hate crime wields its destabilising power (Turpin-Petrosino 2015). It is well-recognised that the harm of hate crime cannot be measured simply by the objective prevalence of individual events. The 'ripple effect' (Perry 2001) of just one racist incident can circulate through local networks and public media to produce feelings of vulnerability, anxiety and anger amongst a group that feels targeted (Chakraborti 2010; Mason 2002). These feelings of injustice come to be directed not just at the prejudice motivated crime itself but also at law enforcement (Macpherson 1999) for downplaying the role of prejudiced motive in violence. If communities are sometimes quick to judge, this is because all too often they have reason to do so.

Nevertheless, the awkward tension between community readiness to label an incident as a hate crime and police hesitancy to apply this label creates significant obstacles for the identification, reporting and investigation of hate crime. In the case of VicPol, however, this friction equally presents an opportunity for a 'partnership approach' (Perry 2010a) to combatting hate crime. Unfettered by the strictures of successful prosecution as a measurable outcome of their PMC Strategy, VicPol has the autonomy to develop a more trusting and symbiotic relationship (Grattet and Jenness 2008) with minority communities and thereby help empower those communities to develop the instrumental voice (Murphy and Cherney 2011) that is essential for a mutual interpretation of prejudice motivated crime. This can only be realised by approaching the strategy as a vehicle, rather than as a hurdle, for consulting directly with those communities where there is a history of long-standing distrust and for striving to accommodate their perceptions of harm and safety (as well as detecting and punishing offenders). This opening to pursue greater police–community consensus on the meaning of prejudice motivated crime, while well-supported in terms of force command structures, coalesces at the operational level where front-line decision-makers need clear, consistent and practical guidance to identify and record prejudice motivated crime.

Under- and over-inclusive approaches at the operational level

Vague terminology and definitions have been recognised as a core challenge in the effective enforcement of hate crime policies, creating problems of identification at the operational level (Boyd *et al.* 1996; Cronin *et al.* 2007). This is heightened for VicPol because it appears to be the only jurisdiction internationally to consistently use the term prejudice motivated crime. Traditionally, police rely on a range of filtering mechanisms and rules of thumb to overcome the operational challenges of identifying hate crime (Bell 1997, 2002; Boyd *et al.* 1996; Cronin *et al.* 2007). These reflect quite different strategic goals and produce divergent recording and investigation practices.

A determination of bias motivation is complex, as police officers may perceive several plausible motives, indicators of bias may be limited at the crime scene and, as hate crimes are infrequent, police officers may lack routine experience in identifying pertinent evidence, producing threefold issues of ambiguity, uncertainty and infrequency (Cronin *et al.* 2007). Hence, many law enforcement agencies have prioritised the need for greater consistency by adopting standardised operational procedures, particularly through checklists that help officers sift facts to assess an offender's motivations (Alberta Police Services 2010; Ontario Hate Crimes Working Group 2007; US Department of Justice 2012). For example, the FBI's Hate Crime Data Collection Guidelines and Training Manual (2015) provides a list of objective facts that may evidence the relevant bias motivation. Such checklists are largely directed towards identifying 'real' hate crime that can lead to successful prosecution. Although there are exceptions (Grattet and Jenness 2005), constitutional and statutory requirements in the US have generated narrow guidelines that focus on evidence of discriminatory group selection on the part of the offender and thereby avoid the criminalisation of hate speech, irrespective of the harm to the victim (Bell 2002; Boyd *et al.* 1996; Cronin *et al.* 2007). In Chapter 3, we characterised such approaches as 'under-inclusive'. By this, we meant that they provide officers with shortcuts to identify prototype situations that do *not* amount to hate crime and thus rule out certain kinds of events, such as the incidents described above against Indian students involving mixed motives. The tension between police and community perspectives is exacerbated by such checklists, which focus police discretion on prosecutorial thresholds in the identification of hate crime. In jurisdictions such as Victoria, where such evidence may be procedurally relevant only at sentencing, this under-inclusive checklist approach is clearly inappropriate and has not been adopted by VicPol. Instead, they have introduced a separate PMC section into the crime report narrative that is designed to make prejudice motivated crime 'more prominent and visible' for officers on a daily basis (Senior Operational Officer, VicPol, interview 6 May 2016).

In Chapter 3, we also characterised some operational approaches to hate crime as 'over-inclusive'. We used this term to refer to policing services that have responded to public sentiment (Fleming and McLaughlin 2010) by classifying events as hate crime largely on victim perception. In seeking to tackle the deep institutional failings exposed by the Stephen Lawrence Inquiry in the 1990s (Macpherson 1999), the UK response to hate crime stands out in this regard. Since 2007, criminal justice agencies in England and Wales have adopted a common definition of hate crime that is rooted in victim/witness perception. Although the 2014 College of Policing guidelines provide police with more detailed instructions to record and investigate hate crimes in a consistent manner (Chakraborti and Garland 2015; Williams and Tregigda 2013), this victim-perception test allows for incidents to be recorded by police, irrespective of whether they meet the legal threshold for prosecution or sentencing under UK hate crime law (Giannasi 2015b). This 'outside-in' method (O'Connor 2010) of defining hate crime makes it more capable than the checklist approach of recognising the processes of human rights violations that lie behind individual and collective experiences of hate crime. This has had a positive effect on reporting practices (Giannasi 2015b). At the same time, however, it has resulted in a recorded rate of hate crime that far outstrips the US and many European jurisdictions (ODIHR 2010). In harnessing perception, this broad approach (ODIHR 2014) has produced a void between victim-centred reporting mechanisms, based on perception, and the evidence-driven prosecution process (Chakraborti and Garland 2015; Williams and Tregidga 2013). As we argued in Chapter 3, an over-inclusive approach to the identification of hate crime creates a number of risks, including a large gap between recording and prosecution that can sap public confidence, unsustainable public expectations for greater say over the provision of policing services (Fleming and McLaughlin 2010), and confusion about the evidence which investigating officers need to gather to meet legal thresholds. In effect, an over-inclusive approach to the identification of hate crime has the potential to damage, rather than strengthen, the legitimacy of policing policy in the public eye by distancing the practical application of that policy from legal standards altogether. Over-inclusive approaches can effectively water down and diminish the force of the law (Hall 2005) and policy.

In sum, Victorian police need to have concrete but flexible markers of prejudice motivated crime for recording purposes and to effectively implement their strategy. There is precedent for a more 'open and indicative' approach to hate crime indicators (CEJI 2012) and, certainly, we are not suggesting that all operational approaches to the identification of hate crime can be easily categorised into one of the above two camps. But there is greater room for reconciliation of the contributions, and drawbacks, of these different approaches. Under-inclusive checklists geared towards the identification of offender liability for the purpose of prosecution have only limited value for VicPol because prosecutions are virtually impossible in the current legal context. Imposing narrow definitions is likely to encourage officers to exclude 'messy' cases that do not fit a legal category, even though they may cause public outrage. This will do little to address the expectations of minority communities for enhanced recognition, fairness and commitment in the policing of hate crime. On the other hand, over-inclusive approaches that give precedence to victim perceptions can exaggerate the nature and extent of the problem, as well as create unrealistic expectations, leading to criticism that the PMC Strategy is merely symbolic. Implementation of VicPol's strategy calls for evidence-based but flexible indicators that enable officers to identify PMC in ways that strike a balance between high community ideals and narrow legal standards.

The five markers of prejudice motivated crime

To reconcile the tension between police and community perspectives on hate crime and avoid the pitfalls of over- or under-inclusion, we developed a series of flexible markers for the identification of hate crime that aim to recognise both community expectations and operational needs of VicPol. These markers seek to bring concrete legal decisions together with community interests to unpack the meaning of PMC. They are not intended to be prescriptive but, rather, are designed to assist VicPol to negotiate with local communities in mapping the amorphous terrain of PMC with a clear eye to legal standards (in this case, those required for sentencing purposes). Our markers echo operational checklists that are used in other jurisdictions but take legal standards as a threshold only for encouraging a more elastic and socially engaged approach that recognises harm to victims and communities, as well as the moral culpability of the offender (i.e. they are geared towards community policing, as well as punishment). In other words, they provide a framework for negotiating common ground between the need for consistency and certainty in law enforcement and the expectation of communities that their voices and experiences will be heard. They also assist in the dissemination of legal remedies to communities in a language they can access and understand (Fathi 2013). They aim to produce more effective shared frameworks of meaning and expectation between communities and VicPol, to support front-line members to 'see' possible evidence of PMC and be confident in their assessments and, in effect, to assist in the work around PMC that 'is still to be done' (Commander, PCD, VicPol, interview 6 May 2016).

Above, we identified two forms of evidence with direct bearing on how the concept of PMC can be operationalised into a set of concrete but flexible marks for front-line officers in Victoria: (i) legal interpretations of prejudice motivated crime in Victoria's *Sentencing Act*; and (ii) inquiries and research that reveal the specific policing needs of Victoria's targeted communities. First, although Victoria does not have a hate crime offence that can be used to prosecute suspects, as discussed in Chapter 4, it does have discretionary sentencing aggravation provisions for offences that are motivated by prejudice (*Sentencing Act 1991* (Vic) s. 5(2)(daaa)). Given that the definition of PMC in VicPol's strategy is taken directly from this *Sentencing Act,* judicial interpretations of this definition provide the logical beginning point – and indeed the only firm legal foundation – for interpreting the meaning of prejudice motivated crime. As two other Australian jurisdictions (New South Wales and the Northern Territory)[1] have similar sentencing provisions, the project began by identifying a total of 25 reported, and available unreported, cases where sentencing courts gave direct consideration to aggravation by prejudice or group hatred. (This included several common law cases that were heard either before these sentencing provisions were enacted or in states that have not codified this motive as an aggravating factor at sentencing.) The cases included both sentencing judgements in the District/County or Supreme Courts, as well as decisions of the courts of criminal appeal. In 20 of these cases, such a motive was proved; in five cases, it was not. We then analysed the nature of the evidence relied upon to establish such a motive beyond reasonable doubt, extracting its core consistent elements.

Second, although these judicial interpretations function as authoritative texts on the scope and meaning of prejudice motivated crime (Jenness and Grattet

2001), in the face of the kinds of community concerns we have identified throughout this book, we could not allow this legal interpretation to stand as the only attribution of meaning. This is especially so given VicPol's relative autonomy from this legislative framework. We therefore augmented this legal threshold with the expectations of Victoria's minority communities, as recapped above. We concluded that the consistent message to emerge from Victoria's vexed history of police–minority relations is that for communities to report hate crime, they need to be confident that their complaints will be recognised and met with a fair and respectful response from police who have publicly committed to social inclusion and human rights.

The markers are thus guided by legal standards – and share some characteristics with conventional checklists – but are modified to accommodate reasonable community expectations and the major tenets of inclusive policing that keep human rights firmly in sight. As articulated by VicPol, a critical challenge is building member awareness, familiarity and confidence to recognise PMC and to apply the framework: 'it's the confidence of the member to understand what the evidence looks like, in order to be able to say this is prejudice motivated' (Commander, PCD, VicPol, interview 6 May 2016). The mapping of this nascent terrain, aimed at enhancing a mutual understanding of prejudice motivated crime between disparate stakeholders, produced five markers related to: (i) suspect/victim difference; (ii) suspect statements; (iii) the circumstances of the offence; (iv) the absence of other motives and; (v) the suspect's history of group victimisation. We consider each in turn below.

Marker 1: suspect/victim group difference

Consistent with most hate crime checklists, the cases in our review make clear that the suspect and victim in PMC cases usually come from different social or cultural groups (e.g. race, religion, sexual orientation, gender). In 'typical' cases, the victim will be from a minority group background and the offender from a majority-group background (e.g. African victims and white offenders in *Holloway* v. *R* [2011] NSWCCA 23). International case law suggests that this group difference is not essential for a crime to be classified as a hate crime (*R* v. *White* [2001] EWCA Crim 216), as people can be prejudiced against those from the same background, but such difference should immediately put investigating officers on alert to start asking the right questions. Several complexities arise for front-line decision-makers here.

First, exactly which forms of group difference, and thus which forms of prejudice, ought to be protected? In most jurisdictions, as we noted in Chapter 2, this question is settled by the legislature which, mirroring categories protected in extant human rights instruments, specifies the characteristics to be protected under the relevant statutory regime. However, in the wake of high-profile cases, where victims were targeted for characteristics not protected by statute, some governments now delegate authority to local area police (HM Government 2012) to decide which forms of prejudice will be recognised and recorded as hate crime; for example, alternative subcultures such as 'goths' are now recognised as a victim group in the Greater Manchester area (Garland and Hodkinson 2014). As VicPol's PMC Strategy contains a non-exhaustive list of victim attributes, they have similar discretion to determine which victim characteristics to protect and which forms of prejudice to record as PMC.

The cases in our review show that race, ethnicity and religion are well-recognised as protected characteristics by police, prosecutors and the courts in Victoria. However, very few cases of violence against gay or lesbian victims have come before the sentencing courts and none that involve victims with disabilities. As the evidence presented at sentencing is dependent on the ability of investigating officers to identify a potential prejudiced motive, the kinds of training discussed in Chapter 6 will play a key future role in assisting investigating officers to identify these obvious groups as potential victims of PMC and to gather the relevant evidence necessary. In contrast, the courts have held that an offence motivated by prejudice against women does fall into the definition of PMC (e.g. severely humiliating and demeaning group sexual assault was held to be motivated by gender prejudice in *R* v. *I.D. and O.N.* [2007] NSWDC 51). While this creates a precedent for VicPol to extend its PMC Strategy and recording categories into the field of gendered violence, it also presents a dilemma in terms of the 'floodgate' argument that has been used in other jurisdictions to reject the categorisation of gendered violence as hate crime (Hodge 2011; see also Maher *et al.* 2015).

Second, PMC can also be committed by members of minority groups against members of majority groups (e.g. Muslim against Christian in *R* v. *Al-Shawany* [2007] NSWDC 141) or by members of minority groups against other minority groups (e.g. African against Indian in *Hussein* v. *The Queen* [2010] VSCA 257, or Sunni Muslim against Shiite Muslim in *R* v. *El Mostafa* [2007] NSWDC 219). Indeed, in approximately two-thirds of the cases in our review, offenders came from racial or religious-minority, refugee, or culturally and linguistically diverse immigrant backgrounds. In Victoria, police are required to record and investigate such incidents as PMC and, while this is consistent with the strategy's broad commitment to respect for all forms of diversity, the over-representation of minority offenders in the courts indicates that police may be more willing or confident to identify PMC when it issues from minority groups.

In a world where suspect/victim difference is potentially limitless and law enforcement resources are limited, officers need principled guidance to identify forms of group difference that are most consistent with the objectives of their hate crime policies. This is difficult to achieve through checklists that interpret neutral statutory definitions of prejudice motivated crime to mean that any form of group difference will suffice – a point which was brought home in two cases in NSW where sentencing aggravation provisions were applied to protect 'paedophiles' as a victim group (*R* v. *Robinson* [2004] NSWSC 465; *Dunn* v. *R* [2007] NSWCCA 312). Police need to look for group difference between suspect and victim that signals not simply benign diversity (e.g. blue versus brown eyes) or vigilantism but, rather, potential inter-group animus grounded in larger social problems of intolerance; that is, unjustified inequality and disrespect towards others because of their assumed difference or vulnerability (Mason 2014). This qualified understanding of suspect/victim difference provides criteria for helping to ensure that recording categories and policy implementations are guided by the goals of social inclusion, human rights and multiculturalism.

Marker 2: statements by the suspect

Insulting or abusive statements made directly to the victim or witnesses are the most obvious alerts that a crime is motivated by prejudice. Such statements may be made before, during or after the event. They include verbal remarks, written comments (e.g. graffiti or Internet posts) or may be in the form of symbols (e.g. swastikas). Examples of statements relied upon by Australian courts that we have reviewed as evidence of a prejudice motive include: 'Fuck off, Japanese cunt, fuck off back to Japan.'; 'Bloody Indians. Fuck off.'; and 'fucking black cunts' (*R* v. *Dean-Willcocks* [2012] NSWSC 107; *Hussein* v. *The Queen; Holloway* v. *R* [2011] NSWCCA 23).

It is important, however, to recognise that such statements do not necessarily signal that the offence is *motivated* by prejudice. The difficulty for police is to distinguish between events where prejudiced statements are: i) proof of the offender's underlying prejudiced motive (e.g. the offender has no other motive); ii) indicative of partial motive in circumstances where the offender is motivated both by prejudice and also by other motives (e.g. where the offender is driven by generalised anger, intoxication and racism to attack a stranger, as in *R* v. *O'Brien* [2012] VSC 592); or iii) merely additional to the offender's motive (e.g. where the offenders made racist comments, having already resolved to rob the victim, as in *R* v. *Thomas* [2007] NSWDC 69). Under-inclusive guidelines, steered by the goal of successful prosecution, tend to record only the first category. They encourage officers to assume that so-called 'ambiguous' cases should not be recorded as a hate crime (Phillips 2009; Turpin-Petrosino 2015), such as those involving circumstances where there is a pre-existing suspect/victim relationship (as tends to be the case in disablist hate crime), or where the statements are made in circumstances involving drugs, traffic accidents or neighbours (Bell 1997, 2002). This focus on proving offender culpability fails to recognise cases of mixed motives, much less distinguish them from incidental prejudice. Over-inclusive approaches, based on victim/witness perceptions, tend to record all three categories as hate crime. Such approaches fail to distinguish between cases of partial motive or incidental prejudice because police are responding less to evidence of the offender's motive and more to public perceptions of the harm that hate speech inflicts on the dignity of the victim and targeted community (Roberts and Hastings 2001).

Police in Victoria have the opportunity to make nuanced distinctions between cases where the suspect uses prejudiced or insulting language in the commission of the crime. Events where prejudice is the only or partial motive (below we discuss how partial a prejudiced motive should be) are clearly included in

VicPol's strategy and recorded as PMC, but events of incidental prejudice are more problematic because the offender's language is not necessarily a sign of his or her motive for committing the crime (and insufficient for sentencing purposes). Nonetheless, such incidents can cause considerable victim and community disquiet. A recording system that enables such distinctions to be made is an important support mechanism for the flexible markers we propose here. For example, an alternative approach would be to adopt a three-tiered system that includes a standard recording category for events where there is initial and compelling evidence of prejudice, such as 'PMC Beyond Reasonable Doubt', as well as a category for 'Perceived' or 'Suspected' PMC. This would enable operational police to recognise incidental prejudice, boosting public confidence that such complaints are taken seriously, while simultaneously providing investigators with the time to gather evidence to determine whether offender statements are probative of actual motive. As other jurisdictions have recognised (ACPO 2010), a further category of 'PMC Incident' similarly helps meet community expectations by allowing abusive or hostile encounters to be recorded as 'incidents' even if they are unlikely to amount to a criminal offence.

Marker 3: circumstances of the offence

The circumstances of the crime may also put police on notice that a prejudiced motive might be involved. For example, if the crime occurred in a well-known gay area or involved an attack on a religious institution (e.g. where the offender set fire to a mosque in *R* v. *Hanlon* [2003] QCA 75), or if there is evidence of severe violence in circumstances where the victim and suspect are from different social or cultural groups (e.g. where a group of white men violently and repeatedly attacked a group of homeless Aboriginal people with fatal consequences, as in *R* v. *Doody* (Unreported, Supreme Court of the Northern Territory, 23 April 2010)). Other factors, such as the cultural make-up and history of the neighbourhood, the extent to which the victim is a minority in the area, the date of the incident or the involvement of organised hate groups, have all been identified as relevant circumstances in international checklists that help determine if the crime has a prejudiced flavour (Alberta Police Services 2010; CEJI 2012; US Department of Justice 2012). Here, as we discussed in Chapter 6, officers need to be trained to recognise and draw upon local community knowledge as a crucial form of intelligence (Hall 2012).

Marker 4: the absence of any other substantial motive

Many cases where the sentencing aggravation provisions were triggered share a feature that is not immediately apparent from individual sentencing decisions: the absence of cogent evidence from which another non-prejudiced motive can be inferred. This feature is made clear when the successful cases are compared to cases where the prosecution was unable to prove a prejudiced motive, despite evidence of offender/victim difference and derogatory statements. The difference in these latter cases is that there was also evidence presented of a possible alternative motive. In most cases, this evidence pointed to the existence of a pre-existing conflict between the parties that had nothing to do with prejudice (e.g. where a white offender fatally wounded an Aboriginal victim over a driving dispute but made boastful and belligerent racial taunts when the fight was over as in *R* v. *Winefield* [2011] NSWSC 337). Contrary to some prosecution-oriented checklists (Boyd *et al.* 1996), police should probe cases of otherwise unexplained inter-group violence, even if there are no accompanying prejudiced statements (e.g. as in *R* v. *Doody* above, where there was no other reason for a group of white men to viciously and repeatedly attack a group of homeless Aboriginal people). Certainly, investigating officers must search for positive evidence of a prejudiced motive and be attuned to the *absence* of a clear motive in circumstances where the offence, especially one of severe violence, is committed by a member of a dominant group against a member of a vulnerable group. As Bowling (1999) has argued, when an alternate explanation is unavailable, discriminatory practices may offer the best framework for understanding the patterns in view.

However, offenders may have multiple motives. Some guidelines, especially for specialist officers who are reviewing initial hate crime identifications, prompt officers to ask whether the incident would have taken place if the victim was from the same cultural group (e.g. see US Department of Justice 2012). The effect is to include only those cases that would not have been committed 'but for' the victim's group membership, that is, to include only events where prejudice is the sole cause of the offence. Clearly, this is too narrow a marker in the Victorian context – and arguably in many other jurisdictions – where both the PMC Strategy and the sentencing legislation specify that partial motive is sufficient. Of course, as argued above, police are justified in exercising caution against hasty characterisations. While the Australian courts have not been consistent in how partial a prejudiced motive must be, our reading of the cases suggests that, for sentencing purposes at least, police should ask a further question: did prejudice or hatred make a *substantial* contribution to the offender's motive, even if it is not the only motive? (Mason and Dyer 2013)

Still, this does not fully resolve those situations where prejudice is a less-than-substantial influence on the offender, but the victim remains unconvinced by the seemingly subtle difference between an offender whose 'real' motive is prejudice and one for whom it is just an offensive afterthought. While the adoption of an expansive 'perception' test, comparable to that used in the UK, is one way of responding to this community concern, we have argued above that this kind of mandatory approach to recording can amplify official statistics in ways that are unhelpful. The category of 'Suspected PMC' or 'Perceived PMC' proposed above might be one way of allowing police to recognise community viewpoints, without committing to a final PMC categorisation before further investigation. Here, the work of hate crime specialist teams or second-tier assessors have a critical role to play in evaluating the relevant evidence, taking responsibility for the final categorisation out of the hands of local police, who need to maintain effective and open lines of communication with community members and, ultimately, feed the reasons for their decision back to victims. In VicPol's case, this function of evaluation and communication is strengthened in some instances by the work of their PCD, which may table incidents for review as a means to 'get direct feedback from the community' about whether the way they have categorised it is 'acceptable or not or how they prefer it to be termed' (Senior Operational Officer, VicPol, interview 6 May 2016). It is too often assumed that victims and communities will be dissatisfied with a police decision to not record or charge a complaint as a hate crime. However, this remains untested. What the research (Babacan *et al.* 2010; Bowling 1999; Joudo Larsen 2010) does show is that communities resent hasty declarations by police that the incident is not a hate crime before all evidence has been carefully weighed (e.g. through public statements that it is merely 'opportunistic'). Flexible markers, supported by granulated recording categories, enable police to demonstrate to the public that they neither 'rule in' nor 'rule out' an incident until it has been thoroughly investigated. They prompt police to carefully liaise with victims and witnesses, building congruent understanding by explaining the evidentiary reasons for their decision. It is counter-intuitive to assume that minority communities will feel safer if more incidents are labelled as hate crime. There is no reason to assume that perceptions of safety cannot be fostered with convincing evidence that an incident was *not* a hate crime.

Marker 5: offenders with a history of group victimisation

If an offender has a history of choosing victims from the same group or if there is evidence that the victim was chosen because of his/her membership in a particular group, this should alert police to investigate prejudice motivation (*R* v. *Gouros* (Unreported, Victorian County Court, 14 December 2009)). As the 'violence against Indian students' issue demonstrated, a spate of targeted incidents can produce community unrest (with political and economic repercussions), even where some of those victims have been chosen not because of deliberate prejudice but, rather, because of assumptions about their vulnerability (e.g. because they are believed to carry valuable items worth stealing or to be unlikely to resist). The drivers (stereotypes of vulnerability rather than intense feelings of animosity) and goals (financial rather than symbolic) of such crime mean that they may not fit the definition of an offence that is *motivated* by prejudice (although they may well fit the discriminatory selection tests that are common to US hate crime laws). Nonetheless, police need to respond sensitively to such patterns of victimisation, if they hope to advance community confidence and enhance reporting practices. Recognition that an offender attacked only victims of Indian appearance is thus a good start. On its own, however, such a pattern of offending is insufficient evidence of a prejudiced motive. The cases in our review (*DPP* v. *Caratozzolo* [2009] VSC 305; *R* v. *Aslett* [2006] NSWCCA 49) suggest that officers should also be prompted to ask: *why* did the offender choose a victim from this group? Are there sufficient signs that this selection was because the offender wanted to harm a member of this group? Again, these further questions are crucial, if police are to gather the evidence necessary to avoid under- or over-classification and be in a position to present communities with convincing evidence about the extent to which prejudice is a driving force in their victimisation, paving the way for apposite intervention.

All in all, these markers represent a more nuanced, discretionary and victim-oriented form of guidance than traditional checklists imposed by legislation and the demands of prosecution. They use the standards of law as a threshold, prompting officers to identify not just the evidence needed to successfully sentence an offender for a hate crime but also the processes of harm experienced by community stakeholders in circumstances that may fall short of legal culpability for the offender. In this way, the 'messy' but socially relevant terrain of atypical victim groups, mixed motives and patterns of group selection are not automatically excluded because they fall into the 'too hard basket' but are actively opened up to police discretion in the operationalisation of the PMC Strategy. The markers are designed to prompt operational police to investigate further by listening to the voices of victims and communities, but without the obligation to automatically record an incident as a prejudice motivated crime based on perception alone, which can divert attention and resources away from where they are needed most. In juggling legal standards with community experience, the markers are appreciative of both, but beholden to neither. Undoubtedly, achieving this balance between under- and over-inclusive approaches sets high demands on front-line officers. In organisational terms, it requires external recognition of the seriousness of the problem and internal commitment to invest in training that equips members with the skills to apply these markers on a case-by-case basis, encouraging an enhanced appreciation of the larger ongoing social processes of victimisation (Bowling 1999) and human rights violations. In terms of police–community relations, the markers also provide a useful touchstone for communities to develop sustainable expectations of police commitment to the problem of prejudice motivated crime – a nascent blueprint for mutual understanding that reaches beyond the symbolism of hate crime policy.

Conclusion

In this chapter, we suggested that VicPol has an opportunity to lead a conversation in the development of legally valid but community-oriented markers for recognising hate crime, thereby avoiding the major pitfalls of under- and over-inclusive approaches to law enforcement: the former are linked to policing which risks giving undue weight to the goal of prosecution, and the latter to policing which risks raising community expectations to unsustainable levels. High-level organisation support for the PMC Strategy needs to be augmented by useful indicators for front-line members which would simultaneously educate and enhance policing knowledge around PMC and embed clear guidelines for recording that can support identification of PMC and prosecution, if warranted.

Drawing upon evidence of both legal interpretations and community interests, we developed a series of flexible, rather than prescriptive, markers to guide front-line decision-makers in the identification of prejudice motivated crime. While echoing alerts and operational checklists in other jurisdictions, these markers are distinctive because they prompt officers to pay attention to the harm that prejudice motivated crime inflicts on victims and communities, as well as the evidence needed to establish the criminal culpability of offenders: they are geared towards community policing ideals, not just the delivery of punishment. Towards this end, the markers actively deter police from making an immediate assessment that an incident is or is not a PMC, unless the evidence for it is compelling. Such assessments are damaging to community confidence if hate crime is ruled 'out' prematurely, whether explicitly or implicitly through the use of camouflaging descriptors (such as 'opportunistic'), and they create long-term problems for data analysis, investigation and public expectations if PMC is ruled 'in' without supporting evidence. The markers are also distinctive because they provide operational police with a triage tool for acknowledging community voices on hate crime *and* minority communities with a framework for understanding the complexities of evidence-based policing, thus helping to build a much-needed sense of fairness and trust.

The markers we have developed through this research do not purport to reflect the existence of a common language between police and minority communities but, instead, provide a balanced set of indicators for the ongoing process of negotiation needed to ultimately arrive at such common ground; in particular: *suspect/victim difference* prompts police to look for larger warning signs of social intolerance; *prejudicial statements* by the suspect encourage police to ask if those statements are probative of motive or merely incidental; *circumstances of the offence*, such as extreme violence or symbolic targets, provide a situational context which helps expose the flavour of the crime; *the absence of an alternative motive* is a signal to police that unexplained inter-group violence needs to be examined more closely for evidence of substantial prejudice; and *a history of group selection* on the part of the suspect sounds an alarm for police to ask why these victims were chosen. Supported by a recording system that prompts rather than hinders further investigation, the goal of these markers is not just to arrive at a legally defendable determination but to take victims and communities on the same evaluative path, so that the reasons for classifying an event either way are understood by all parties. Further, we suggest that demonstrating that a given incident is not a hate crime may be just as comforting to communities, if not more comforting, than demonstrating that it is. In Victoria, the consistent opportunity provided by the PCD for review and enhanced engagement between VicPol and its communities offers a clear pathway for this discussion to occur.

As operational indicators, these markers exhibit organisational commitment to the problem of hate crime that is practical as well as symbolic. Together, they steer the process for achieving a negotiated understanding of PMC that is meaningful to communities but tied to legal standards that are essential for credibility in the eyes of front-line police (and sentencing courts, where relevant). While the markers were developed with the Victorian jurisdiction in mind, they make a contribution to the field by demonstrating that it is possible to advance the implementation of hate crime policy through strategies that are responsive to both legal standards and public expectations.

Note

1 See also *Crimes (Sentencing Procedure) Act 1999* (NSW) s. 21A(2)(h); *Sentencing Act 1995* (NT) s. 6A(e). Judicial interpretations of these provisions represent the end point of a chain of criminal justice actors, starting with police, and are thus the cumulative product of law enforcement agencies and advisers.

Part IV

Conclusion

9 Conclusion

Deep diving

The concept of hate crime is constantly under construction (Perry 2016a). It is a practical way of describing a very real problem but, equally, it is a changing conceptual tool. Joanna Perry argues that we can only use a concept such as hate crime to its best effect when we recognise that the meanings that we attribute to it are grounded in the specific contexts and cultures within which it is used. This produces 'strong and often conflicting opinions' about hate crime between diverse communities and the law enforcement agencies charged to serve them. These stakeholders need an 'equal and meaningful stake in this process of construction, as opposed to it being "delivered" to them as a pre-determined set of laws, procedures or approaches' (ibid.). For example, recent research in the UK (Trickett 2015) suggests that front-line police officers (response officers, beat managers and community support officers) feel that training does not equip them adequately for identifying hate crime and gathering evidence, especially in cases involving 'messy' and less clear cut circumstances or particular forms of vulnerability, such as disability and 'mate crime'. The research concludes that officers need more exposure to the victims of hate crime, and the groups who represent these communities, to increase their knowledge and understanding. It is this process of negotiation over the recognition and meaning of 'hate crime' that we have sought to explore and advance in this book.

Another way of looking at this is that legitimacy in the policing of hate crime demands a 'dialogue' (Bottoms and Tankebe 2016). Here, we are thinking of both the legitimacy of the concepts through which we acknowledge and understand the problem of hate crime – prejudice motivated crime, bias crime, targeted crime – and the legitimacy of law enforcement responses to this problem: the two are interdependent. The legitimacy of hate crime policing policies comes to rest on an alignment between community values and the values of law enforcement agencies. Such dialogue does not only arise from cordial and respectful police–community relations. Somewhat perversely, the identification of a deficit in police legitimacy can be a powerful motivating force for community dialogue and the opportunity to produce 'momentous change' (Bottoms and Tankebe 2012). The transformation in the policing of hate crime in the United Kingdom following the Stephen Lawrence Inquiry (Macpherson 1999) is a perfect example of the way in which the public exposure of serious institutional bias and failure can jolt a law enforcement agency and government into action. But, ultimately, 'dialogue' requires such deficits in trust and confidence to be compellingly countered by effectual agency commitment to prejudice-sensitive policing policy and practice, one that embeds a human rights culture and values instrumental engagement with community voices. This demands police–community conversation capable of engendering mutual understandings of hate crime.

The territory encompassed by the concept of hate crime has expanded dramatically over the last 30 years. Purpose-built hate crime laws have proliferated in Western countries. 'Protected' characteristics have multiplied, both in terms of legal and policy recognition by criminal justice agencies and in claims for such recognition by stakeholder groups. Dedicated public and school-based educational campaigns have intensified and media attention, while waxing and waning, is certainly more informed than it once was. Some policing agencies have been at the forefront of these developments, while others have lagged behind. As more and more actors, formal and informal, have entered the debate about the significance and implications of hate crime, it may be that the ground upon which we attribute meaning to hate crime has splintered more than it has solidified. As we pointed out in Chapter 2, this is no longer a contained debate over the relative merits of different terminology, about which much has been written. Terminology has become less important as the years have revealed that the real contestation lies in the meaning that criminal justice stakeholders attribute, and are prepared to attribute, to the victimisation of people on the basis of group hostility and animosity.

This is now a debate about the capacity of these stakeholders to come together to work towards a mutual perspective on the harm and culpability intrinsic to such victimisation. Hence, it is not for us, as the authors of this book, to define prejudice motivated crime, hate crime, bias crime or targeted crime. It is up to law enforcement and communities to work together to negotiate common ground that gives meaning and relevance to hate crime at the local level.

There is no universal understanding of or meaning to terms such as 'hate crime', 'bias crime', 'targeted crime' or 'prejudice motivated crime', even as they are operationalised by law enforcement agencies. This is not just about the divergences *between* these different concepts. It is also about the fact that even *within* a given concept, there is no singular denotation. 'Hate crime' provides a label to denounce the violation of one's right to be free from hostility, animosity and intimidation based on one's membership of a particular group or association with a particular identity category. This hostility is experienced differently within and between victim groups. Representatives of criminal justice agencies also understand it differently, both on an institutional and individual basis. As Iganski (2008) has argued, the attribution of meaning to a concept such as hate crime varies from domain to domain: legal, policy, social, academic. The histories and processes that shape community experiences of hate crime may be quite distinct from the needs of law enforcement to define, identify, investigate and prosecute such behaviour. Yet, at some point, the two must meet. They must meet at the local level. While global forces inevitably shape the expectations and interests that each bring to this negotiation, this meeting of values and experiences needs to take place on the ground, so to speak, where neighbourhood and regional, not just national and international, priorities can be recognised.

It is the potential force that comes with negotiating a mutual understanding of hate crime that we highlight in our analysis of Victoria Police's approach to hate crime throughout this book. There are now excellent manuals and protocols for the policing of hate crime which provide comprehensive guides for individual police services to 'revisit and develop their own policy approaches and tactical options' for policing hate crime (ACPO 2005). Collectively, these guides (for example, ACPO 2005; CEJI 2012; College of Policing 2014; FRA 2013, 2016; FBI 2015; Greater Manchester Police 2014; ODIHR 2012, 2014; Wiltshire Police 2013) seek to provide consistent and holistic approaches to the identification, recording, investigation and prevention of hate crime, emphasising:

- leadership that displays ownership of the problem, rejects internal prejudice and establishes consistent corporate standards
- intelligence-gathering that is attuned to local communities and stakeholders
- sensitive and informed investigation
- accurate and timely data recording from police and justice agencies of reported cases, prosecutions and sentences
- ongoing monitoring mechanisms
- early, integrated, ongoing and community-engaged training
- dedicated staff through the establishment of hate crime investigators and units
- victim-directed campaigns and strategies to both encourage reporting and make the process of reporting easier and more accessible, as well as policies to provide follow-up
- the establishment and utilisation of close, problem-solving partnerships with communities and external agencies (including media).

These guides represent an ongoing commitment by governments and law enforcement agencies to address the specific needs of hate crime victims and affected communities (Perry 2016b). For example, the OSCE/ODIHR has sought to strengthen the policing response to hate crimes via the Training against Hate Crimes for Law Enforcement programme (ODIHR 2012). Our analysis has benefited greatly from these protocols, and we have drawn on them as appropriate. Given the comprehensive and methodical guidance they now offer collectively, however, we have not sought to replicate this approach. Instead, our goal has been to complement the extant manuals and protocols by offering context-specific insights and lessons from one research partnership in a rapidly evolving policing environment. There has been a recognised 'lack of synergy between academics and policy makers' (Perry *et al.* 2016) that we have attempted to address through our engagement with VicPol. We believe that many of the challenges faced within our case study are shared by other policing agencies, to

greater and lesser degrees, and that their responses to these hurdles, and our analysis in turn, are transferable across policing contexts. But, as we have pointed
out above, this knowledge transfer requires interpretation and adaptation to local
variables, particularly the history of police relations with marginalised and vulnerable communities, the nature and pace of cultural change within policing
agencies, and the particular make-up and experiences of targeted communities.

The challenges of policing hate crime, particularly in the Australian state of
Victoria, that we have identified in this book circulate around organisational,
operational and relational matters. Organisational matters refer to the internal
aspects of cultural change, leadership, structure and the deployment of resources.
Operational factors refer to practical policing matters, such as recording, identifying and investigating hate crime, as well as training. By relational matters, we
mean the relationship between the police and targeted communities, especially
the history of distrust that exists with some vulnerable and marginalised communities. In the following sections, we use this tripartite framework to bring
together the major challenges for policing hate crime that we have identified
throughout this book and propose some modest and context-specific strategies
for overcoming these hurdles. The 'exit' interviews we conducted with senior
VicPol personnel some years after the launch of their PMC Strategy prove particularly illuminating now, as seasoned police reflect on the impediments and
achievements of implementing the strategy. At this point in the book, it should
come as no surprise that we see the third aspect of policing – police–community
relations – as formative of all others when it comes to hate crime.

Organisational issues

Police culture and change

Hate crime has become core business for law enforcement agencies. Its policing
calls for distinct approaches, grounded in an appreciation of both the global
environment of intensifying social division and local patterns of group-based
animosity. Historically, police have responded to hate crimes as detached incidents, without recognising the impact of these broader social contexts on the
experiences of communities that are most vulnerable to targeted violence. For
many policing organisations, re-orientation of this kind requires significant cultural change or, in some cases, reaffirmation and advancement of changes that
have already started to take place. Yet, policing organisations and aspects of
police culture are often resistant to the values that underpin the hate crime
agenda.

Naming the problem, through dedicated policies and protocols, for instance,
is an essential first step to achieving cultural change that moves away from past
practice, especially where that practice tended to express entrenched prejudice
by responding to some minority communities as if they were primarily in need
of control rather than protection. This requires police to deploy terminology and
language that explicitly, not just indirectly, names and denounces hate crime.

VicPol clearly recognises the value of such nomenclature in strengthening community expectations of police: 'the community has a language and can have an expectation that police will respond. I think that's great' (Commander, PCD, VicPol, interview 6 May 2016).

The language used by law enforcement agencies is complicit in informing and shaping public opinion, expressing ideology, eliciting empathy, and framing police and other criminal justice responses. It has a role to play in building trust and confidence between police and vulnerable communities. As our focus group research in Chapter 5 reveals, however, police cannot afford to be complacent about the terminology and concepts they deploy. 'Hate crime' was the favoured term amongst stakeholder groups in Victoria, with 'prejudice motivated crime' receiving a far from enthusiastic embrace. It may be that minority communities are less enamoured of convoluted phrases such as 'prejudice motivated crime' when they have no pre-existing currency or political purchase with that community or with the public at large. A term that does not resonate with vulnerable communities as one that captures their experience is unlikely to be a term that members of those communities will confidently call on to name and define a complaint to police.

Law enforcement agencies would do well to liaise with targeted communities about the relative merits of adopting different terms *before* they integrate those terms into corporate values, strategies, protocols and the procedures, such as recording, that guide routine policing. Furthermore, while umbrella terms such as 'hate crime' have significant strategic value and practical impact, police services need to acknowledge that some communities may more readily understand more specific terms such as anti-Semitism or homophobia. If vulnerable and marginalised communities are to feel they have an active voice in the policing of hate crime, mutual agreement on the language through which that victimisation is labelled and identified is infinitely preferable to the top-down imposition of linguistic frameworks.

At the end of the day, however, our research shows that it matters not so much *what* the problem is called but, rather, that the bigotry and animosity that drives the problem *is* called – called out and denounced at the highest level of law enforcement. It is the way in which meaning is attributed to the relevant concepts that strikes a chord of importance with both targeted communities and law enforcement. Moreover, we need to remember that these meanings are not static. As VicPol Command puts it, 'a lot has happened in five years to change the way our whole – and I'm not just talking organisation, I'm talking about our whole community – views some really complex issues' (Commander, PCD, VicPol, interview 6 May 2016). For example, although the PMC Strategy has been a key mechanism through which VicPol have sought to gain a better understanding of hate crime, they recognise that this does not mean that 'the language we used three years ago is actually still right now' (Commander, PCD, VicPol, interview 6 May 2016). Like terminology, the meanings that law enforcement attribute to 'hate crime' need to be refreshed on a regular basis.

Much has already been written about the damaging nature of policies and protocols that merely pay lip service to cultural change (Giannasi 2015; Hall 2013; Jenness and Grattet 2005). Without rehearsing those critiques again, it is important to emphasise that cultural change at the top of the command chain needs to be supported by consistent internal and external messaging towards institutional values that demonstrate a genuine commitment to the interests of vulnerable and marginalised communities. There are ongoing debates about whether hate crime itself is helpfully understood as a violation of human rights (Brudholm 2015). Putting these to one side, a human rights framework is undoubtedly beneficial in the context of law enforcement. Responding to victimisation demands that police approach members of targeted communities free from discrimination and prejudice. This right to impartial and respectful policing is consistent with the values of fairness and dignity that are integral to procedural justice and essential in overcoming the mistrust with which many minority communities continue to view police (despite the important inroads that some law enforcement agencies have already made). While the incorporation of human rights into policing policy does not automatically embed these values into everyday policing, it does go a long way towards helping front-line members to 'get' the 'overall principles of respect and treating people with dignity' (Senior Operational Officer, VicPol, interview 6 May 2016). Operational officers will not place value on best practice in the policing of hate crime if their commanders, and the force they represent, do not. The kind of change that is necessary for individual officers to treat hate crime seriously and sensitively calls for the integration of human rights principles at the level of the institution itself.

Strategy: a conduit

The VicPol experience demonstrates that police do not need to wait for the legislature to introduce hate crime laws to develop a policing strategy and approach (and certainly VicPol are not the only policing agency to be proactive in this way). Unfortunately, it is the often the case, as it was in Victoria, that public and media outcry over high-profile cases of targeted violence provide the impetus for police to take the initiative in this domain. Nonetheless, to paraphrase the aims of VicPol's strategy, a dedicated policy provides a 'flagship', a 'tool' and a 'springboard' (Commander, PCD, VicPol, interview 6 May 2016) for enhancing police understanding of hate crime and, ultimately, reducing its incidence. It is thus a benchmark against which to measure outcomes. The VicPol experience also demonstrates that the introduction of a dedicated hate crime strategy plays a formative role in achieving the kind of internal cultural change we refer to above and implementing the kind of operational change we discuss below. It creates a 'direct conduit' between central command and operational police, a structure to follow for communication and understanding within the institution (Senior Operational Officer, VicPol, interview 6 May 2016). It is at this central or corporate level that VicPol sees its own strategy as having had its greatest impact.

While the absence of a legal imperative can make it more onerous for police to define hate crime, it also offers an opportunity for police to take the experience of victim and community harm, not just the legal liability of the offender, as a defining feature of hate crime. Instead of providing an exhaustive definition for identifying the kinds of behaviour that amount to hate crime, the criminal law in this context need only provide an indicative framework that enables police to pay closer attention to the experiences and interests of targeted communities in formulating the meaning of hate crime. This assists law enforcement organisations to reconceptualise their traditional role as gatekeepers of the criminal justice system, becoming more active agents in the delivery of social change and the protection of human rights.

In addition to being a conduit between management and operational officers, a dedicated strategy should also operate as a conduit to the community. It can help enact a qualitative shift in engagement between police, victims and communities. For example, it should prompt front-line officers to be more 'mindful in the very first instance' that an incident may be a hate crime and should be recorded as such, so that 'actually listening to a person' becomes part of 'how they view their interaction with the diverse community' (Commander, PCD, VicPol, interview 6 May 2016). In other words, a strategy provides a reason for officers 'to recognise that this is prejudice motivated … not just an opportunistic assault' (ibid.).

While much attention has been placed on the importance of confidence amongst victim communities in the policing of hate crime, it is worth remembering that individual police officers also need to feel confident, and comfortable, in naming and identifying hate crime. A strategy encourages police to have 'the confidence … to understand what the evidence looks like, in order to be able to say this is prejudice motivated crime', especially in interactions with victims who may not always explicitly describe it in these terms:

> So, where a victim of a prejudice motivated crime may be quite confident that that's what it is for them, they may not be articulate in describing what that looks like. And where it's been done well, is the member being cognisant that that's what it could be and having that discussion with that person, rather than looking at all the other possibilities and then coming to a PMC if they're reminded of it?
>
> (Commander, PCD, VicPol, interview 6 May 2016)

In effect, a dedicated strategy, supported by cultural change and commitment from leadership, provides a platform from which police can be assisted to see hate crime as the first port of call, if the circumstances warrant it, not the last.

Embedding hate crime: a victim-centred orientation

The interviews we conducted with VicPol personnel five years after the introduction of the PMC Strategy brought home the importance of positioning hate crime policy within wider victim-centred portfolios in the organisation. Hate crime strategies have a natural home within victim commands, which can assist in developing a 'whole of organisation' response to the problem. In the case of VicPol, without this larger cultural change, it is unlikely that the problem of prejudice motivated crime, and the aims of the PMC Strategy, would have gained the same degree of internal traction. And within this environment, VicPol's PMC Strategy has had success in raising awareness at all levels of the agency.

A core ingredient of this success has been resisting a siloed approach to the policing of hate crime. Concerns about the narrow framing of police relations with minority communities have been raised by other researchers who suggest, for example, that hate crime is best positioned within the larger spectrum of vulnerability and diversity (Bartkowiak-Theron and Asquith 2015). For their part, VicPol has chosen to embed responsibility for hate crime within the Priority Communities Command, which oversees the work that police do with diverse communities as a whole. This underscores the logical link between best-practice responses to hate crime and the larger imperative to resist racial profiling, prejudice and other discriminatory forms of policing. This victim-centred domain helps make the application of human rights obligations a core component in the delivery of justice to victims as well as offenders:

> We used to be very focused on the offender, getting the offender, you know, taking the report from the victim, getting the offender and that was our focus. Cool, locked up, done, you know. Justice served. And the victim is sitting there not knowing the outcome, not really understanding the process that's just occurred. So I think now the members are much more aware and there are certain obligations on them now in terms of how they engage with the victim … that has been a huge shift for the organisation and that you can definitely see on the front line.
>
> (Senior Operational Officer, VicPol, interview 6 May 2016)

At the same time, however, an embedded approach does run the risk that the specific hate crime message will be overshadowed by wider institutional performance indicators, operational imperatives or community tensions, especially where there is no dedicated hate crime unit to ensure compliance. For example, research suggests that in-service hate crime training for police can get lost within training modules that address larger issues of diversity and equality (Trickett and Hamilton 2015). We return to this point below.

Resourcing

Victoria Police has invested significant financial and human resources into its Priority Communities Command (The Age 2014). Adequate resourcing not only ensures that the work gets done, but it also demonstrates corporate commitment to the issue. The establishment of training programmes, specialised units, tailored victim-referral services, and so on, all cost money and this outlay is, without a doubt, essential to the success of any hate crime initiative.

Operational matters

Existing research (FRA 2013; Giannasi 2015b; Grattet and Jenness 2005; Hall 2013) has convincingly demonstrated that it is the actual implementation of hate crime policy and law into everyday policing that has proven most elusive, with questions arising around: how front-line police gain their knowledge of hate crime; how they translate legal requirements for prosecution or sentencing into routine practices; how they accurately record hate crime; and how resistance to implementing yet another policy can be overcome amongst busy and overworked officers. This implementation gap is well-evidenced in the case of VicPol which, despite the organisational advances it has made since launching the PMC Strategy, readily recognises that 'inaction by members' is an 'ongoing problem' about which vulnerable communities are rightly concerned (Commander, PCD, interview, 6 May 2016). This inaction occurs on several fronts and stems from several sources.

Reporting and recording

Under-reporting is a challenge both for law enforcement agencies that have recently begun to recognise hate crime and for those that have a long history of initiatives in this area. In turn, accurate recording of victim reports is key to effective, inclusive policing that meets the objectives of hate crime policy and law. Careful classification and recording by police, along with sympathetic treatment of victims, also help build trust by signalling to impacted communities that police are operating in a non-discriminatory manner and listening to their complaints.

Robust data that speaks to the type of incidents that are occurring, where they are occurring, who is committing them, who is being targeted, and the surrounding social context within which they occur is essential, not just to gain an accurate picture of the problem but also to form an evidence base from which to strategically direct resources and preventative interventions where they are most needed. For its part, and as we discussed in Chapter 7, this is an area where VicPol has struggled to achieve real progress. Reporting rates have not increased since the implementation of the strategy and, indeed, have declined overall, with the exception of sexual-orientation and gender-identity hate crimes. While a number of reasons for this decline are canvassed in Chapter 7, VicPol acknowledges that under-reporting, entwined with limited understanding at the front line, is one of the greatest operational difficulties it faces. This is a particular concern given that increased reporting is a central goal of the PMC Strategy. Nonetheless, as we hope we have demonstrated in this book, recording is not the only benchmark of success when it comes to prejudice-sensitive policing.

Low reporting and recording rates are likely to stem from both community reticence to report – fuelled by a trust deficit and a lack of certainty over the meaning of terms such as 'prejudice motivated crime' – and a lack of proficiency, confidence and commitment amongst police to identify and record complaints as motivated by a particular form of prejudice. This combination of community and police ambiguity can coalesce into a larger quagmire of confusion that makes it all too hard for both parties to formally recognise and classify an incident as a prejudice motivated crime.

Hate crime policy needs to be fed from within. While embedding such policy within larger victim-oriented commands helps spread and normalise its message, as we have pointed out above, it also risks diluting its potency as a tool for operational change amongst the larger demands of policing multicultural and diverse communities. Wherever they are located in an organisational structure, hate policies need to be continually and explicitly nurtured at the operational level. This normally requires a dedicated unit – ideally within a larger community-oriented command – to oversee compliance with the implementation of policy objectives, recording criteria, operating procedures, and so on. Despite all of the lessons learnt since law enforcement agencies first started explicitly responding to the problem of hate crime, low reporting rates are a clear indicator of the resilient nature of the implementation gap between policy and practice. In our view, it is also a clear indicator of the need to promote and invest in police–community conversation geared towards minimising ambivalence and maximising joint accord.

Identification

A second operational challenge in the policing of hate crime, and one which is intimately connected to recording practices, lies in identifying the kinds of criminal conduct that amount to a prejudice motivated crime. This comes down to the extent to which individual officers understand what hate crime actually *is*; this, in turn, has a powerful impact on their capability to record it accurately and collect supporting evidence. VicPol also identify this as one of their greatest challenges: 'I'd say the biggest challenge would still be the front-line members.... If you surveyed them or asked them, they would still struggle to understand' (Senior Operational Officer, VicPol, interview 6 May 2016).

Our research shows that individual VicPol officers continue to be confused about what constitutes prejudice motivated crime and thus do not record and investigate as they should:

> We still do have challenges ... with people misinterpreting what would be prejudice motivated crime or not and sometimes ... knowing what the specific categories are and what they mean can cause confusion for members, so that's still an ongoing piece of work.
>
> (Senior Operational Officer, VicPol, interview 6 May 2016)

While VicPol see this as less of a problem for officers who have recently been through hate crime training at the academy (a point we qualify below), it clearly applies to long-term members:

> All the members going through the academy, if you surveyed them, they would probably have a really good understanding. If you surveyed some of my members that have worked the van for the last 30 years and the last time they went to the academy was probably to do their firearms qualification or whatever it might be, I think it would be a different story.
>
> (Senior Operational Officer, VicPol, interview 6 May 2016)

In a very practical sense, even with the best training, this kind of understanding only comes from familiarity and on-the-job practice. For busy beat officers, hate crime has to be one of the first scenarios that come to mind when responding to vulnerable and marginalised communities:

> There are so many balls for operational officers to juggle, that in a constantly changing diverse community, it has to be one of the very first responses that you think of in being able to triage what's in and what's out.
>
> (Commander, PCD, VicPol, interview 6 May 2016)

To achieve this, operational officers, who often feel 'overwhelmed' by the sheer number of organisational policies and protocols, need to be provided with digestible markers and visible prompts that assist them to keep hate crime at the forefront of their minds, 'as opposed to ... thinking that front-line members will actually read a strategy and have that at the forefront of their mind' (Senior Operational Officer, VicPol, interview 6 May 2016).

The identification of hate crime thus remains a principal challenge for VicPol and, indeed, for all police forces who take an active approach to the problem. Effective identification requires agencies such as VicPol to make prejudice motivated crime 'more prominent and visible' for front-line officers to readily understand what hate crime *looks* like (Senior Operational Officer, VicPol, interview 6 May 2016). In addition, as has been recognised in other literature, specialised, second-tier or review units are essential to confirm or correct identification and support investigation.

While punchy checklists are convenient mechanisms for time-poor officers, they also tend to encourage police to quickly rule out a diversity of 'messy' or ambiguous circumstances that may not immediately fit the mould. Although the evidential signs of hate crime may vary somewhat between locales, depending on local histories and current tensions, our research suggests that operational police need legally grounded but community-oriented markers that offer practical guidance for identifying and investigating hate crime: guidance that is flexible, rather than prescriptive, in the sense that it has been developed with active input from community stakeholders. The markers we proposed for VicPol in Chapter 8 represent a more nuanced, discretionary and victim-oriented form of guidance than traditional checklists, dominated by legislation and the demands of prosecution. They use the standards of law as a threshold, prompting officers to identify not just the evidence needed to successfully sentence an offender for a hate crime but also the processes of harm experienced by community stakeholders in circumstances that may fall short of legal requirements. Checklists are an important tool in shaping discretion and assisting front-line police to identify prejudice motivated incidents, but checklists that are developed solely by police without input from stakeholder communities can be overly narrow and largely geared towards facts that provide the evidence for successful prosecution or sentencing. While this may constitute the preferred meaning of hate crime from a law enforcement perspective, it does little to accommodate the more process-oriented experiences of victims and their communities.

Arriving at an understanding of hate crime that is genuinely agreed upon by both police and vulnerable communities may be a long way off for many law enforcement agencies. However, the development of community-cognisant systems of identification provides a means of working towards greater congruence – between the need for consistency and certainty in law enforcement and the expectations of communities that their voices and experiences are instrumental in identifying hate crime.

Training

It is apparent from Chapter 6 that training needs to overcome a plethora of well-recognised barriers to the implementation of hate crime policies amongst rank and file officers, including: indifference to following protocols because it is simply one more thing that busy officers need to do; resistance due to bias, both unconscious and conscious, amongst officers; and a lack of understanding about the meaning of concepts such as prejudice motivated crime that, in turn, diminishes the ability of front-line officers to accurately recognise such crime and respond consistently and effectively. If police are to comprehend the nature of hate crime, its significance to minority communities and its centrality to larger goals of crime prevention and community safety, training needs to reinforce the message that hate crime is 'real' crime, not simply a soft, social-welfare or low-priority policing activity.

Our research with recruits in Victoria shows that prejudice motivated crime has multiple meanings for operational officers and that these meanings conflict with their own prejudices and shift according to the quality of the training and the extent to which it is embedded in larger institutional standards and rules of professional conduct. This ambiguity has a direct impact on the ability of officers to quickly and effectively identify and record hate crime. While much has been made of the lack of trust amongst minority communities towards police, our survey research suggests that this lack of trust is likely to be reciprocated by new officers when they meet members of minority groups for the first time. This compounded 'trust deficit' is a major hurdle for the implementation of hate crime training, making it unsurprising that our survey results also reveal that training – especially if too piecemeal and too complex – does not always improve officers' capacity or preparedness to recognise and classify hate crime. On the one hand, VicPol sees the progress that has been made in developing the knowledge of its front-line officers around hate crime as one of its training successes. Yet, on the other hand, it recognises that there is still a long way to go in skilling officers with a genuine and ongoing understanding of the problem and its interaction with larger issues of policing diverse communities: 'Our frontline members [have] a knowledge of it, and there's peaks and troughs to the depth of that knowledge. And that's where I see our challenge.... There's a lot of work that's yet to be done' (Commander, PCD, VicPol, interview 6 May 2016).

Going forward, hate crime training needs to be finely calibrated, stimulating, fleshed out through personal experience, contextualised within larger victim-centred approaches; it must speak to officers' intelligence, align with standards of professional conduct, and be overt about the ways in which it is integrated into larger performance indicators, such as human rights principles and the enhancement of institutional legitimacy. Training and guidelines benefit from narrative (which can be written and visual) and human experiences to communicate the personalised, multi-dimensional and sometimes contradictory face of hate crime: training and resources should equip officers with the skills, confidence and ethics to ask the right questions of victims and witnesses. This needs to be delivered as a part of formal training programmes but also reinforced through regular capacity-building processes, such as internal communication and media systems. As we have already suggested, training needs be extended beyond new recruits to 'hard to engage' members (Senior Operational Officer, VicPol, interview 6 May 2016). Nonetheless, adopting the very best practice in training will not be sufficient to achieve significant cultural and operational advances where there is dissonance between the world-view of police officers and the key underpinnings or organisational view of hate crime. An essential first step in achieving greater congruence between community, institutional and individual officer perspectives on hate crime requires clear leadership on the question of *why* such training is being undertaken and how its desired outcomes contribute to organisational values and service delivery to targeted communities. Only when these elements are in place can the question of *how* training is to be done be comprehensively addressed.

Relational matters

Developing community trust: addressing internal prejudice

Suspicion and a lack of trust amongst vulnerable and marginalised communities towards police emerged as key findings from our research. The tension that we see in the Australian state of Victoria between a police force with an avowed commitment to community policing and human rights, yet a history of prejudice, profiling and excessive use of force in their dealings with minority communities, is a tension that is replicated in many policing agencies around the world. As we noted earlier, the introduction of a hate crime strategy or policy is an opportunity for police to take a leading role in social change and address the trust deficit that exists with these communities. Yet, Australian and international research shows that minority and non-minority groups hold the perception that police both unfairly target some minorities, such as ethnic minorities, as potential suspects and neglect or trivialise the victimisation of these same communities. As we pointed out in Chapters 3 and 4, this undermines the perceived credibility and legitimacy of the police in the eyes of these communities, producing a contradiction between police as champions of social justice or human rights and police as the source of discriminatory treatment and brutality. The continued tendency of police to see engagement with minority communities as an opportunity to gather intelligence rather than genuinely engage with those communities also underscores the resilience of police attitudes that are prone to seeing some marginalised communities through a criminalising lens.

Encouraging reporting and co-operation from minority communities is not just a matter of having the best concepts, recording systems and investigation protocols. If prejudice-sensitive policing is to be 'the best', it must incorporate generic policing measures that prioritise procedural justice. Such measures – that require police to treat all citizens with impartiality, respect and dignity – align with human rights principles that are now incorporated into the governing structures for many police forces, including VicPol: 'If everyone treats everyone with respect and dignity and has a victim-centric approach … you should have a positive outcome for the victim when they're dealing with Police and … justice at the end of the day' (Senior Operational Officer, VicPol, interview, 6 May 2016). The integration of these values into training and everyday policing is essential to ameliorate the historical alienation that some victim communities feel towards law enforcement agencies and thereby encourage hate crime reporting. When police do initiate and commit to prejudice-sensitive policing this can, in turn, boost confidence more broadly within marginalised communities.

Perception versus evidence

Hate crime is about victimisation as well as offending, about victims and not just offenders. It requires policing initiatives that are capable of integrating the perceptions and experiences of victim communities, not just those that are driven by legalistic definitions of offender culpability or the imperatives of prosecution. We have, however, expressed some reservations in this book about policing protocols and guidelines that seek to do this by handing all decision-making to the victim, or other witnesses, for deciding whether an event is to be recorded as a hate crime or not, for example through a 'perception' test. The appropriateness of using such an expansive test hinges, in part, on the legislative environment within which police are operating and may, for instance, be more suitable where police are also working with a relatively wide legal definition of hate crime itself. In environments such as the Australian state of Victoria, where the legal definition of hate crime under sentencing law is flexible in only some regards (such as protected characteristics) but restricted to offences where there is compelling evidence of the offender's prejudicial *motive*, it must be recognised that there is the potential for significant divergence to emerge between recorded hate crime and offences which can actually be proceeded against as hate crime (whether through prosecution or sentencing). In effect, this comes down to a tension between the need for police to pay attention both to community perceptions and experiences of hate crime and to evidence of the perpetrator's reasons and motives for committing that offence.

While adopting a broad test for recording practices certainly helps ease community feelings of mistrust in police decision-making processes, it risks creating a disconnect between official statistics and legal standards, potentially undermining the commitment of front-line officers to follow through and investigate such incidents as hate crime. While we are fully cognisant of the institutional failures that have necessitated these kinds of operational shifts, so profoundly documented in inquiries such as the Macpherson Report (1999) in the UK, our concern is that this approach risks substituting genuine community–police dialogue about where the hate crime threshold should lie with the relocation of responsibility for identifying hate crime to members of the public alone. One way around this may be for recording systems to distinguish between hate crime and hate incidents. While some law enforcement agencies already do this, including VicPol, it is normally done to distinguish between events that meet the threshold of criminal behaviour (i.e. a breach of the criminal law) and events that do not meet this threshold but nonetheless are distressing to victims (i.e. verbal insults). The category of hate incidents could also encompass situations where victims or witnesses perceive the presence of prejudicial hostility, but there is no evidence to support this. This may enable hate crime to be more effectively understood as an ongoing social process that implicates lived experiences of patterns of prejudice and the harmful cumulative effects of everyday 'low-level' incidents.

Despite decades of solidification in some regions, the ongoing ambiguity of the concept of hate crime, including the gap between what might legally count as a hate crime and what might be experienced as a hate crime by the victim or community, challenges the effective implementation of hate crime policy and law. At the same time, however, it is these challenges that make it imperative for police to engage in dialogue that builds mutual understanding with vulnerable or marginalised communities. This process of negotiation provides the platform upon which the voices of communities become instrumental in defining and demarcating the meaning of hate crime and thereby are accorded respect in police decision-making. It is through this negotiation that trust is built.

The diversity of victimisation

In this book, we have entwined current law enforcement responses with key debates on the meaning of hate crime. One of the most contested issues to have emerged in the hate crime field is the question of which characteristics are to be recognised by law enforcement and by the criminal justice system more broadly. Many police forces see themselves as restricted by legal definitions of hate crime and the groups that are specifically protected under hate crime statutes and thus they record only these categories. Yet, others have responded to community pressure by extending classification systems to characteristics not formally recognised in law. Still others, who operate in a legislative environment that does not pre-determine protected characteristics, such as VicPol, have the discretion to decide which forms of group identity and difference to acknowledge in their recording processes and investigation practices. While there is no necessary imperative for police recording categories to be restricted by statutory limits – and demonstrating preparedness to classify hostility towards less traditional forms of difference is a key way in which police can build trust with alternative communities – there is increasing concern about the disparity that this opens up between the incidents that are recorded as hate crime and those that can actually be prosecuted or sentenced as hate crime. Though there are many guiding principles police can use to decide which forms of prejudice and hostility should be recorded as hate crime (Chakaraborti and Garland 2012), pre-existing human rights instruments and anti-discrimination measures certainly provide a beginning point and framework (Mason 2014; Perry 2016b; Schweppe 2012) for police to have these conversations with communities that feel vulnerable to targeted crime.

Diving deep into the meaning of hate crime

In the Introduction to this book, we identified 'understanding' as a fundamental challenge facing VicPol in the policing of hate crime: understanding the meaning of prejudice motivated crime and understanding how to respond. This requires police to make a qualitative shift in the value they place on engagement with targeted communities. Quite simply, telling officers '"you must tick this box" … doesn't engage them' (Senior Operational Officer, VicPol, interview 6 May 2016). Such engagement only comes if the workforce understands the 'principles behind' it, that is, if they 'believe and understand why' they must listen to victims and communities (Senior Operational Officer, VicPol, interview 6 May 2016). To reinforce a point made in Chapter 6, police will not develop an 'authentic' understanding of what hate crime means until they have

> lifted the arrogance and understand what absolute value community can have in us testing our tools, our strategies, our policies, our education programs, whatever it is, in a much more beneficial way.
> (Commander, PCD, VicPol, interview 6 May 2016)

This more 'authentic' approach to community engagement – one that feeds off multiple pathways and does not assume that police always know best – is vital at the developmental stage before one-sided definitions and procedures become entrenched. It can help minimise the gap between community and organisational expectations, adding value to both. It also proffers an unintended benefit or side effect: genuine efforts to respond effectively to hate crime can strengthen not just the policing of hate crime itself but also the underlying relations between police and diverse communities more generally. While hate crime policies and procedures are crucial tools for this engagement, they are ever only a vehicle through which to achieve a 'greater depth of trust and approachability – to community and from community'. In other words, it is the 'underlying relationship' between police and the communities they serve that is key to generating confidence in the organisation and its individual members (Commander, PCD, VicPol, interview 6 May 2016).

Law enforcement agencies can effect cultural change at the organisation level, and they can enact best practice at the operational level 'but it doesn't really translate unless there is a really deep dive into community' (Commander, PCD, VicPol, interview 6 May 2016). It is this 'deep dive' into the world-view of diverse communities that enables a police force to move beyond the rhetoric of hate crime policy and procedure, by negotiating over where the threshold should be set for identifying the type of behaviour, the kind of prejudice and the depth of animosity that amounts to a hate crime. Mismatches in perspective and experience can undermine confidence, both from communities towards police and amongst police to name and identify hate crime. An effective dialogue requires authentic conversation, a process of law enforcement officers speaking *with*, not *at*, victims and vulnerable communities:

> It's a two way thing: it's building the confidence of community to understand that we will act, and it's also about reinforcing, to our members, the importance of acting.
>
> (Commander, PCD, VicPol, interview 6 May 2016)

Diving deep into affected communities to develop a mutuality of understanding lies at the heart of legitimate policing of hate crime.

References

Aaronson, T. (2013) *The Terror Factory: Inside the FBI's Manufactured War on Terrorism*. New York: Ig Publishing.

ABC Television (2009) 'Police deny Indian attacks racist', ABC News, 9 June 2009. Retrieved from www.abc.net.au/news/stories/2009/06/09/2592953.htm.

ABC News (2014) 'Number of Indian students applying to Australian universities more than doubles', ABC News, 28 July 2016. Retrieved from www.abc.net.au/news/2014-02-12/an-indian-students-rising-hold/5242504.

The Age (2014) 'Victoria Police's Priority Communities Division: real change or just more talk?', April 29, 2014. Retrieved from: www.theage.com.au/victoria/victoria-polices-priority-communities-division-real-change-or-just-more-talk-20140429-37fq2.html.

Alberta Police Services (2010) 'Guidelines for the investigation of hate/bias crime and incidents', Alberta: Alberta Police Services.

Alfieri, A. V. (2013) '"He is the darkey with the glasses on": race trials revisited' *North Carolina Law Review*, **91**, pp. 1497–1512.

Allen, M. (2014) 'Police-reported hate crime in Canada, 2012', Canadian Centre for Justice Statistics, Juristat. Retrieved from www.statcan.gc.ca/pub/85-002-x/2014001/article/14028-eng.pdf.

Alpert, G. P. , Dunham, R. G. and Smith, M. R. (2007) 'Investigating racial profiling by the Miami-Dade Police Department: a multimethod approach' *Criminology and Public Policy*, **6**(1), pp. 25–55.

Anderson, J. F., Dyson, L. and Brooks Jr., W. (2002) 'Preventing hate crime and profiling hate crime offenders' *The Western Journal of Black Studies*, **26**(3), pp. 140–148.

Angelari, M. (1994) 'Hate crime statutes: a promising tool for fighting violence against women' *American University Journal of Gender and Law*, **1994**(2), pp. 63–105.

Ashworth, A. (2013) 'Hate crime', *Criminal Law Review*, **9**, pp. 709–710.

Ashworth, A. (2014) 'Moving against hate crime' *Criminal Law Review*, **7**, pp. 475–476.

Asquith, N. (2004) 'In terrorem: with their tanks and their bombs, and their bombs and their guns, in your head' *Journal of Sociology*, **40**(4), pp. 400–416.

Asquith, N. L. (2015) 'A governance of denial: hate crime in New Zealand and Australia' in Hall, N., Corb, A., Giannasi, P. and Grieve, J. (eds) *Routledge International Handbook on Hate Crime*. London: Routledge, pp. 174–189.

Association of Chief Police Officers (ACPO) UK (2000) 'Guide to identifying and combating hate crime', London: Home Office Police Standards Unit.

Association of Chief Police Officers (ACPO) UK (2005) 'Hate crime: delivering a quality service – good practice and tactical guidance', London: Home Office Police Standards Unit.

Australian Department of Education and Training (2015) 'The value of international education to Australia' Canberra: ACT.

Australian Human Rights Commission (2012) 'National anti-racism strategy'. Retrieved from:www.humanrights.gov.au/sites/default/files/National%20Anti-Racism%20Strategy.pdf.

Baas, M. (2015) 'The question of racism: how to understand the violent attacks on Indian students in Australia?' *Cosmopolitan Civil Societies: An Interdisciplinary Journal*, 7(3), pp. 37–60.

Babacan, H., Pyke, J., Bhathal, A., Gurjeet, G., Grossman, M., and Bertone, S. (2010) 'The community safety of international students in Melbourne: a scoping study', Institute for Community, Ethnicity and Policy. Melbourne: Victoria University.

Bakalis, C. (2015) 'Legislating against hatred: the Law Commission's report on hate crime' *Criminal Law Review*, 3, pp. 192–207.

Balboni, J. M. and McDevitt, J. (2001) 'Hate crime reporting: understanding police officer perceptions, departmental protocol, and the role of the victim: is there such a thing as a "love" crime?' *Justice Research and Policy*, 3(1), pp. 1–27.

Barnes, A. and Ephross P. H. (1994) 'The impact of hate violence on victims: emotional and behavioral responses to attacks' *Social Work*, 39(3), pp. 247–251.

Bartkowiak-Theron, I. and Corbo Crehan, A. (2010) 'A new movement in community policing? From community policing to vulnerable people policing' in Putt, J. (ed.), *Community Policing in Australia*, AIC Reports Research and Policy Series 111, Canberra: Australian Institute of Criminology, pp. 16–23.

Bartkowiak-Theron, I. and Asquith, N. (2015) 'Policing diversity and vulnerability in the post-Macpherson era: unintended consequences and missed opportunities' *Policing: A Journal of Policy and Practice*, 9(1), pp. 89–100.

Bartosiewicz, P. (2012), 'Deploying informants, the FBI stings Muslims', *The Nation*, 14 July 2012. Retrieved from www.thenation.com/article/168380/deploying-informants-fbi-stings-muslims.

Bayley, D. and Shearing, C. (2001) 'The new structure of policing: description, conceptualization, and research agenda'. Washington, DC: US Department of Justice, Office of Justice Programs, National Institute of Justice.

Becker, A. B. (2014) 'Employment discrimination, local school boards, and LGBT civil rights: reviewing 25 years of public opinion data' *International Journal of Public Opinion Research*, edu003.

Beetham, D. (1991) *The Legitimation of Power*. London: Macmillan.

Bell, J. (1997) 'Policing hatred: police bias units and the construction of hate crime' *Michigan Journal of Race and Law*, 2, pp. 421–460.

Bell, J. (2002) 'Deciding when hate is a crime: the first amendment, police detectives, and the identification of hate crime' *Rutgers Race and Law Review*, 4, pp. 33–76.

Bell, J. (2004) *Policing Hatred: Law Enforcement, Civil Rights, and Hate Crime*. New York: NYU Press.

Bensinger, G. J. (1992) 'Hate crimes: a new/old problem' *International Journal of Comparative and Applied Criminal Justice*, 16(1), pp. 115–124.

Berk, R. A. (1990) 'Thinking about hate-motivated crimes' *Journal of Interpersonal Violence*, 5(3), pp. 334–349.

Beyer, L. (1993) 'Community policing: lessons from Victoria' *Australian Studies in Law, Crime and Justice*. Canberra: Australian Institute of Criminology.

Beyond Barriers (2003) 'First out … report of the findings of the Beyond Barriers survey of lesbian, gay, bisexual and transgender people in Scotland', Edinburgh: Beyond Barriers.

Bishop, J. (2007) 'Addressing hate crime as a regional security threat: an overview of the ODHIHR Law Enforcement Officer Programme', Office for Democratic Institutions and Human Rights.

Blee, K. M. (2007) 'The microdynamics of hate violence: interpretive analysis and implications for responses' *American Behavioral Scientist*, **51**(2), pp. 258–270.

Blumberg, D. M., Giromini, L. and Jacobson, L. B. (2015) 'Impact of police academy training on recruits' integrity' *Police Quarterly*, pp. 1–24. DOI: 10.1177/109861111 5608322.

Boeckmann, R. J. and Turpin-Petrosino, C. (2002) 'Understanding the harm of hate crime' *Journal of Social Issues*, **58**(2), pp. 207–225.

Bottoms, A., and Tankebe, J. (2012) 'Beyond procedural justice: a dialogic approach to legitimacy in criminal justice' *The Journal of Criminal Law and Criminology*, pp. 119–170.

Bowling, B. (1999). *Violent Racism: Victimization, Policing and Social Context*. Oxford: Oxford University Press.

Boyd, E. A., Berk, R. A. and Hamner, K. M. (1996) 'Motivated by hatred or prejudice: categorization of hate-motivated crimes in two police divisions' *Law and Society Review*, **30**(4), pp. 819–850.

Bradford, B. (2014) 'Policing and social identity: procedural justice, inclusion and cooperation between police and public' *Policing and Society*, **24**(1), pp. 22–43.

Bradford, B., Murphy, K., and Jackson, J. (2013) 'Officers as mirrors: policing, procedural justice and the (re)production of social identity', Oxford Legal Studies Research Paper No. 86/2013. SSRN. Retrieved from: http://ssrn.com/abstract=2337913.

Bradley, D. (2015) 'Human rights in policing: a global assessment' *Policing and Society*, **25**(5), pp. 540–547.

Bradley, K. and Connors, E. (2007) 'Training evaluation model: evaluating and improving criminal justice training', National Institute of Justice. Retrieved from: www.evaw-intl.org/Library/DocumentLibraryHandler.ashx?id=550.

Brewer, P. R. (2014) 'Public opinion about gay rights and gay marriage' *International Journal of Public Opinion Research*, **26**(3), pp. 279–282.

Brooks, L. W. (2001) 'Police discretionary behavior: a study of style', in Dunham, R. and Alpert, G. (eds) *Critical Issues in Policing: Contemporary Readings*. Prospect Heights, IL: Waveland Press, Inc., pp. 71–131.

Brudholm, T. (2015) 'Hate crimes and human rights violations' *Journal of Applied Philosophy*, **32**(1), pp. 82–97.

Bullock, K. and Johnson, P. (2011) 'The impact of the Human Rights Act 1998 on policing in England and Wales' *British Journal of Criminology*, **52**(3) pp. 630–650.

Burke, K. and Leben, S. (2007) 'A white paper of the American Judges Association, the voice of the judiciary (R): procedural fairness: a key ingredient in public satisfaction' *Court Review*, **44**, pp. 4–164.

Burnap, P., Williams, M. L., Sloan, L., Rana, O., Housley, W., Edwards, A., and Voss, A. (2014) 'Tweeting the terror: modelling the social media reaction to the Woolwich Terrorist Attack' *Social Network Analysis and Mining*, **4**(1), pp. 1–14.

Byers, B. and Zeller, R. (1997) 'An examination of official hate crime offense and bias motivation statistics for 1991–1994' *Journal of Crime and Justice*, **20**(1), pp. 91–106.

Caldero, M. A. and Crank, J. P. (2011) *Police Ethics: The Corruption of Noble Cause*. Burlington, MA: Elsevier, Inc.

California Commission on Peace Officer Standards and Training (2008) 'Hate crimes policy guidelines'. Retrieved from: http://lib.post.ca.gov/Publications/hate_crimes.pdf.

Campbell, R. (2014) 'Not getting away with it: linking sex work and hate crime in Merseyside', in Chakroborti, N. and Garland, J. (eds), *Responding to Hate Crime: The Case for Connecting Policy and Research*. Bristol: The Policy Press.

CEJI (2012) 'Making hate crimes visible: facing facts project'. Retrieved from: www. ceji.org/media/Guidelines-for-monitoring-of-hate-crimes-and-hate-motivated-incidents-PROTECTED.pdf.

Chakraborti, N. (2009) 'A glass half full? Assessing progress in the policing of hate crime' *Policing*, 3(2), pp. 121–128.

Chakraborti, N. (ed.) (2010) *Hate crime: concepts, policy, future directions*. Cullompton: Willan.

Chakraborti, N. (2015) 'Framing the boundaries of hate crime' in Hall, N., Corb, A., Giannasi, P. and Grieve, J. (eds) *Routledge International Handbook on Hate Crime*. London: Routledge, pp. 13–23.

Chakraborti, N. and Garland, J. (2009/2015) *Hate Crime: Impact, Causes and Responses*. London: Sage Publications.

Chakraborti, N. and Garland, J. (eds) (2014) *Responding to Hate Crime: The Case for Connecting Policy and Research*. Bristol: Policy Press.

Chakraborti, N., Garland, J. and Hardy, S. J. (2014) 'The Leicester Hate Crime Project: findings and conclusions'. Retrieved from: www2.le.ac.uk/departments/criminology/hate/documents/fc-full-report.

Chakraborti, N. and Zempi, I. (2012) 'The veil under attack: gendered dimensions of Islamophobic victimization' *International Review of Victimology*, 18(3), pp. 269–284.

Chandra, M. (2012) 'Social profiling: the root causes of racial discrimination against North East Indians', North East Support Centre and Helpline. Retrieved from http://nehelpline.net/?p=702.

Chapman, A. and Kelly, K. (2005) 'Australian anti-vilification law: a discussion of the public/private divide and the work relations context' *Sydney Law Review*, 27(2), pp. 203–236.

Clarke, G. and Sevak, P. (2013) 'The disappearing gay income penalty' *Economics Letters*, 121(3), pp. 542–545.

Clement, S., Brohan, E., Sayce, L., Pool, J. and Thornicroft, G. (2011) 'Disability hate crime and targeted violence and hostility: a mental health and discrimination perspective' *Journal of Mental Health*, 20(3), pp. 219–225.

College of Policing (2014a) 'National policing (2014) hate crime strategy'. Retrieved from: http://library.college.police.uk/docs/college-of-policing/National-Policing-Hate-Crime-strategy.pdf.

College of Policing (2014b) 'College of Policing (2014) hate crime operational guidance'. Retrieved from: http://library.college.police.uk/docs/college-of-policing/Hate-Crime-Operational-Guidance.pdf.

College of Policing (2015) 'Implementation framework: disability hate crime'. Retrieved from: www.college.police.uk/What-we-do/Support/Equality/Pages/Implementation-framework.aspx.

Cordner, G. (1995) 'Community policing: elements and effects' *Police Forum*, 5(3), pp. 1–8.

Cowdery, N. (2009) 'Review of laws of vilification: criminal aspects', Roundtable on Hate Crime and Vilification Law: Developments and Directions, Sydney Institute of Criminology. Retrieved from: http://sydney.edu.au/law/criminology/ahcn/docs_pdfs/Cowdrey_Antivilification_Roundtable_Usyd_2009.pdf.

Crawshaw, R., Cullen, S. and Williamson, T. (2007) *Human Rights and Policing* (Vol. 5). Martinus Nijhoff Publishers.

Cronin, S. W., McDevitt, J., Farrell, A. and Nolan, J. J. (2007) 'Bias-crime reporting organizational responses to ambiguity, uncertainty, and infrequency in eight police departments' *American Behavioral Scientist*, **51**(2), pp. 213–231.

Crown Prosecution Service (2013–14) 'Hate crime and crimes against older people report'. Retrieved from: www.cps.gov.uk/publications/docs/cps_hate_crime_report_2014.pdf.

Crown Prosecution Service (2014) 'Conviction rate for hate crime at all-time high'. Retrieved from: www.cps.gov.uk/news/latest_news/conviction_rate_for_hate_crime_at_all-time_high/index.html.

Cunneen, C. (2001) *Conflict, Politics and Crime: Aboriginal Communities and the Police*. Sydney: Allen and Unwin.

Cunneen, C. (2009) 'Hate crime' in Wakefield, A. and Fleming, J. (eds), *The Sage Dictionary of Policing*. London: Sage, pp. 132–135.

Cunneen, C., Fraser, D. and Tomsen, S. (eds) (1997) *Faces of Hate: Hate Crime in Australia*. Sydney: Hawkins Press.

Cunneen, C. and White, R. (2002) 'Ethnic minority young people', in *Juvenile Justice: Youth and Crime in Australia*. Melbourne: Oxford University Press, pp. 184–199.

Davis, M. (2006) 'Globalisation and the new racism: a short history', paper presented at The New Racisms, New Anti-Racisms Conference, Research Institute for Humanities and Social Sciences, Human Rights and Equal Opportunity Commission, Department of Anthropology, University of Sydney, 3–4 November 2006. Retrieved from: www.humanrights.gov.au/new-racisms-new-anti-racisms.

Duckitt, J., Callaghan, J. and Wagner, C. (2005) 'Group identification and outgroup attitudes in four South African ethnic groups: a multidimensional approach' *Personality and Social Psychology Bulletin*, **31**(5), pp. 633–646.

Duggan, M. (2015) 'Sectarianism and hate crime in Northern Ireland' in Hall, N., Corb, A., Giannasi, P. and Grieve, J. (eds), *Routledge International Handbook on Hate Crime*. London: Routledge, pp. 117–128.

Dunham, R. G., Alpert, G. P., Stroshine, M. S. and Bennett, K. (2005) 'Transforming citizens into suspects: factors that influence the formation of police suspicion' *Police Quarterly*, **8**(3), pp. 366–393.

Dunn, K. (2003) 'Racism in Australia: findings of a survey on racist attitudes and experiences of racism', paper presented at The Challenges of Immigration and Integration in the European Union and Australia, University of Sydney, Sydney. Retrieved from: https://openresearch-repository.anu.edu.au/bitstream/1885/41761/4/dunn_paper.pdf.

Dunn, K. in Noble, G. (2009) 'Performing Australian Nationalisms at Cronulla', in *Lines in the Sand: The Cronulla Riots, Multiculturalism and National Belonging*, Sydney: Sydney Institute of Criminology Monograph Series, pp. 76–94.

Dunn, K. M., Klocker, N. and Salabay, T. (2007) 'Contemporary racism and Islamophobia in Australia: racializing religion' *Ethnicities*, **7**(4), pp. 564–589.

Elliott, I., Thomas, S. D. M. and Ogloff, J. R. P. (2011) 'Procedural justice in contacts with the police: testing a relational model of authority in a mixed methods study' *Psychology, Public Policy and Law*, **17**(4), pp. 592–610.

Executive Council of Australian Jewry (2014) '2014 Report on antisemitism in Australia', Executive Council of Australian Jewry, 2014, NSW.

Fathi, S. (2013) 'Bias crime reporting: creating a stronger model for immigrant and refugee populations' *Gonzaga Law Review*, **49**, pp. 249–262.

Federal Bureau of Investigation (1996) 'Training guide for hate crime data collection: uniform crime reporting', US Department of Justice.

Federal Bureau of Investigation (2015) 'Hate crime data collection guidelines and training manual', US Department of Justice. Retrieved from: www.fbi.gov/about-us/cjis/ucr/hate-crime-data-collection-guidelines-and-training-manual.pdf.

Federal Bureau of Statistics (2004) 'Hate crime'. Retrieved from: www2.fbi. gov/ucr/cius_04/offenses_reported/hate_crime/.

Feenan, D. (2006) 'Religious vilification laws: quelling fires of hatred?' *Alternative Law Journal*, **31**(3), pp. 153–158.

Finn, P. (1988) 'Bias crime: difficult to define, difficult to prosecute' *Criminal Justice*, **3**, pp. 19–23, 47–48.

Fitzroy Legal Service (2010) '"Boys, you wanna give me some action?": interventions into policing of racialised communities in Melbourne', Melbourne: Fitzroy Legal Service. Retrieved from: www.fitzroy-legal.org.au/cb_pages/files/LegalAid_Racial-Adol_FA2.pdf.

Fleming, J. (2010) 'Community policing: the Australian connection' in Putt, J. (ed.), *Community Policing in Australia*, AIC Reports Research and Policy Series 111, Canberra: Australian Institute of Criminology, pp. 1–7.

Fleming, J. and McLaughlin, E. (2010) '"The public gets what the public wants?" Interrogating the "public confidence" agenda' *Policing: a Journal of Policy and Practice*, **4**(3), pp. 199–202.

Flemington Legal Service (2013) 'Information on the *Haile-Michael* v. *Konstantinidis* race discrimination settlement case', Flemington Legal Service. Retrieved from: www.communitylaw.org.au/flemingtonkensington/cb_pages/race_discrimination_case_documents.php.

Flitton, D. (2010) 'UN panel's race crime rebuke', *The Age*, 10 August 2010. Retrieved from: www.theage.com.au/victoria/un-panels-race-crime-rebuke-20100829-13xmw.html.

Forbes-Mewett, H., McCulloch, J. and Nyland, C. (2015) *International Students and Crime*. New York: Palgrave Macmillan.

Foster, J., Newburn, T. and Souhami, A. (2005) *Assessing the Impact of the Stephen Lawrence Inquiry*. London: Home Office.

FRA (European Union Agency for Fundamental Rights) (2013) 'Fundamental rights-based police training: a manual for police trainers', Luxembourg: Publications Office of the European Union. Retrieved from: http://fra.europa.eu/sites/default/files/fra-2013-fundamental-rights-based-police-training_en_0.pdf.

FRA (European Union Agency for Fundamental Rights) (2016) 'Ensuring justice for hate crime victims: professional perspectives', Luxembourg: Publications Office of the European Union. Retrieved from: http://fra.europa.eu/sites/default/files/fra_uploads/fra-2016-justice-hate_crime-victims_en.pdf.

Fraser, D., Melhem, M. and Yacoub, M. (1997) 'Violence against Arab Australians' in Cunneen, C., Fraser, D. and Tomsen, S. (eds) *Faces of Hate: Hate Crime in Australia*. Bellflower, CA: Hawkins Press, pp. 75–96.

Freilich, J. D. and Chermak, S. M. (2013) 'Hate crime', Center for Problem-Oriented Policing. Retrieved from: www.popcenter.org/problems/pdfs/hate_crimes.pdf.

Gadd, D. and Dixon, B. (2012) 'Look before you leap: hate crime legislation reconsidered' *South African Crime Quarterly*, **40**, pp. 25–30.

Garland, J. (2010) '"It's a mosher just been banged for no reason": assessing targeted violence against goths and the parameters of hate crime' *International Review of Victimology*, **17**(2), pp. 159–177.

Garland, J. (2012) 'Difficulties in defining hate crime victimization' *International Review of Victimology*, **18**(1), pp. 25–37.

Garland J. M. (2014) 'Reshaping hate crime policy and practice: lessons from a grassroots campaign', in Chakraborti, N. and Garland, J. (eds), *Responding to Hate Crime: the Case for Connecting Policy and Research*. Bristol: Policy Press One, pp. 39–54.

Garland, J. and Chakraborti, N. (2009) *Hate Crime: Impact, Causes, and Consequences.* London: Sage.

Garland, J. and Chakraborti, N. (2012) 'Divided by a common concept? Assessing the implications of different conceptualisations of hate crime in the European Union' *European Journal of Criminology*, **9**(1), pp. 38–51.

Garland, J. and Hodkinson, P. (2014) '"F**king freak! What the hell do you think you look like?" Experiences of targeted victimization among goths and developing notions of hate crime' *British Journal of Criminology*, **54**, pp. 613–631.

Gelber, K. (2000) 'Hate crimes: public policy implications of the inclusion of gender', *Australian Journal of Political Science*, **35**(2), pp. 275–289.

Gerstenfeld, P. B. (2013) *Hate Crimes: Causes, Controls, and Controversies*. Thousand Oaks, CA: Sage.

Giannasi, P. (2014) 'Academia from a practitioner's perspective: a reflection on the changes in the relationship between academia, policing and government in a hate crime context' in Chakraborti, N. and Garland, J. (eds), *Responding to Hate Crime: The Case for Connecting Policy and Research*. Bristol: Policy Press One, pp. 27–38.

Giannasi, P. (2015a) 'Hate crime in the United Kingdom' in Hall, N., Corb, A., Giannasi, P. and Grieve, J. (eds) *Routledge International Handbook on Hate Crime*. London: Routledge, pp. 105–116.

Giannasi, P. (2015b) 'Policing and hate crime' in Hall, N., Corb, A., Giannasi, P. and Grieve, J. (eds), *Routledge International Handbook on Hate Crime*. London: Routledge, pp. 331–342.

Gill, A. K. and Mason-Bish, H. (2013) 'Addressing violence against women as a form of hate crime: limitations and possibilities' *Feminist Review*, **105**(1), pp. 1–20.

Godin, E. (2015) 'The European extreme right', in Hall, N., Corb, A., Giannasi, P. and Grieve, J. (eds), *Routledge International Handbook on Hate Crime*. London: Routledge, pp. 138–152.

Goodrich, P. (1984) 'Law and language: an historical and critical introduction' *Journal of Law and Society*, **11**(2), pp. 173–206.

Grattet, R. (2009) 'The urban ecology of bias crime: a study of disorganized and defended neighborhoods' *Social Problems*, **56**(1), pp. 132–140.

Grattet, R. and Jenness, V. (2003) 'The birth and maturation of hate crime policy in the United States', in Perry, B. (ed.) *Hate and Bias Crimes: A Reader*. London: Routledge, pp. 389–408.

Grattet, R. and Jenness, V. (2005) 'The reconstitution of law in local settings: agency discretion, ambiguity, and a surplus of law in the policing of hate crime' *Law and Society Review*, **39**(4), pp. 893–941.

Grattet, R. and Jenness, V. (2008) 'Transforming symbolic law into organizational action: hate crime policy and law enforcement practice' *Social Forces*, **87**(1), pp. 501–528.

Gray, B., Leonard, W. and Jack, M. (2006) 'With respect: a strategy for reducing homophobic harassment in Victoria', discussion paper for the consideration of the Victorian Attorney General. Retrieved from: www.notohomophobia.com.au/wp-content/uploads/2012/08/With-Respect-A-Strategy-for-Reducing-Homophobic-Harassment-in-Victoria.pdf.

Graycar, A. (2010) 'Racism and the tertiary student experience in Australia', occasional paper 5/2010, Canberra: The Academy of Social Sciences in Australia.

Greater Manchester Police (2014) 'Hate crime policy and procedure'. Retrieved from: www.gmp.police.uk/content/WebAttachments/A902DDDD4CD8149180257CED0050 D768/$File/GMP%20Hate%20Crime%20Policy%20January%202014%20updated% 20May%202014.pdf.

Green, D. P., McFalls, L. H. and Smith, J. K. (2001) 'Hate crime: an emergent research agenda' *Annual Review of Sociology*, **27**, pp. 479–504.

Griffiths, E. (2014) 'George Brandis defends "right to be a bigot" amid government plan to amend Racial Discrimination Act', ABC News, 24 March 2014. Retrieved from: www.abc.net.au/news/2014-03-24/brandis-defends-right-to-be-a-bigot/5341552.

Grundy, D. (2011) 'Friend or fake? Mate crimes and people with learning disabilities' *Journal of Learning Disabilities and Offending Behaviour*, **2**(4), pp. 167–169.

Hall, B. (2013) 'Minister wants boat people called illegals', The Sydney Morning Herald, 20 October 2013. Retrieved from: www.smh.com.au/federal-politics/political-news/ minister-wants-boat-people-called-illegals-20131019-2vtl0.html.

Hall, N. (2005) *Hate Crime*. Devon: Willan Publishing.

Hall, N. (2012) 'Policing hate crime in London and New York City: some reflections on the factors influencing effective law enforcement, service provision and public trust and confidence' *International Review of Victimology*, **18**(1), pp. 73–87.

Hall, N. (2013) *Hate Crime*. London: Routledge.

Hall, N. (2014) 'The adventures of an accidental academic in "policy-land": a personal reflection of bridging academia, policing and government in a hate crime context' in Chakraborti, N. and Garland, J. (eds) *Responding to Hate Crime: The Case for Connecting Policy and Research*. Bristol: Policy Press One, pp. 13–26.

Hall, N., Corb, A., Giannasi, P. and Grieve, J. (eds), *Routledge International Handbook on Hate Crime*. London: Routledge.

Hamilton, P. and Trickett, L. (2015) 'Disability hostility, harassment and violence in the UK: a "motiveless" and "senseless" crime?' in Hall, N., Corb, A., Giannasi, P. and Grieve, J. (eds) *Routledge International Handbook on Hate Crime*. London: Routledge, pp. 207–225.

Harlow, C. W. (2005) 'Hate crime reported by victims and police', US Department of Justice, Office of Justice Programs, Bureau of Justice Statistics.

Heard, C. (2013) 'Sentencing hate crime' *Archbold Review*, **8**, pp. 5–6.

Heard, C. (2014) 'Sentencing hate crime' *Archbold Review*, **7**, pp. 4–5.

Herek, G. M., Gillis, J. R. and Cogan, J. C. (1999) 'Psychological sequelae of hate-crime victimization among lesbian, gay, and bisexual adults' *Journal of Consulting and Clinical Psychology*, **67**(6), pp. 945–951.

Hindustan Times (2009) 'PM "appalled" at attacks on Indian students in Australia', *Hindustan Times*, 9 June 2009. Retrieved from: www.hindustantimes.com/indians-abroad/ india/PM-appalled-at-attacks-on-Indianstudents-in-Australia/420480/Article1-419564. aspx.

HM Government (2012) 'Challenge it, report it, stop it: the government's plan to tackle hate crime'. Retrieved from: www.gov.uk/government/uploads/system/uploads/ attachment_data/file/97849/action-plan.pdf.

Hodge, J. P. (2011) *Gendered Hate: Exploring Gender in Hate Crime Law*. Boston: Northeastern University Press.

Hodkinson, P. (2002) *Goth: Identity, Style and Subculture*. Oxford: Berg Publishers.

Home Office (2013–2014) 'Hate crimes, England and Wales, 2013/14', Home Office

Statistical Bulletin. Retrieved from: www.report-it.org.uk/files/home_office_hate_crime_data_201314.pdf.

Home Office (2014) 'Challenge it, report it, stop it: delivering the government's hate crime action plan'. Retrieved from: www.gov.uk/government/publications/hate-crime-action-plan-challenge-it-report-it-stop-it.

Home Office, Office for National Statistics and Ministry of Justice (2013) 'An overview of hate crime in England and Wales'. Retrieved from: www.gov.uk/government/uploads/system/uploads/attachment_data/file/266358/hate-crime-2013.pdf.

Home Office Police Standards Unit (2005) 'Hate crime: delivering a quality service: good practice and tactical guidance', Home Office Police Standards Unit and Association of Chief Police Officers, London. Retrieved from: www.bedfordshire.police.uk/pdf/tacticalguidance.pdf.

Hoong, C., Sanah, S. and Khanna, S. M. (2012) 'Police readiness for tackling hate crime against people with learning disabilities – areas for improvement and examples of good practice' *Safer Communities*, **11**(3), pp. 145–153. Retrieved from: http://dx.doi.org/10.1108/17578041211244058.

Hopkins, T. (2009) 'VLF report: effective investigation', Melbourne: Victorian Law Foundation. Retrieved from: www.communitylaw.org.au/flemingtonkensington/cb_pages/files/VLF%20REPORT%20-Effective%20Investigation.pdf.

Hough, M., Jackson, J., Bradford, B., Myhill, A. and Quinton, P. (2010) 'Procedural justice: trust and institutional legitimacy' *Policing: a Journal of Policy and Practice*, **4**(3), pp. 203–210.

Human Rights and Equal Opportunity Commission (HREOC) (1991) 'Racist violence: report of the National Inquiry into Racist Violence in Australia', Canberra: Australian Government Publishing Service. Retrieved from: www.humanrights.gov.au/sites/default/files/document/publication/NIRV.pdf.

Human Rights and Equal Opportunity Commission (HREOC) (2004) 'IsmaU – Listen: national consultations on eliminating prejudice against Arab and Muslim Australians'. Retrieved from: www.humanrights.gov.au/isma-listen-national-consultations-eliminating-prejudice-against-arab-and-muslim-australians.

Human Rights Watch/Columbia Law School, Human Rights Institute (2014) 'Illusions of justice: human rights abuses in US terrorism prosecutions', Human Rights Watch. Retrieved from: www.hrw.org/report/2014/07/21/illusion-justice/human-rights-abuses-us-terrorism-prosecutions.

Hunt, R. and Martinez, T. (2015) 'Lessons from a hate crime detective: a guide for law enforcement'. Washington, DC: Office of Community Oriented Policing Services.

Huq, A. Z., Tyler, T. R. and Schulhofer, S. J. (2011) 'Why does the public cooperate with law enforcement? The influence of the purposes and targets of policing' *Psychology, Public Policy and Law*, **17**(3), p. 419.

Iganski, P. (2007) 'Too few Jews to count? Police monitoring of hate crime against Jews in the United Kingdom' *American Behavioral Scientist*, **51**(2), pp. 232–245.

Iganski, P. (2008) *Hate crime and the city*. Bristol: Policy Press.

Iganski, P. and Smith, D. (2011) 'Rehabilitation of hate crime offenders', Equality and Human Rights Commission, Scotland.

Iganski, P. and Levin, J. (2015) *Hate Crime: A Global Perspective*. London: Routledge.

Ivanov, V. and Kilian, L. (2001) 'A practitioner's guide to lag order selection for vector autoregressions', CEPR discussion paper no. 2685. London: Centre for Economic Policy Research. Retrieved from: www.cepr.org/pubs/dps/DP2685.asp.

Jacobs, J. B. and Potter, K. (1998) *Hate Crimes: Criminal Law and Identity Politics*. Vol. 67. New York: Oxford University Press.

Jakubowicz, A. and Monani, D. (2015) 'Mapping progress: human rights and international students in Australia' *Cosmopolitan Civil Societies: An Interdisciplinary Journal*, 7(3), pp. 61–80.

James, Z. (2014) 'Policing hate against Gypsies and Travellers: dealing with the dark side', in Chakraborti, N. and Garland, J. (eds), *Responding to Hate Crime: The Case for Connecting Policy and Research*. Bristol: Policy Press One, pp. 215–229.

James, Z. (2015) 'Hate crimes against Gypsies, Travellers and Roma in Europe' in Hall, N., Corb, A., Giannasi, P. and Grieve, J. (eds), *Routledge International Handbook on Hate Crime*. London: Routledge, pp. 237–248.

Jenness, V. (2001) 'The hate crime canon and beyond: a critical assessment' *Law and Critique*, 12, pp. 279–308.

Jenness, V. (2002) 'Contours of hate crime politics and law in the United States', in Ignaski P. (ed.) *The Hate Debate: Should Hate Be Punished as a Crime?* London: Profile Books.

Jenness, V. (2003) 'Engendering hate crime policy: gender, the "dilemma of difference" and the creation of legal subjects' *Journal of Hate Studies*, 2, pp. 73–97.

Jenness, V. (2007) 'The emergence, content and institutionalization of hate crime law: how a diverse policy community produced a modern legal fact' *Annual Review of Law and Social Science*, 3, pp. 141–160.

Jenness, V. and Grattet, R. (2001) *Making Hate a Crime: From Social Movement to Law Enforcement*. New York: Russell Sage Foundation.

Jenness, V. and Grattet, R. (2005) 'The law-in-between: the effects of organizational perviousness on the policing of hate crime' *Social Problems*, 52(3), pp. 337–359.

Johnson, H. (2005a) 'Experiences of crime in two selected migrant communities' *Trends and Issues in Criminal Justice*, Australian Institute of Criminology, 302, pp. 1–6.

Johnson, H. (2005b) *Crime Victimisation in Australia: Key Findings of the 2004 International Crime Victimisation Survey*. Canberra: Australian Institute of Criminology.

Johnson, K. R. and Cuevas Ingram, J. E. (2012) 'Anatomy of a modern-day lynching: the relationship between hate crimes against Latina/os and the debate over immigration reform' *North Carolina Law Review*, 91, pp. 1613–1656.

Joudo Larsen, J. (2010) 'Community policing in culturally and linguistically diverse communities' in Putt, J. (ed.), *Community Policing in Australia*, AIC Reports Research and Policy Series 111, Canberra: Australian Institute of Criminology, pp. 24–31.

Joudo Larsen, J., Payne, J. and Tomison, A. (2011) *Crimes against International Students in Australia: 2005–09*. Canberra: Australian Institute of Criminology.

Kelly, A. (2016) 'Victoria Police working to shift away from old-school culture', *The Age*, 23 March 2016. Retrieved from: www.theage.com.au/comment/victoria-police-working-working-to-shift-away-from-oldschool-culture-20160322-gno4ig#ixzz43mlX20iL.

Kielinger, V. and Paterson, S. (2007) 'Policing hate crime in London' *American Behavioral Scientist*, 51(2), pp. 196–204.

Kim, L. K. Y. (2011) 'Matthew Shepard and James Byrd, Jr. Hate Crimes Act: the interplay of the judiciary and congress in suspect classification analysis' *Loyola Journal of Public Interest Law*, 12, pp. 495–529.

Law Commission (UK) (2014) 'Hate crime: should the current offences be extended?' Retrieved from: http://lawcommission.justice.gov.uk/docs/lc348_hate_crime.pdf.

Lawrence, F. (1999) *Punishing Hate: Bias Crimes under American Law*. Cambridge: Harvard University Press.

Lee, M. and McGovern, A. (2014) *Policing and Media: Public Relations, Simulations and Communications*. London: Routledge.

Levin, B. (1999) 'Hate crimes: worse by definition' *Journal of Contemporary Criminal Justice*, **15**(1), pp. 6–21.

Levin, B. (2002) 'From slavery to hate crime laws: the emergence of race and status-based protection in American criminal law' *Journal of Social Issues*, **58**(2), pp. 227–245.

Levin, J. and McDevitt, J. (1993) *Hate Crimes: The Rising Tide of Bigotry and Bloodshed*. New York: Plenum.

Levin, J., Rabrenovic, G., Ferraro, V., Doran, T. and Methe, D. (2007) 'When a crime committed by a teenager becomes a hate crime: results from two studies' *American Behavioral Scientist*, **51**, pp. 246–257.

Lewis, P. and Evans, R. (2013) *Undercover: The True Story of Britain's Secret Police*. London: Faber and Faber.

Linden, A. (2014) 'ITSA: Stata module to perform interrupted time series analysis for single and multiple groups'. Retrieved from: https://ideas.repec.org/c/boc/bocode/s457793.html.

Linden, A. (2015) 'Conducting interrupted time-series analysis for single- and multiple-group comparisons' *Stata Journal*, **15**(2), pp. 480–500.

Lyons, C. J. (2008) 'Defending turf: racial demographics and hate crime against blacks and whites' *Social Forces*, **87**(1), pp. 357–385.

Lyons, C. J. and Roberts, A. (2014) 'The difference "hate" makes in clearing crime: an event history analysis of incident factors' *Journal of Contemporary Criminal Justice*, **30**(3), pp. 268–289.

Macpherson, W. (1999) 'The Stephen Lawrence inquiry: report of an inquiry by Sir William Macpherson of Cluny', Stationery Office, Parliamentary Papers, London.

MacVean, A. and Cox, C. (2012) 'Police education in a university setting' *Policing*, **6**(1), pp. 16–25.

Maher, J., McCulloch, J. and Mason, G. (2015) 'Punishing gendered violence as hate crime: aggravated sentences as a means of recognising hate as motivation for violent crimes against women' *Australian Feminist Law Journal*, **41**(1), pp. 177–193.

Martin, S. E. (1995) 'A cross-burning is not just an arson: police social construction of hate in Baltimore County' *Criminology*, **33**(3), pp. 303–326.

Martin, S. E. (1996) 'Investigating hate crimes: case characteristics and law enforcement responses' *Justice Quarterly*, **13**(3), pp. 455–480.

Martin, S. E. (1999) 'Police and the production of hate crimes: continuity and change in one jurisdiction' *Police Quarterly*, **2**(4), pp. 417–437.

Mason, G. (1993) 'Violence against lesbians and gay men', Violence Prevention Series No. 2, Canberra: Australian Institute of Criminology.

Mason, G. (2001a) 'Recognition and reformulation' *Current Issues in Criminal Justice*, **13**(3), pp. 251–268.

Mason, G. (2001b) 'Not our kind of hate crime' *Law and Critique*, **12**(3), pp. 253–278.

Mason, G. (2002) *The Spectacle of Violence: Homophobia, Gender and Knowledge*. London: Routledge.

Mason, G. (2005) 'Hate crime and the image of the stranger' *The British Journal of Criminology*, **45**(6), pp. 837–859.

Mason, G. (2009a) 'Hate crime laws in Australia: are they achieving their goals?' *Criminal Law Journal*, **33**(6), pp. 326–340.

Mason, G. (2009b) 'The penal politics of hatred', J. V. Barry Memorial Lecture, *Australian and New Zealand Journal of Criminology*, **42**(3), pp. 275–286.

Mason, G. (2010) 'Violence against Indian students in Australia: a question of dignity' *Current Issues in Criminal Justice*, **21**(3), pp. 461–466.

Mason, G. (2012a) 'Naming the "R" word in racial victimization: violence against Indian students in Australia' *International Review of Victimology*, **18**(1), pp. 39–56.

Mason, G. (2012b) '"I am tomorrow": violence against Indian students in Australia and political denial' *Australian and New Zealand Journal of Criminology*, **45**(1), pp. 4–25.

Mason, G. (2014) 'Victim attributes in hate crime law' *British Journal of Criminology*, **54**, pp. 161–179.

Mason, G. (2015) 'Legislating against hate' in Hall, N., Corb, A., Giannasi, P. and Grieve, J. (eds) *Routledge International Handbook on Hate Crime*. London: Routledge, pp. 59–67.

Mason, G. and Dyer, A. (2013) '"A negation of Australia's fundamental values": sentencing prejudice-motivated crime' *Melbourne University Law Review*, **36**(3), pp. 872–917.

Mason, G. and Pulvirenti, M. (2013) 'Former refugees and community resilience "papering over" domestic violence' *British Journal of Criminology*, **53**, pp. 401–418.

Mason, G., McCulloch, J. and Maher, J. (2012) 'Working paper 1: The Victoria Police Prejudice Motivated Crime Strategy: contexts, aims and comparisons', unpublished paper.

Mason, G., McCulloch, J. and Maher, J. (2014) 'Policing prejudice motivated crime: a research case study', in Chakraborti, N. and Garland, J. (eds) *Responding to Hate Crime: The Case for Connecting Policy and Research*. Bristol: Policy Press One, pp. 199–214.

Mason, G., McCulloch, J. and Maher, J. (2015) 'Policing hate crime: markers for negotiating common ground in policy implementation' *Policing and Society*, (ahead-of-print), pp. 1–18.

Mason-Bish, H. (2013) 'Examining the boundaries of hate crime policy considering age and gender' *Criminal Justice Policy Review*, **24**(3), pp. 297–316.

Mason-Bish, H. (2015) 'Beyond the silo', in Hall, N., Corb, A., Giannasi, P. and Grieve, J. (eds), *Routledge International Handbook on Hate Crime*. London: Routledge, pp. 24–33.

Mazerolle, L., Antrobus, E., Bennett, S. and Tyler, T. R. (2013) 'Shaping citizen perceptions of police legitimacy: a randomized field trial of procedural justice' *Criminology*, **51**(1), pp. 33–63.

Mazerolle, L., Wickes, R., Cherney, A., Murphy, K., Sargeant, E. and Zahnow, R. (2012) *Community Variations in Crime: A Spatial and Ecometric Analysis Wave 3*. Brisbane: ARC Centre of Excellence in Policing and Security.

McCulloch, J. (2001) *Blue Army: Paramilitary Policing in Australia*. Carlton: Melbourne University Press.

McDevitt, J., Balboni, J. M., Bennett, S., Weiss, J. C., Orchowsky, S. and Walbolt, L. (2003) 'Improving the quality and accuracy of bias crime statistics nationally' in Perry, B., *Hate and Bias Crime: A Reader*. London: Routledge, p. 77.

McDevitt, J., Levin, J., Nolan, J. and Bennett, S. (2010) 'Hate crime offenders' in Chakraborti, N. (ed.) *Hate Crime: Concepts, Policy, Future Directions*. Devon: Willan Publishing, pp. 125–145.

McKernan, H. and Weber, L. (2016) 'Vietnamese Australians' perceptions of the trustworthiness of police' *Australian and New Zealand Journal of Criminology*, **49**(1), pp. 9–29.

McNamara, L. (2002) *Regulating Racism: Racial Vilification Laws in Australia.* Sydney: University of Sydney Institute of Criminology.

Meagher, D. (2006) 'So far no good: the regulatory failure of criminal racial vilification laws in Australia' *Public Law Review*, **17**, pp. 213–232.

Meli, L. (2014) 'Hate crime and punishment: why typical punishment does not fit the crime' *University of Illinois Law Review*, pp. 921–965.

Metropolitan Police Service (2010) 'Hate crime policy', London Metropolitan Police Service.

Metropolitan Police Service (2013) 'Equality impact assessment'. Retrieved from: www. met.police.uk/foi/pdfs/policies/hate_crime_impact.pdf.

Meyer, D. (2010) 'Evaluating the severity of hate-motivated violence: intersectional differences among LGBT hate crime victims' *Sociology* **44**(5), pp. 980–995.

Meyerson, D. (2009) 'The protection of religious rights under Australian law' *Brigham Young University Law Review*, pp. 529–553.

Miles-Johnson, T. (2013) 'Confidence and trust in police: how sexual identity difference shapes perceptions of police' *Current Issues in Criminal Justice*, **25**, pp. 685–702.

Miles-Johnson, T. (2015) 'Perceptions of group value: how Australian transgender people view policing' *Policing and Society*, pp. 1–22.

Miles-Johnson, T. (2016) 'Policing diversity: examining police resistance to training reforms for transgender people in Australia' *Journal of Homosexuality*, **63**(1), pp. 103–136.

Miles-Johnson, T., Mazerolle, L., Pickering, S. and Smith, P. (2016) 'Police perceptions of prejudice: how police awareness training influences the capacity of police to assess prejudiced motivated crime' *Policing and Society*, pp. 1–17. DOI: 10.1080/ 10439463.2016.1206099.

Milne, A., Cambridge, P., Beadle-Brown, J., Mansell, J. and Whelton, B. (2013) 'The characteristics and management of elder abuse: evidence and lessons from a UK case study' *European Journal of Social Work*, **16**(4), pp. 489–505.

Mkhize, N., Bennett, J., Reddy, V. and Moletsane, R. (2010) *The Country We Want to Live In: Hate Crimes and Homophobia in the Lives of Black Lesbian South Africans.* Cape Town: HSRC Press.

Moran, L. and Sharpe, A. (2002) 'Policing the transgender/violence relation' *Current Issues in Criminal Justice*, **13**(3) pp. 269–285.

Moran, L. (2015) 'LGBT hate crime' in Hall, N., Corb, A., Giannasi, P. and Grieve, J. (eds), *Routledge International Handbook on Hate Crime.* London: Routledge, pp. 266–277.

Moran, L. J. and Sharpe, A. N. (2004) 'Violence, identity and policing: the case of violence against transgender people' *Criminal Justice*, **4**(4), pp. 395–417.

Morgan, J. (2002) 'US hate crime legislation: a legal model to avoid in Australia' *Journal of Sociology*, **38**(1), pp. 25–48.

Moss, I. (1991) 'The report of the National Inquiry into Racist Violence', Human Rights Commission, Canberra, Australian Government Publishing Service.

Mouzos, J. and Thompson, S. (2000) 'Gay-hate related homicides: an overview of major findings in New South Wales' *Trends and Issues in Crime and Criminal Justice*, Australian Institute of Criminology, **155**, pp. 1–6.

Muir, W. K. (1979) *Police: Streetcorner Politicians.* Chicago: University of Chicago Press.

Murphy, K. and Barkworth, J. (2014) 'Victim willingness to report crime to police: does procedural justice or outcome matter most?' *Victims and Offenders*, **9**(2), pp. 178–204.

Murphy, K. and Cherney, A. (2011) 'Fostering cooperation with the police: how do ethnic minorities in Australia respond to procedural justice-based policing?' *Australian and New Zealand Journal of Criminology*, **44**(2), pp. 235–257.

Murphy, K. and Cherney, A. (2012) 'Understanding cooperation with police in a diverse society' *British Journal of Criminology*, **52**, pp. 181–201.

Murphy, K., Hinds, L., and Fleming, J. (2008) 'Encouraging public cooperation and support for police' *Policing and Society*, **18**(2), pp. 136–155.

Myhill, A. and Bradford, B. (2013) 'Overcoming cop culture? Organizational justice and police officers' attitudes toward the public' *Policing: An International Journal of Police Strategies and Management*, **36**(2), pp. 338–356.

NineMSN (2005) 'Australia not racist, says Howard', 9 News, 12 December 2005. Retrieved from: http://news.ninemsn.com.au/national/77009/australia-not-racist-says-howard.

NSW Attorney General's Department (2003) '"You shouldn't have to hide to be safe": a report on homophobic hostilities and violence against gay men and lesbians in New South Wales', New South Wales Attorney General's Department, Crime Prevention Division.

NSW Government (2007) *Strategic Framework 2007–2012 – Working Together: Preventing Violence against Gay, Lesbian, Bisexual and Transgender People.* Sydney, NSW: Network of Government Agencies.

NSW Police Force (2011a) 'Policy on sexuality and gender diversity 2011–2014: working with gay, lesbian, bisexual, transgender and intersex people', NSW Police Force. Retrieved from: www.police.nsw.gov.au/__data/assets/pdf_file/0007/195154/Sexuality_and_Gender_Policy_Doc_LRES.pdf.

NSW Police Force (2011b) 'Culturally, linguistically and religiously diverse society: and multicultural policies and services forward plan 2011–2014', NSW Police Force. Retrieved from: www.police.nsw.gov.au/__data/assets/pdf_file/0004/73156/Internet_-_MPSP_Plan_2011-14.pdf.

NSW Police Force (2012) 'Community safety – preventing homophobic crime', NSW Police Force. Retrieved from: www.police.nsw.gov.au/community_issues/gay,_lesbian_and_transgender_issues/community_safety_-_preventing_homophobic_crime.

NSW Police Force (2014) 'Bias crimes', NSW Police Force. Retrieved from: www.police.nsw.gov.au/community_issues/bias_crimes.

Newburn, T. and Matassa, M. (2002) 'Policing hate crime' *Criminal Justice Matters*, **48**(1), pp. 42–43.

Neyroud, P. (2009) 'Squaring the circles: research, evidence, policy-making, and police improvement in England and Wales' *Police Practice and Research: An International Journal*, **10**(5–6), pp. 437–449.

Nicholls, T. (2014) 'Victoria Police apologise for 1994 raid on Tasty Nightclub to makeup for "sins of the past"', ABC News, 5 August 2014. Retrieved from: www.abc.net.au/news/2014-08-05/victoria-police-apologise-for-1994-tasty-nightclub-raid/5649498.

Nixon, C. and Chandler, J. (2011) *Fair cop.* Melbourne: Victory Books.

Noble, G. (2009) 'Where the bloody hell are we?' in Noble, G. (ed.), *Lines in the Sand: The Cronulla Riots, Multiculturalism and National Belonging.* Sydney: Institute of Criminology, pp. 1–22.

Nolan, J. J. and Akiyama, Y. (1999) 'An analysis of factors that affect law enforcement participation in hate crime reporting' *Journal of Contemporary Criminal Justice*, **15**(1), pp. 111–127.

Nolan, J. J. and Akiyama, Y. (2002) 'Assessing the climate for hate crime reporting in law enforcement organizations: a force-field analysis' *The Justice Professional*, **15**(2), pp. 87–103.

Nolan, J. J., Akiyama, Y. and Berhanu, S. (2002) 'The Hate Crime Statistics Act of 1990: developing a method for measuring the occurrence of hate violence' *American Behavioral Scientist*, **46**(1), pp. 136–153.

Nolan, J. J., McDevitt, J., Cronin, S. and Farrell, A. (2004) 'Learning to see hate crimes: a framework for understanding and clarifying ambiguities in bias crime classification' *Criminal Justice Studies*, **7**(1), pp. 91–105.

Oakley, R. (2005) 'Policing racist crime and violence: a comparative analysis', Europe Monitoring Centre on Racism and Xenophobia. Retrieved from: http://fra.europa.eu/sites/default/files/fra_uploads/542-PRCV_en.pdf.

O'Connor, D. (2010) 'Performance from the outside-in' *Policing: A Journal of Policy and Practice*, **4**, pp. 152–156.

Office for Democratic Institutions and Human Rights (ODIHR) (2009) 'Hate crime laws: a practical guide', OSCE Office for Democratic Institutions and Human Rights, Warsaw. Retrieved from: www.osce.org/odihr/36426?download=true.

Office for Democratic Institutions and Human Rights (ODIHR) (2010) 'ODIHR and the battle against hate crime: factsheet', OSCE Office for Democratic Institutions and Human Rights, Warsaw. Retrieved from: http://addresshatecrime.eu/materialdocs/OSCE%20Guides/ODIHR%20and%20hate%20crime.pdf.

Office for Democratic Institutions and Human Rights (ODIHR) (2012) 'Training against hate crimes for law enforcement'. Retrieved from: www.osce.org/odihr/tahcle.

Office for Democratic Institutions and Human Rights (ODIHR) (2013) 'Hate crimes in the OSCE region: incidents and responses, annual report for 2012'. Retrieved from: http://tandis.odihr.pl/hcr2012/pdf/Hate_Crime_Report_full_version.pdf.

Office for Democratic Institutions and Human Rights (ODIHR) (2014) 'Hate crime data-collection and monitoring mechanisms: a practical guide', OSCE Office for Democratic Institutions and Human Rights, Warsaw. Retrieved from: www.osce.org/odihr/datacollectionguide?download=true.

Office for National Statistics (2013–2014) 'Crime in England and Wales, year ending June 2014', CSEW. Retrieved from: http://webarchive.nationalarchives.gov.uk/20160105160709/http://www.ons.gov.uk/ons/rel/crime-stats/crime-statistics/period-ending-june-2014/stb-crime-stats--year-ending-june-2014.html.

Oliver, W. M. (2001) *Community-Oriented Policing: A Systemic Approach to Policing*, (2nd ed.) Upper Saddle River, NJ: Prentice Hall.

Ontario Hate Crimes Working Group (2007) 'Responding to hate crime: a police officer's guide to investigation and prevention'. Ontario: Ontario Police College.

Organisation for Security and Co-operation in Europe (OSCE) (2009) 'Hate crime laws: a practical guide', Office for Democratic Institutions and Human Rights, Organisation for Security and Co-operation in Europe, Warsaw. Retrieved from: www.osce.org/odihr/36426?download=true.

Perry, B. (2001) *In the Name of Hate: Understanding Hate Crimes*. London: Routledge.

Perry, B. (2003a) 'Where do we go from here? Researching hate crime' *Internet Journal of Criminology*, **3**, pp. 45–47.

Perry, B. (2003b) 'Accounting for hate crime' in Perry, B., *Hate and Bias Crime: A Reader*. London: Routledge.

Perry, B. (2010a) 'Policing hate crime in a multicultural society: observations from Canada' *International Journal of Law, Crime and Justice*, **38**(3), pp. 120–140.

Perry, B. (2010b) 'A crime by any other name: the semantics of "hate"' *Journal of Hate Studies*, **4**(1), pp. 121–137.

Perry, B. (2015) 'Exploring the community impacts of hate crime' in Hall, N., Corb, A., Giannasi, P. and Grieve, J. (eds), *Routledge International Handbook on Hate Crime*. London: Routledge, pp. 47–58.

Perry, J, (2016a) 'An interdisciplinary thought about hate crime', International Network for Hate Studies, blog post, 28 April 2016. Retrieved from: www.internationalhate studies.com/3033-2/.

Perry, J. (2016b) 'A shared global perspective on hate crime?' *Criminal Justice Policy Review*, **27**(6), pp. 610–626.

Perry, B., Perry, J., Schweppe, J. and Walters, M. (2016) 'Introduction: understanding hate crime: research, policy, and practice' *Criminal Justice Policy Review*, **27**(6), pp. 571–576.

Petersen, J. (2011) *Murder, the Media, and the Politics of Public Feelings: Remembering Matthew Shepard and James Byrd Jr.* Bloomington: Indiana University Press.

Phillips, C. and Bowling, B. (2012) 'Ethnicities, racism, crime and criminal justice' in Maguire, M., Morgan, R. and Reiner, R. (eds) *The Oxford Handbook of Criminology*. Oxford: Oxford University Press, pp. 421–460.

Phillips, N. (2009) 'The prosecution of hate crime: the limitations of hate crime typology' *Journal of Interpersonal Violence*, **24**(5), pp. 883–905.

Phillips, S. and Grattet, R. (2000) 'Judicial rhetoric, meaning-making, and the institution-alization of hate crime law' *Law and Society Review*, pp. 567–606.

Pickering, S. J., McCulloch, J. and Wright-Neville, D. P. (2008) *Counter-terrorism Policing: Community, Cohesion and Security.* New York: Springer Verlag.

Poynting, S. (2002) 'Bin Laden in the suburbs: attacks on Arab and Muslim Australians before and after 11 September' *Current Issues in Criminal Justice*, **14**(1), pp. 43–64.

Poynting, S. and Mason, V. (2007) 'The resistible rise of Islamophobia: anti-Muslim racism in the UK and Australia before 11 September 2001' *Journal of Sociology*, **43**(1), pp. 61–86.

Poynting, S. and Noble G. (2004) 'Living with racism: the experience and reporting by Arab and Muslim Australians of discrimination, abuse and violence since 11 September 2001', Report to the Human Rights and Equal Opportunity Commission, 19 April 2004. Retrieved from: http://citeseerx.ist.psu.edu/viewdoc/download?doi=10.1.1.511.2 683&rep=rep1&type=pdf.

Prenzler, T. (2004) 'Chief Commissioner Christine Nixon, Victoria: Australia's first female police chief' *Police Practice and Research*, **5**(4–5), pp. 301–315.

Putt, J. (2010) Foreword in Putt, J. (ed.) *Community Policing in Australia*, AIC Reports Research and Policy Series 111. Canberra: Australian Institute of Criminology, pp. iii–ix.

Queensland Police Service (2011a) 'Queensland Police Service multicultural action plan 2011–2012', Queensland Government, Queensland. Retrieved from: www.police.qld. gov.au/corporatedocs/reportsPublications/other/Documents/Multicultural%20 Action%20Plan%202011-2012.pdf.

Queensland Police Service (2011b) 'Queensland Police Service good practice guide for interaction with transgender clients', Queensland Government, Queensland. Retrieved from: www.police.qld.gov.au/programs/community/lgbti/Documents/Good%20Practice% 20Guide%20Interaction%20with%20Transgender%20Clients%20V12.pdf.

Ray, L. and Smith, D. (2001) 'Racist offenders and the politics of "hate crime"' *Law and Critique*, **12**, pp. 203–221.

Reiner, R. (2010) *The Politics of the Police*. Oxford: Oxford University Press.

Rennie, R. (2009) 'Attacks on students "clearly racist": Overland', 10 June 2009. Retrieved from: www.theage.com.au/national/attacks-on-students-clearly-racist-overland-20090609-c2l9.

Rich, D. (2015) 'Global antisemitism', in Hall, N., Corb, A., Giannasi, P. and Grieve, J. (eds), *Routledge International Handbook on Hate Crime*. London: Routledge, pp. 129–137.

Roberts, J. V. and Hastings, A. J. (2001) 'Sentencing in cases of hate-motivated crime: an analysis of subparagraph 718.2 (a)(i) of the Criminal Code' *Queen's Law Journal*, **27**, pp. 93–103.

Roberts, C., Innes, M., Williams, W., Tregidga, J. and Gadd, D. (2013) 'Understanding who commits hate crime and why they do it', Welsh Government Social Research, Number 38/2013. Retrieved from: http://gov.wales/docs/caecd/research/130711-understanding-who-commits-hate-crime-and-why-they-do-it-en.pdf.

Robinson, A. L. and Williams, M. (2003) *Counted Out*. Wales: Stonewall Cymru.

Rosenberg, M. (1979) *Conceiving the Self*. New York: Basic Books.

Rowe, M. (2013) 'Race and policing', in Brown, J. (ed.), *The Future of Policing*. Abingdon: Routledge, pp. 120–134.

Rowe, M. and Garland, J. (2013) *Police Diversity Training: A Silver-Bullet Tarnished? Policing beyond Macpherson – Issues in Police, Race and Society*. Collumpton: Willan, pp. 43–65.

Royal Commission into Aboriginal Deaths in Custody (1991) National Report Volumes 1 and 2. Retrieved from: www.austlii.edu.au/au/other/IndigLRes/rciadic/national/vol1/.

Rubenstein, W. B. (2003) 'The real story of US hate crimes statistics: an empirical analysis' *Tulane Law Review*, **78**, p. 1213.

Rule, A. and Silvester, J. (2010) 'He fought the law and the law won', *The Age*, 27 November 2010. Retrieved from: www.theage.com.au/victoria/he-fought-the-law-and-the-law-won-20101126-18aql.html.

Russell, E. (2016) 'A "fair cop": queer histories, affect and police image work in Pride March', Crime, Media, Culture: 1741659016631134.

Salisbury, H. and Upson, A. (2004) 'Ethnicity, victimisation and worry about crime: findings from the 2001/02 and 2002/03 British Crime Survey', Home Office Research Findings No. 237. London: Home Office Research Development and Statistics Directorate.

Sandroussi, J. and Thompson, S. (1995) *Out of the Blue: A Police Survey of Violence and Harassment against Gay Men and Lesbians*. Sydney: New South Wales Police Service.

Sargeant, E., Murphy, K. and Cherney, A. (2014) 'Ethnicity, trust and cooperation with police: testing the dominance of the process-based model' *European Journal of Criminology*, **11**(4), pp. 500–524.

Schulhofer, S. J., Tyler, T. R. and Huq, A. Z. (2011) 'American policing at a crossroads: unsustainable policies and the procedural justice alternative' *The Journal of Criminal Law and Criminology*, pp. 335–374.

Schweppe, J. (2012) 'Defining characteristics and politicising victims: a legal perspective' *Journal of Hate Studies*, **10**(1), pp. 173–198.

Scrivens, R. (2011) 'Police officers' perceptions of gender-motivated violence in Canada', unpublished thesis. Oshawa: University of Ontario Institute of Technology.

Segrave, M. and Wilson, D. (2011) 'The station study report – Victoria Police and victims of crime: police perspectives and experiences from across Victoria', Victoria: Monash School of Social Sciences.

Sentas, V. (2014) *Traces of Terror: Counter-terrorism Law, Policing, and Race*. Oxford: Oxford University Press.

Sentencing Advisory Council (Victoria) (2009) 'Sentencing for offences motivated by hatred or prejudice', July 2009. Retrieved from: www.sentencingcouncil.vic.gov.au/sites/default/files/publication-documents/Sentencing%20for%20Offences%20Motivated%20by%20Hatred%20or%20Prejudice.pdf

Sharma, S. (2015) 'Caste-based crimes and economic analysis: evidence from India' *Journal of Comparative Economics*, **43**(1), pp. 204–226.

Shaw, M. (2002) 'Preventing hate crimes: international strategies and practice', International Centre for the Prevention of Crime, Canada. Retrieved from: www.crime-prevention-intl.org/fileadmin/user_upload/Publications/2005-1999/2002.ENG. Preventing_Hate_Crimes_International_Strategies_and_Practice.pdf.

Sherry, M. (2010) *Disability Hate Crimes: Does Anyone Really Hate Disabled People?* Farnham: Ashgate.

Shirlow, P., Taylor, L. K., Merrilees, C. E., Goeke-Morey, M. C. and Cummings, E. M. (2013) 'Hate crime: record or perception?' *Space and Polity*, **17**(2), pp. 237–252.

Sin, C. H. (2015) 'Hate crime against people with disabilities', in Hall, N., Corb, A., Giannasi, P. and Grieve, J. (eds), *Routledge International Handbook on Hate Crime*. London: Routledge, pp. 193–206.

Sin, C. H., Hedges, A., Cook, C., Mguni, N., and Comber, N. (2009) 'Disabled people's experiences of targeted violence and hostility', Manchester, NH: Equality and Human Rights Commission. Retrieved from: https://lemosandcrane.co.uk/resources/sin%202009%20ehrc.pdf.

Sin, C. H., Mguni, N., Cook, C., Comber, N. and Hedges, A. (2010) 'Targeted violence, harassment and abuse against people with learning disabilities in Great Britain', *Tizard Learning Disability Review*, **15**(1), pp. 17–27.

Singh, H., Singh, J. and Singh P. (2013) 'A systems approach to identifying structural discrimination through the lens of hate crimes', *Asian American Law Journal*, **20**, pp. 107–138.

Skolnick, J. H. and Fyfe, J. J. (1993) *Above the Law: Police and the Excessive Use of Force*. New York: Free Press.

Smith, H. J., Tyler, T. R., Huo, Y. J., Ortiz, D. J. and Lind, E. A. (1998) 'The self-relevant implications of the group-value model: group membership, self-worth, and treatment quality' *Journal of Experimental Social Psychology*, **34**(5), pp. 470–493.

Smith, M. R. and Alpert, G. P. (2007) 'Explaining police bias: a theory of social conditioning and illusory correlation' *Criminal Justice and Behavior*, **34**(10), pp. 1262–1283.

Smith, S. (2010) Commonwealth of Australia, Parliamentary Debates, House of Representatives, 9 February 2010, 834 (Stephen Smith, Member for Perth, Minister for Foreign Affairs). Retrieved from: http://parlinfo.aph.gov.au/parlInfo/search/display/display.w3p;db=CHAMBER;id=chamber%2Fhansardr%2F2010-02-09%2F0029;query=Id%3A%22chamber%2Fhansardr%2F2010-02-09%2F0000%22

Spalek, B. and O'Rawe, M. (2014) 'Researching counterterrorism: a critical perspective from the field in the light of allegations and findings of covert activities by undercover police officers' *Critical Studies on Terrorism*, **7**(1), pp. 150–164.

Stanko, E. A. (2001) 'Re-conceptualising the policing of hatred: confessions and worrying dilemmas of a consultant' *Law and Critique*, **12**(3), pp. 309–329.

Stanko, E. A. (2004) 'Reviewing the evidence of hate: lessons from a project under the Home Office Crime Reduction Programme' *Criminal Justice: The International Journal of Policy and Practice*, **4**(3), pp. 277–286.

Stonewall (2014) 'Homophobic hate crime: the gay British crime survey 2013', London: Stonewall. Retrieved from: www.stonewall.org.uk/sites/default/files/Homophobic_Hate_Crime__2013_.pdf.

Storry, K. (2000) 'The implications of the Macpherson Report into the death of Stephen Lawrence' *Current Issues in Criminal Justice*, **12**(1), pp. 106–113.

Strike Force Neil (2006) 'Cronulla riots: review of the police response', Vol. 1, Sydney: NSW Police. Retrieved from: www.abc.net.au/mediawatch/transcripts/ep38cronulla1.pdf.

Stroshine, M., Alpert, G. and Dunham, R. (2008) 'The influence of "working rules" on police suspicion and discretionary decision making' *Police Quarterly*, **11**(3), pp. 315–337.

Sullivan, A. (1999) 'What's so bad about hate?', *New York Times*, 26 September 1999. Retrieved from: www.nytimes.com/1999/09/26/magazine/what-s-so-bad-about-hate.html.

Sunshine, J. and Tyler, T. R. (2003) 'The role of procedural justice and legitimacy in shaping public support for policing' *Law and Society Review*, **37**(3), pp. 513–548.

Tankebe, J. (2013) 'Viewing things differently: the dimensions of public perceptions of police legitimacy' *Criminology*, **51**(1), pp. 103–135.

Taras, R. (2013) '"Islamophobia never stands still": race, religion, and culture' *Ethnic and Racial Studies*, **36**(3), pp. 417–433.

Tasmania Police (2011) 'Tasmania Police: lesbian, gay, bisexual, transgender and intersex (LGBTI) liaison officers'. Retrieved from: www.police.tas.gov.au/what-we-do/lesbian-gay-bisexual-transgender-intersex-lgbti-liaison-officers/.

Thompson, S. (1993) 'Homophobic violence: a NSW Police response', 17 June 1993, paper presented at the Second National Conference on Violence, Canberra: Australian Institute of Criminology.

Times Now (2009) 'Australia finally admits its racism', *Times Now*, 16 September 2009. Retrieved from: www.timesnow.tv/videoshow/4327476.cms?frm=mailtofriend.

Tomsen, S. (2002) 'Hatred, murder and male honour: anti-homosexual killings in New South Wales', Research and Public Policy Series No. 43, Canberra: Australian Institute of Criminology.

Tomsen, S. (2010) *Violence, Prejudice and Sexuality*. London: Routledge.

Topsfield, J. (2009) 'Indians told to keep low profile', *The Age*, 19 February 2009. Retrieved from: www.theage.com.au/national/indians-told-to-keep-low-profile-20090218-8bjz.html.

Torres-Reyna, O. (n.d.) Time series. Retrieved from: http://dss.princeton.edu/training/TS101.pdf.

Trickett, L. (with Hamilton, P.) (2015) 'The policing of hate crime in Nottinghamshire', Nottingham Law School, Nottingham Trent University. Retrieved from: http://report-it.org.uk/files/nottinghamshire_police_final_draft.pdf.

Trickett, L. and Hamilton, P. (2015) 'Policing hate crime in Nottingham: lessons for police training', Police Foundations Conference, Policing and Protecting Vulnerability', 5 November 2015. Retrieved from: www.slideshare.net/CSSaunders/dr-loretta-trickett-how-do-we-deal-with-hate-crime-effectively.

Trojanowicz, R. C. and Bucqueroux, B. (1990) *Community Policing: A Contemporary Perspective*. Cincinnati: Anderson Publishing Company.

Turpin-Petrosino, C. (2015) *Understanding Hate Crimes: Acts, Motives, Offenders, Victims, and Justice.* Abingdon: Routledge.

Twenge, J. M., Sherman, R. A. and Wells, B. E. (2016) 'Changes in American adults reported same-sex sexual experiences and attitudes, 1973–2014' *Archives of Sexual Behavior*, pp. 1–18.

Tyler, T. R. (1990) *Why People Obey the Law.* New Haven, CT: Yale University Press.

Tyler, T. R. (2003) 'Procedural justice, legitimacy, and the effective rule of law' *Crime and Justice*, **30**, pp. 283–357.

Tyler, T. R. and Huo, Y. (2002) *Trust in the Law: Encouraging Public Cooperation with the Police and Courts.* New York: Russell Sage Foundation.

Tyler, T. R. and Murphy, K. (2011) 'Procedural justice, police legitimacy and cooperation with the police: a new paradigm for policing', Australian Research Council Centre of Excellence in Policing and Security briefing paper, May issue. Brisbane: Griffith University.

Tyler, T. R. and Wakslak, C. J. (2004,) 'Profiling and police legitimacy: procedural justice, attributions of motive, and acceptance of police authority' *Criminology*, **42**(2), pp. 253–282.

Tyler, T. R., Boeckmann, R. J., Smith, H. J. and Huo, Y. J. (1997) *Social Justice in a Diverse Society.* United States: Westview Press.

Tyler, T. R., Schulhofer, S. and Huq, A. Z. (2010) 'Legitimacy and deterrence effects in counterterrorism policing: a study of Muslim Americans' *Law and Society Review*, **44**(2), pp. 365–402.

US Department of Justice, 'National hate crimes training curricula'. Retrieved from: www.ncjrs.gov/pdffiles1/nij/186784.pdf.

US Department of Justice, Federal Bureau of Investigation (2012) 'Hate crime data collection guidelines and training manual', Criminal Justice Information Services Division, Uniform Crime Reporting Program. Retrieved from: http://risp.ri.gov/documents/UCR/Hate_Crime_Data_Collection_Guidelines_rev2012.pdf.

University of Leicester (2014) 'Leicester Hate Crime Project'. Retrieved from: www2.le.ac.uk/departments/criminology/research/current-projects/hate-crime.

University of Melbourne Graduate Student Association (2009), press release, 30 May 2009. Retrieved from: www.gsa.unimelb.edu.au/artman2/uploads/1/GSA-MR-Stud Attacks.pdf.

Van Dijk, T. (1992) 'Discourse and the denial of racism' *Discourse and Society*, **3**(1), pp. 87–118.

Van Maanen, J. (2005) 'The asshole' in Newburn T. (ed.), *Policing: Key Readings*, Cullompton. Devon: Willan Publishing, pp. 280–296.

Victoria Department of Justice (2010) 'Hate crime review: review of identity motivated hate crime (consultation issues)'. Melbourne: Department of Justice.

Victorian Equal Opportunity and Human Rights Commission (VEOHRC) (2010) 'Review of identity-motivated hate crime'.

Victoria Equal Opportunity and Human Rights (VEOHR) (2012) 'Anti-hate spray'. Retrieved from: www.antihate.vic.gov.au.

Victoria Equal Opportunity and Human Rights (VEOHR) (2013) 'Reporting racism: what you say matters'. Retrieved from: www.humanrightscommission.vic.gov.au/media/k2/attachments/Reporting_Racism_Web_low_res.pdf.

Victoria Police (2007) 'The way ahead 2008–2013', Melbourne, Victoria. Retrieved from: http://trove.nla.gov.au/work/35264455?selectedversion=NBD42694307.

Victoria Police (2009a) 'Police and Indian group to tackle crime', media release, 21

January 2009. Retrieved from: www.police.vic.gov.au/content.asp?Document_ID=18830.

Victoria Police (2009b) 'Chief commissioner discusses assaults on Indian students', Victoria Police News – Our Say, 2 June 2009. Retrieved from: www.vicpolicenews.com.au/our-say/547-our-saychief-commissioner-discusses-assaults-on-indian-students.html.

Victoria Police (2010) 'Prejudice Motivated Crime Strategy', Corporate Strategy and Governance Department. Melbourne: Victoria Police.

Victoria Police Diagnosis Paper (2010) 'Prejudice Motivated Crime Strategy: diagnosis paper', Crime Strategy Group. Melbourne: Victoria Police.

Victoria Police (2011) 'Prejudice Motivated Crime', brochure, Corporate Strategy and Governance Department, Victoria Police, Melbourne. Retrieved from: www.police.vic.gov.au/content.asp?document_id=32278.

Victoria Police (2013) 'Equality is not the same', report, Victoria Police response to community consultation and reviews, Melbourne: Victoria Police. Retrieved from: www.police.vic.gov.au/content.asp?Document_ID=39350.

Victoria Police (2015) 'Future directions for victim-centric policing', Melbourne: Victoria Police. Retrieved from: www.police.vic.gov.au/retrievemedia.asp?Media_ID=111511.

Waddington, P. A. J. (2000) Book review of Bowling, B. (1998) *Violent Racism: Victimization, Policing and Social Context* in *The British Journal of Criminology*, Oxford University Press, **40**(3), pp. 532–552. www.jstor.org.ezproxy1.library.usyd.edu.au/stable/23638947.

Walker, S. E. and Archbold, C. A. (2013) *The New World of Police Accountability* (2nd edn). Los Angeles: Sage Publications.

Walker, S. and Katz, C. M. (1995) 'Less than meets the eye: police department bias-crime units' *American Journal of Police*, **14**(1), pp. 29–48.

Wang, L. (1994) *Hate Crime Laws*. New York: Clark, Boardman, Callaghan.

Weber, L., Fishwick, E. and Marmo, M. (2014) *Crime, Justice and Human Rights*. Basingstoke: Palgrave Macmillan.

Weber, M. (1978) *Economy and Society: An Outline of Interpretive Sociology*. Los Angeles: University of California Press.

Wells, H. and Polders, L. (2006) 'Anti-gay hate crimes in South Africa: prevalence, reporting practices, and experiences of the police' *Agenda: Empowering Women for Gender Equality*, **20**(67), pp. 20–28.

Whine, M. (2015) 'Hate crime in Europe' in Hall, N., Corb, A., Giannasi, P. and Grieve, J. (eds), *Routledge International Handbook on Hate Crime*. London: Routledge, pp. 95–104.

Wickes, R., Pickering, S., Mason, G., Maher, J. and McCulloch, J. (2015) 'From hate to prejudice: does the new terminology of prejudice motivated crime change perceptions and reporting actions?' *British Journal of Criminology*. DOI: 10.1093/bjc/azv041.

Wickes, R., Sydes, M., Benier, K. and Higginson, A. (2016) '"Seeing" hate crime in the community: do resident perceptions of hate crime align with self-reported victimization?' *Crime and Delinquency*, January 2016.

Williams, M. L. and Robinson, A. L. (2004) 'Problems and prospects with policing the lesbian, gay and bisexual community in Wales' *Policing and Society*, **14**(3), pp. 213–232.

Williams, M. L. and Robinson, A. L. (2007) 'Counted in! The All Wales Survey of lesbian, gay and bisexual people', Stonewall. Retrieved from: http://orca.cf.ac.uk/60693/.

Williams, M. L. and Tregidga, J. (2013) 'All Wales Hate Crime Research Project research overview and executive summary'. Retrieved from: www.refweb.org.uk/files/Wales%20Hate%20Crime%20Report.pdf.

Williams, M. L. and Tregidga, J. (2014) 'Hate crime victimization in Wales: psychological and physical impacts across seven hate crime victim types' *British Journal of Criminology*, **54**(5), pp. 946–967.

Wilson, L. (2010) 'Police smeared in Indian newspaper as "Ku Klux Klan"', The Australian, 8 January 2010. Retrieved from: www.theaustralian.com.au/news/nation/police-smeared-in-indian-newspaper-as-ku-klux-klan/story-e6frg6nf-1225817145020.

Wilson, M. M. (2014) 'Hate crime victimization, 2004–2012', statistical tables. US Department of Justice, NCJ, 244409. Retrieved from: www.bjs.gov/content/pub/pdf/hcv0412st.pdf.

Wiltshire Police (2015) 'Wiltshire Police Force policy and procedure: hate crime'. Retrieved from: www.wiltshire.police.uk/information/documents/publication-scheme/policies-and-procedures/crime-reduction-and-delivery/280-hate-crime-policy/file.

Wisler, D. and Onwudiwe, I. D. (eds) (2009) *Community Policing: International Patterns and Comparative Perspectives*. CRC Press.

Wong, K. (2009) 'Do the right thing: the Stephen Lawrence Inquiry Report 10 years on' *Safer Communities*, **8**(3), pp. 10–13.

Wong, K. and Christmann, K. (2008) 'The role of victim decision-making in reporting of hate crimes' *Safer Communities*, **7**(2), pp. 19–35.

Woods, J. B. and Herman, J. L. (2015) 'Anti-transgender hate crime', in Hall, N., Corb, A., Giannasi, P. and Grieve, J. (eds), *Routledge International Handbook on Hate Crime*. London: Routledge, pp. 278–288.

Zaykowski, H. (2010) 'Racial disparities in hate crime reporting' *Violence and Victims*, **25**(3), pp. 378–394.

Zempi, E. C. (2014) 'Unveiling Islamophobia: the victimisation of veiled Muslim women', doctoral dissertation, Department of Criminology, University of Leicester. Retrieved from: http://hdl.handle.net/2381/28962.

Legislation and conventions

Charter of Human Rights and Responsibilities Act 2006 (Vic)
Crimes (Sentencing Procedure) Act 1999 (NSW)
Crime and Disorder Act 1998 (UK)
Criminal Justice Act 2003 (UK)
International Covenant on Civil and Political Rights 1966 (ICCPR)
Public Order Act 1986 (UK)
Racial and Religious Tolerance Act 2001 (Vic)
Sentencing Act 1995 (NT)
Sentencing Act 1991 (Vic)

Case law

DPP v. *Caratozzolo* [2009] VSC 305
Dunn v. *R* [2007] NSWCCA 312
Holloway v. *R* [2011] NSWCCA 23
Hussein v. *The Queen* [2010] VSCA 257

R v. *Al-Shawany* [2007] NSWDC 141

R v. *Aslett* [2006] NSWCCA 49

R v. *Dean-Willcocks* [2012] NSWSC 107

R v. *Doody* (Unreported, Supreme Court of the Northern Territory, 23 April 2010)

R v. *El Mostafa* [2007] NSWDC 219

R v. *Gouros* (Unreported, Victorian County Court, 14 December 2009)

R v. *Hanlon* [2003] QCA 75

R v. *I.D. and O.N.* [2007] NSWDC 51

R v. *O'Brien* [2012] VSC 592

R v. *Robinson* [2004] NSWSC 465

R v. *Thomas* [2007] NSWDC 69

R v. *White* [2001] EWCA Crim 216

R v. *Winefield* [2011] NSWSC 337

Index

Page numbers in *italics* denote tables, those in **bold** denote figures.

.

Made in the USA
Middletown, DE
08 July 2023

34722459R00124